Dear Mom and Dad,
Love from Vietnam

DESERT BUGLE PRESS

©2014 Joseph E. Abodeely
All rights reserved. Printed in the United States of America. No part of this book may be used or reproduced in any manner whatsoever without written permission except in the case of brief quotations embodied in critical articles and reviews. For information address inquiries to:

Desert Bugle Press
P.O. Box 1065
Maricopa, AZ 85139
www.DesertBuglePress.com

Abodeely, Joe, Dear Mom and Dad, Love from Vietnam
13-Digit ISBN: 978-0-9915286-0-8
Library of Congress Control Number: 2014936082
Copyright information available upon request.
v. 1.0

Cover layout by Mark Saloff Designs
Interior layout by J. L. Saloff

All images are from the author's collection with the following exceptions:

The water color painting on the cover and p. 12, "Here Comes the Cavalry," was painted by Alexander Pekala (©2013).

Images from Wikipedia include: p. 46, U.S.S. New Jersey, photographed by PH2 Monty L. Tipton, Naval Historical Center, PD; p. 97, LZ Calu, Operation Pegasus, photographed by Icemanwcs, Creative Commons; p. 98, B-52 bomber, photographed by United States Air Force; National Museum of the USAF collection, PD; p. 108, Situation Room: Walt Rostow shows President Lyndon B. Johnson a model of the Khe Sanh area, 02/15/1968, US Archiv ARCWEB, PD.

Images from the Robert Lutz collection, used with permission: 1st Cavalry troops in Operation Pegasus, p. 104; NVA mortar rounds and arms, p. 105, Nardi and Lutz with sign, p. 114; plane crash, p. 118; crashed helicopter at LZ Pepper, p. 125; Chinook hovering at LZ Pepper, p.126; punji pit, p. 140.

Note: *Names have been changed.

First Edition

This compilation of my Vietnam diary, letters, and memoirs is dedicated to my mother, Grace, and to my father, Edward, who helped make me who I was and who I am.

It is also dedicated to my wife, Donna, who has been with me for nearly half a century through our trials and tribulations.

Lastly, and very importantly, this is dedicated to all who honorably served in the Vietnam War—especially the "grunts"—the "sky troopers" of the 1st Air Cavalry Division. *Garry Owen.*

Dear Mom and Dad,
Love from Vietnam

Joe Abodeely

DESERT BUGLE PRESS

I Was Prescient

There is no "only one" Vietnam experience—there are as many as there are those who went to Vietnam—but this is mine—the combat, the excitement, the discomfort, the fear, the accomplishments, the hubris, the politics, the challenges, and the sex. This is 1968—MY Vietnam experience.

The United States made a solemn commitment by the SEATO Treaty in 1955 to come to the aid of the Republic of Vietnam (South Vietnam) in defense of its freedom from Communist aggression consistent with nonaggression principles of the UN Charter.

In the 1960s, Americans sensed that a war was looming in Southeast Asia. American advisors were sent to the Republic of Vietnam (RVN)—the correct name for South Vietnam—to fight Communist insurgency. John F. Kennedy pledged to the world: "Let every nation know, whether it wishes us well or ill, that we shall pay any price, bear any burden, meet any hardship, support any friend, oppose any foe to assure the survival and the success of liberty." In August 1964, Congress enacted the Southeast Asian Resolution by a combined vote of 504-2.

It was an interesting time—"sex, drugs, and rock-and-roll." I drank alcohol but never did drugs because I was an athlete (played football and wrestled in high school and college). It was a time of the Kennedys, J.F.K. and Jackie—our "Camelot." I had never been interested in politics, but I liked J.F.K. (our first Catholic President and I was Catholic) who said we should defend South Vietnam. My high school senior class in Tucson, Arizona, elected four of us to give graduation speeches. As a 17-year-old young man in 1961, in part of my speech, I said:

"Lenin may have said something significant in his prophesies. Communism already has Eastern Europe, most of Asia; and it's starting in the Western hemisphere in Cuba. The threat is no longer a 'prophesy'—it's very real, and it's at our back door. We are our nation's future, our nation's hope. Our way of life must prevail over that of Communism. And our generation must be the one to curb the ever-growing threat, Communism, in order to ensure that the free world does prevail..."

I obviously sensed that the expansion of Communism was a serious threat then.

In 1963, I was a sophomore at the University of Arizona, and I gave a "persuasive" speech in my Speech Course about how and why America should send more troops to South Vietnam rather than simply using "advisors," who were outmanned and outgunned by enemy forces. It was just a required speech to "persuade" on any issue, and I chose that. In just a few years, I was sensing the international dynamics of the times.

ROTC was mandatory for the first two years, but the advanced program was an opportunity to earn a commission in the military. I was a wrestler on the university's wrestling team and had always been a leader, and going into the Army as an officer sounded appealing and exciting. I was a Distinguished Military Graduate in the advanced ROTC program in 1965 when I graduated from the University of Arizona and was commissioned a 2nd Lieutenant, Infantry.

Ma and me at my graduation and commissioning on May 26, 1965.

The Army granted me an excess leave to attend law school at the University of Arizona, which I did. After my first year, I had to reexamine in a course to remain eligible for my leave, so I changed my course of study for a semester by attending Graduate School in Business.

The Vietnam War was on and young men waited with great anxiety for announcements from the lottery. Some got drafted or enlisted. Others protested against the war, burned their draft cards, or ran off to Canada. If you changed your academic program or changed your course of study for which you got a deferment, Uncle Sam took you. Some young men got several academic deferments or got married to avoid going to Vietnam. It is interesting that two-thirds of those who served in Vietnam enlisted; one-third was drafted. In World War II, the reverse was true—one-third enlisted while two-thirds were drafted.

When I first entered active duty in 1967, I went to Fort Benning, Georgia, for Combat Platoon Leaders Course (CPLC). After a short leave, I went to my first assignment at Fort Polk, Louisiana, where my first job was Assistant Adjutant (S-1), Headquarters Special Troops.

It was an interesting administrative job, reviewing a lot of paperwork, personnel actions, reports of survey (lost or damaged property), line of duty investigations (personal injuries), Courts and Boards actions (administrative actions), and answering Congressional inquiries. Of course, I was an infantry officer, so I eventually was assigned to train troops at "Tiger Land" there at Fort Polk—training them in basic infantry tactics and skills (obstacle course, weapons familiarization, shooting, hand grenades, physical training, patrolling, hand-to-hand combat, bayonet training, etc.). I was in good physical shape and personally led much of the training. It was athletic and enhanced my leadership skills.

Sign entering Fort Polk.

Tiger Land training brigade sign where I trained troops.

I got my orders to "go across the pond" which assigned me to the 199th Light Infantry Brigade of the Americal Division. I had 30 days leave and went back to Tucson before I went to Vietnam. I met Kathleen, then, who became a close friend and pen pal. Mike and Phil were old law school classmates, so before I departed for Vietnam, I left my LPs (long-playing records)—The Doors, The Rolling Stones, The Jefferson Airplane, The Animals, Henry Mancini, etc., the kind of music I still love today—with Phil. I wound up in Vietnam at the beginning and height of the Tet Offensive in January 1968. I went to Vietnam to help the South Vietnamese people fight the Communist invasion from North Vietnam and Communist Vietcong insurgents. I believed in that cause then and I still do now. My dad gave me the "1968 Yearbook" from Arizona Trust Company in Tucson, Arizona, and suggested I keep a diary, which I started in Tucson. I wrote letters home on paper made available to us, and I received mail periodically, brought out to us with other supplies.

Disclaimer

The following are entries in my diary and letters home. I forgot to enter the time of entry a few times, but this is 99.9% of the exact entries in the diary and letters, except for some minor punctuation changes, spelling corrections, and name changes of referenced people.

The photos are mine except as otherwise noted. Some of the photos were made from Super 8 movies which I took in Vietnam. The less than perfect clarity is due to the technology of the time and my inexperience in taking movies.

The commentaries are my recollections, and sometimes I added comments or facts based on contemporary research. Many entries may appear to be "robotic" as I did not always have the luxury to feel emotions—but consider the circumstances.

The "experience" was almost surrealistic at times, but it was "real" then and is embedded in my being, still, today. I want to share this experience because I want people to better understand and to care about Vietnam veterans.

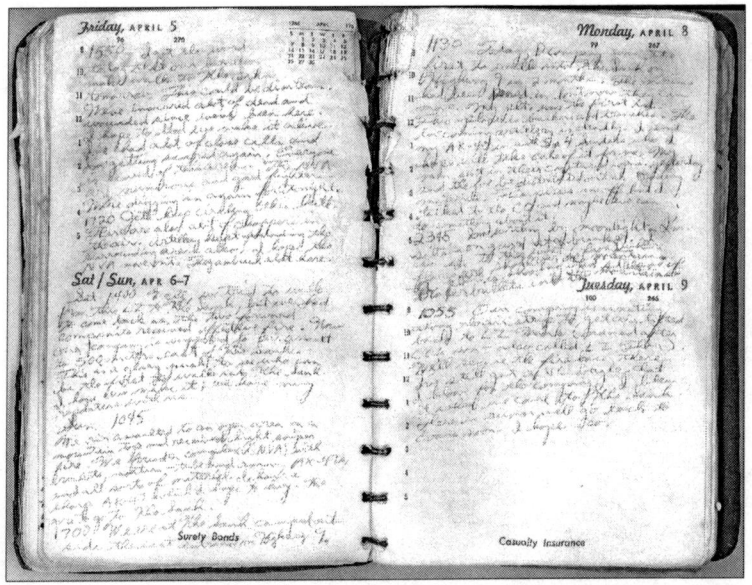

My 1968 diary written while in Vietnam.

January, 1968

Monday, January 1

Today I will start to keep this diary. I'm sleepy now as it is 12:30 a.m. of 2 January but it seems proper to make an entry for 1 January to start things at the beginning. I have a lot to do tomorrow for preparation for my trip.

[I was so busy getting ready for my Odyssey that I forgot to make a timely first entry.]

Tuesday, January 2

I bought a pocket flashlight. Tonight, Mike, Phil, our dates, and I are going to see "Camelot." I'm anxious to get under way on my new adventure. At times I feel apprehensive, realizing the situation I'm heading toward, but most of the time I feel the excitement and anxiety for this new and, I hope, profitable experience.

[I was excited to embark on "my new adventure," while at the same time realizing that I could get killed. It was all becoming more real to me now that I was actually on my way to Vietnam.]

Wednesday, January 3

I saw "Camelot" last night. It was very romantic, well acted, beautifully filmed, and an enjoyable movie. I am packing now and just waiting for time to go by.

Remember, the Kennedys were our "Camelot." It was a time of "idealism." The Kennedys were a romantic, idealized, almost "royal" couple. It was a time of "Camelot." I went to Vietnam to help the South Vietnamese people. I was a knight on a quest, as in Camelot. That idealism would later evaporate.

I flew from Tucson to Travis Air Force Base in the San Francisco Bay area via commercial flight, and from Travis AFB I flew to the Republic of Vietnam on a military aircraft—I believe a C-130. It was a long flight with many other soldiers. It was uncomfortable and bumpy and we had to rest and sleep on our duffel bags. I think the trip was about 11 hours.

Saturday, January 6

Today is 6 January 68. I am now in RVN. We landed at Bien Hoa and took buses to Long Bien where I am now. It is hot and humid. I've seen a lot of guys who were in my CPLC at Fort Benning. I've got a bad cold from San Francisco, but that's the least of my worries. The area reminds me of Nogales, with beat-up houses and poor people walking the streets. Right now I'm in a base camp at Long Bien. I'll know my assignment by tomorrow.

[CPLC was Combat Platoon Leaders Course at Fort Benning, Georgia. ROTC-commissioned officers attended this eight-week program as a "refresher" course on how to be a combat leader. I was remembering Nogales, Mexico, south of Tucson just across the Arizona-Mexico border, which I had visited numerous times.]

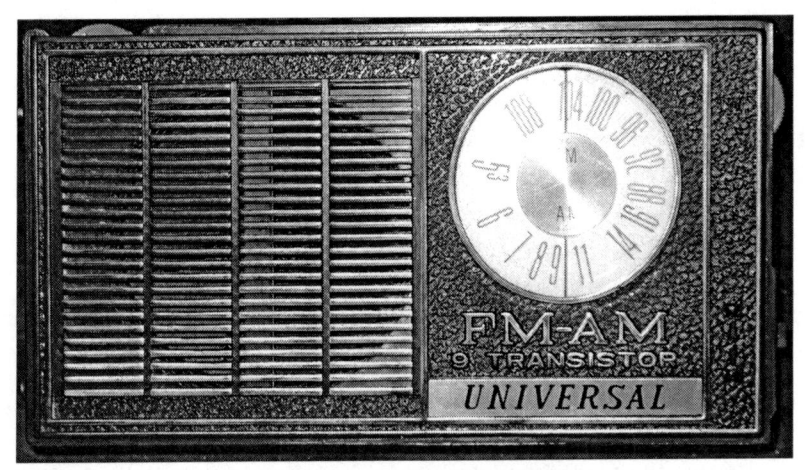

The radio I had in Vietnam.

1615 hrs. I slept awhile and then attended an orientation. We are waiting for our assignments to be confirmed. My buddies are playing cards and listening to my transistor radio. I'm going to sleep some more.

[My dad gave me a black transistor radio which periodically provided entertainment for my comrades and me. We listened to the music of the times—"Satisfaction," "California Dreaming," "Light My Fire," "Nights in White Satin," "Whiter Shades of Pale," "Purple Haze," "I Can See for Miles," "Somebody to Love," etc.]

Sunday, January 7

I waited all day for confirmation of assignment. I checked with operations and the Sgt said I'm assigned to the 1st Cavalry Division. That means I fly north after midnight tonight or tomorrow night. I'm a little scared at the change of assignment and the thought of flying north. I slept and listened to my transistor radio today. It's humid so I'll take a shower and be ready to move out tonight.

[I was originally assigned to the 199th Light Infantry Brigade (Americal Division).]

2100 hrs. Dear Mom and Dad,

I've been here in Bien Hoa (near Saigon) since yesterday waiting for confirmation or change in my assignment. They frequently change the assignments here because of the needs of the various units. It so happens that my orders were changed so now I'm assigned to the 1st Cavalry Division which is up north at An Khe. I've met a lot of my old buddies from Fort Benning. They, too, are assigned to various infantry units.

Right now we are in Bien Hoa in a large compound. There are barb wire and sandbagged bunkers all around. I slept in a bunk with the protective mosquito net last night. It's hot and humid. I've been listening to my transistor radio a lot. There are a couple of stations from Saigon.

Well, I still don't really know what's happening. There's a lot of activity during the day. Trucks with troops are constantly moving. At night our artillery and mortars fire rounds. I'll leave either tonight or tomorrow night for my unit. One of my buddies just told me that he's assigned to the 1st Cavalry, too. This unit is an air assault unit. They have a lot of helicopters organic to the unit. It should be interesting, but I'll probably see a lot of action. I don't know yet but I should find out my job when I report to the unit in a day or two. Meanwhile, I'm just waiting to be told what to do. I'm still a little apprehensive but excited, too. Well I'll sign off for now. I guess my original APO is still good for my mail but it will probably be better if you wait for my next letter with my new address. Don't worry about me even if I write that I'm scared because all of us here feel that way--especially infantry officers. The unit I am going to is a good unit and has a lot of support --fire and logistical--because of its helicopter organic makeup. I'll get this letter off and I'll try to write as soon as I get to my unit.

Love, Joe

The 1st Air Cav, as it was often called, excelled in the traditional cavalry missions to reconnoiter, screen, delay, and conduct raids over wide terrain. The 1st Cavalry Division (Airmobile) was an organization of about 15,000 men. It had its own infantry, artillery, logistics, and other division support capabilities, but most importantly, it had its own aviation assets directly assigned to the division to provide aerial reconnaissance, troop transport, aerial rocket artillery fire support, and logistical transport. It integrated attack, transport, and observation aircraft with the fighting elements of the division. The "combat air assault" was the zenith of the attack phase of air mobility. A combat air assault, as a tactical mission, was more than merely transporting troops from point A to point B by helicopters. Once the enemy was located and contact was made, often by scout helicopters escorted by gunships, air cavalry troops could be swiftly deployed by helicopters from less critical situations and could be quickly concentrated at the point of battle.

Huey lift flights, usually four to six helicopters, picked up the cavalry troopers and transported them to the mission's landing zone. As the Hueys approached, artillery pounded the LZ (landing zone), ending with a white phosphorus round impact that let the helicopter pilots know to start their descent. Huey or Cobra gunships would first strafe the LZ with suppressing fire, in case enemy troops planned an ambush, before the lift ships would then land and the troopers dismounted to continue their mission.

Instant radio communications enabled commanders, who were often in their command-and-control helicopters, to monitor scout ship transmissions and to direct responsive air landings in the midst of fluid combat situations. As the infantrymen deployed from the helicopters with rifles and machine guns blazing, gunships patrolled overhead providing close-in covering fire with rockets and machine guns. Rapid helicopter airlift of howitzers and ordnance assured that infantry fighting for

Watercolor painting--"Here Comes the Cavalry" by Alexander Pekala (2013).

remote and isolated landing zones would have sustained artillery fire support. Enemy opposition was often stunned and overwhelmed by this swiftly executed initial aerial onslaught. Of course, I did not know all of this about the Cav then, but I experienced and participated in much of what I just described and learned about what a great unit the 1st Air Cavalry was from research after the war.

Monday, January 8

It's 1030 hrs. and most of my buddies from the CPLC here left for their units or are waiting to leave in an hour or so. I'll leave tonight. Everyone tells me that the 1st Cavalry Division sees a lot of action and this scares me somewhat to think that I may not come back. This abstract word "death" now has some meaning, but I feel I'm doing something worthwhile. Two Vietnamese maids are here and I think I'll talk to them to kill time. I sure wish people in the U.S.A. really could appreciate what's happening in this country, but our nation has grown soft and selfish.

I was a believer. I believed in our cause in Vietnam then, and I still believe today in the justice of our cause to defend the South Vietnamese from Communist aggression. History has proven that it was NOT beneficial to the South Vietnamese for Communist domination. Ask the "Boat People" or those who were imprisoned in the "reeducation camps" or the survivors in Cambodia and the "killing fields." Ask those who lost their families and property to the Communists. Ask those whose family members were sold into slavery. I remember when Congress voted to stop funding support to the South Vietnamese military, thereby allowing the Communist North Vietnam to invade the South again in violation of the 1973 Geneva Peace Accords. I remember how the Vietnam veteran was blamed for "losing" the Vietnam War and was maligned and disrespected for his meritorious service, which actually won the war of U.S. involvement in 1973.

Tuesday, January 9

It is 0300 hrs. I got up one hour ago. I am now at the airfield at Bien Hoa waiting for the plane to An Khe. I met another lieut. from Cedar Rapids, Iowa. He knows the Abodeely family. In a few hours I should be at An Khe and at my new assignment. I keep experiencing alternating feelings of anxiety, apprehension, excitement, and boredom. It's hard to believe I'm on the other side of the world in a combat zone, but the Army Jeep escort of the buses to the airfield helps to remind us.

1515 hrs. I'm at the admin station in An Khe. We packed onto a cargo plane like sardines and had a roller-coaster flight here. Now I'm just waiting to find out where I go for my assignment. They were impressed with my education and adjutant experience, but I'm still not ready not to be a platoon leader. It's rainy and muddy here. A lot of helicopters keep circling this base.

Wednesday, January 10
0917 hrs. Dear Mom and Dad,

    Well, I don't know where to begin but I'll try and cover as best I can what I've done and what I'm told I'll be doing. When I left Tucson, I got to San Francisco where I took a bus to Travis AFB. I got there around midnight waiting to report between 0400 and 0700 to the desk as my order stated. The plane was delayed so I stayed up all night and finally left at 1430 (2:30 p.m.) that day. The plane was a Trans International Airways charter flight for military personnel. I flew to Hawaii where I bought you some jewelry, Ma, which I'll try to send when it's convenient for me. After Hawaii I stopped at Wake Island, and then one more stop at Clark AFB in the Philippines. Then we arrived at Bien Hoa at an AFB. From there we took buses to Long Bien which is a reception station where we waited for confirmation for changes in our orders. Both Bien Hoa and Long Bien are near each other and fairly near Saigon.

    Anyhow, I met a lot of old buddies from my CPLC (Combat Platoon Leaders Course) at Fort Benning. We all talked about the infantry school and just waited for news of our orders. It so happened that the 199th Infantry Brigade had its allocations filled; so they took only two captains and one lieut. Thus, my orders were changed to the 1st Air Cavalry. This is one of the main combat units up here. Now don't worry about all the stuff I'm going to be telling about the unit and where and how they operate because I'm just going to keep you people informed so you won't be surprised by any outside news. When I got my orders at Long Bien, I was taken back to Bien Hoa and flown to An Khe which is where I am now

--up north in the Central Highlands. The flight was in a cargo plane and all of us--officers and enlisted men--and our luggage were crammed in like sardines. The flight was rough and I almost got airsickness. Yesterday, we processed again at the 1st Cavalry admin center to get our assignments. A couple of the clerks said I'd probably get an adjutant's job later because of my background; but right now I'm assigned to D Company, 7th Battalion, 2nd Brigade (sic), of the 1st Cav Division as a combat platoon leader. The 1st Cav is a highly regarded division here in Vietnam. It has the best kill ratio of any unit--it kills the most VC with the least possible losses itself. It is an airmobile division which means that it has helicopter units as part of its organic makeup. That means we fly by helicopter to our assault positions and we have helicopter support for transportation, for logistical (ammo and food), and for a Medevac (rescue). We also have helicopter gunship fire support. If I could have made a choice as to the combat unit I could be in, it would probably have been this one.

    Yesterday, another lieut. and I were greeted by a capt. who told us what the 1st Cav is doing. Within the next day or two, I'll go to the four-day school to get some general info on the 1st Cavalry and review some tactics. Then I'll go to Phan Thiet. This is back down again near Saigon. There will be a base camp there and I'll work out of there going to different LZs (landing zones for helicopters) and patrolling out from them. The platoon leaders of these units are pretty independent and we run our platoons. Of course, we're broken in gradually, but we have to know our stuff. This is the real thing and the capt. said we will see plenty of action.

Mom and Dad, please try and get as good a map of Vietnam as you can so you'll know where I am when I give locations. I'm at An Khe now but as I said I'll be sent down south again to around Phan Thiet. This letter will take about 5 days to reach you and I probably won't get any mail for two weeks because of my dislocation. I'll try and keep you informed where I am so you can communicate with me. They had us fill out a card which says you'll be notified if I'm lightly wounded. Don't worry about it because if you are notified it just means I received the wound for which I was treated by an aid station and it's not serious. Eventually I am going to have to send back some stuff because I don't have room for it. I was issued my field gear and jungle fatigues and boots. This unit is well supplied and taken care of. The weather here at An Khe is nice and cool. Farther south around Saigon, it's hot and humid. I'm in a fairly well built-up base camp with helicopters flying overhead both day and night. The food is good but there are the normal wartime inconveniences such as foul-smelling outhouses and makeshift showers and just dirt and mud in unbuilt-up areas.

This year's going to be a real experience. I don't mind saying that I'm really pretty damn scared, but there's nothing I can do about it. I hope I learn fast and that I have good help from everywhere. Don't worry because people over here know their jobs. With some luck and other things, I'll be all right. I'll write later when I get time or maybe when I get to Phan Thiet.

My address is Lieut. Abodeely, 05710979, D2/7 Cav, APO SF 96490

Love, Joe

[I misstated my unit of assignment. I was assigned to D Company, 2nd Battalion, 7th Cavalry, 1st Cavalry Division (Airmobile) or D/2/7 Cav. My comment about the platoon leaders running their platoons was correct as my further experience verified. It has been accurately said that Vietnam was a platoon leaders' and company commanders' war.]

Wednesday, January 10, (cont.)

1345 hrs. I am packing stuff to send home. Tomorrow I'll attend a four-day school of tactics review. I wrote Mom and Dad a letter today. I'm worried about the danger at times, but most of the time I feel confident and have a "give a damn" attitude.

Friday, January 12

2030 hrs. Another Lieut. (Richard Vineyard) and I just came back from an officers' club. Yesterday we attended a class which involved our going outside the perimeter. The VC could've attacked us at any time. Last night I slept on the perimeter. I surely like the M-16 if it just won't ever jam on me. Here's hoping. I'm listening to my transistor radio now. Tomorrow is a free day. I think I'll go into the city of An Khe. Constantly I hear "choppers" and artillery fire searching the outside area. Whenever a 175 mm artillery fires, it rocks this room.

Saturday, January 13

0820 hrs. I was awakened this morning by artillery fire. The guns usually fire a few rounds to scare the VC out of the brush, but apparently this morning some VC were spotted by a patrol or by the two choppers circling the area. The artillery had a fire mission and just kept pumping rounds off for about 10 to 15 minutes.

1845 hrs. I went into An Khe today. They have a little whorehouse section called "sin city." I just looked around and didn't patronize. I met a Lieut. Wells from the company, whom I'm replacing. He has a skin infection and is restricted from the field. I'll take over his platoon.

The town of An Khe was near Camp Radcliff—the 1st Air Cavalry Division's headquarters location. As in war zones throughout history, An Khe had its "red-light district" where soldiers could meet prostitutes. The Army knew about it, had MPs keep the peace in the area, and often had medics check the "girls" for disease. The "world's oldest profession" was endorsed, at least implicitly, by the Army. I was a single young man of 24 who would eventually patronize the brothels.

Sunday, January 14

2028 hrs. I attended classes for my four-day orientation again today. Tomorrow I fly to Qui Nhon to have my eyes checked. We had a lot of artillery and machine gun fire on the perimeter early this morning. It was routine searching fire into the boonies looking for VC.

I wore glasses and later contact lenses before I went to Vietnam. The wind, heat, dust, and lack of sanitary conditions were not conducive to wearing contacts in-country. I went to have my eyes checked to get issued Army glasses. I still have those glasses as part of my Vietnam memorabilia.

Monday, January 15

0925 hrs. I've just boarded an Army Caribou. It's taking off now heading to Qui Nhon where I'll have my eyes checked. The plane is shaking while I'm writing. It's a troop transport plane and I'm loaded on with other troops sitting across from each other. We're taking off now. We're in the air now and it's a rough flight—we're dipping and fishtailing as we go.

1315 hrs. I've had my eyes checked. I'm now on a C-130 heading back to An Khe. This is going to be a rough ride.

2000 hrs. Dear Mom and Dad,

Well, today I finalized a brief four-day course or orientation about the 1st Air Cavalry. I also flew to Qui Nhon to have my eyes checked for glasses. The glasses will be sent to the field in about 3 weeks. I sent home some of my fatigues and other things as I won't be needing them. They should reach you in about 2 or 3 weeks (by boat).

Tomorrow, I go to Phan Thiet which I guess will be my home for about the next 6 to 8 months. There is an LZ (landing zone for choppers) near Phan Thiet and two other LZs nearby. A Company works out of the LZs. I'll be platoon leader of D Company, 2nd Battalion, of the 7th Cavalry of the 1st Air Cavalry division. Each platoon rotates activities, but one platoon will be on the LZ to defend in a perimeter defense. Another platoon will go out on a long-range patrol looking for VC and setting up ambushes. And another platoon will conduct air assaults by helicopters.

Now that I've been in An Khe awhile, I developed more confidence. I'm actually looking forward to getting to my platoon tomorrow. I talked to a Lieut. Wells, whom I am replacing because he has a skin infection and can't work in the field anymore, and he said that when he reported in, the very next day he led his platoon on an air assault. Hell, I might get to see some action tomorrow or the day after for sure. I'm so bored waiting to get to my unit that I'm looking for action now. Phan Thiet is supposed to be a pretty area and guys in other units say that everyone wants to get in 2nd of the 7th (my unit) because of the area and because the VC have small units there (guerrillas, VC, not regiments but a couple of battalions).

    I'm going to leave some of my stuff here at this rear area because we are supplied with everything in the field from shaving equipment to fatigues and socks and one hot meal a day. Because we are the airmobile division--choppers --we get things the other divisions don't. I think I'm going to like this job, but I'll have to see. In case you've been writing to me, I haven't and won't receive any mail until about another week or so.

    So much for me. How are things at home? Are you two getting along now? How's the teaching job going, Dad? Oh, I checked with finance and I'll have my money sent to you, Dad. Please save it for me. I'm keeping $50/month and this is still too much to keep because I don't need any money. There is this program I can put my money in savings at 10% interest, but I can't withdraw anything until I get home. I may later change to this.

    Bob's birthday is on 28 January and I'll try to get him something but if I'm busy or in or on a mission, I'm not going to worry about it.

    Have to get up early tomorrow so I'll hit the hay now. I'm sleeping in a sleeping bag on a bunk. It's warm as the Central Highlands are cool at night.

    Love, Joe

[When I referred to Bob, I was talking about my brother who was still in college].

Tuesday, January 16

0807 hrs. I'm in the battalion orderly room with Lieut. Vineyard and the adjutant. All three of us are flying to Phan Thiet today. It's drizzly outside now. In Phan Thiet it's supposed to be hot. I'll find out soon.

I remember reporting in to a colonel with Richard Vineyard. The colonel had a patch over one eye like a pirate. He welcomed us to the 1st Cavalry Division and made some comments I still remember. He said that when the shooting started, we should get down. He said the men would respect us if we got down and properly assessed the situation. He also said that the 1st Air Cavalry had a lot of helicopters, but they were hard to replace. He said we should not lose any helicopters, and that 2nd Lieutenants were easier to replace than were helicopters. That is when I first realized that I was expendable.

1530 hrs. False alarm! I'm back at 2/7 BOQ. We got at the airfield at 0900 and waited until 1500. Many planes came in and departed carrying troops but none to Phan Thiet. I'm going to have to get a camera to record the many sights I've seen already and will see.

[BOQ means Bachelor Officers' Quarters—a term for billets for single officers.]

2015 hrs. Tomorrow we'll try and get another flight to Phan Thiet. It's cool outside and in here as this wooden room has screens for windows. Thank goodness for my sleeping bag which I have on the bunk. It's really warm at night even though I'm sleeping completely naked except for my dog tags. I haven't been wearing underwear either as it is customary with many of the field troops.

[It may have been cool at night, but I was very warm in the "mummy" bag.]

DEAR MOM AND DAD, LOVE FROM VIETNAM | 21

Wednesday, January 17

1030 hrs. Well, here we are again at An Khe airfield trying to get a flight to Phan Thiet. Flights keep getting delayed or canceled—this one is grounded because of bad weather at Phan Thiet.

1100 hrs. I'm finally on a C-130. The weather is bad in Phan Thiet but here goes.

1550 hrs. We got to Phan Thiet (here) at 1300. I'm with 1st Lieut. Lutstein who is XO of the company. The 2/7 (my unit) is moving up north to the Pershing AO (area of operations). It's a lot of action up there. Tonight I fly to LZ Bartlett.

Thursday, January 18

1500 hrs. Last night I slept on LZ Bartlett. I took my first ride in a chopper; it's great as the side doors are open and I can see for miles. I met my platoon sgt.—Sgt. Stoddard, who has 23 years' service, is a very capable man, but drinks literally all the time. He was high when I met him. He somewhat resents me taking over his platoon but I think we'll do all right. Phan Thiet is near the South China Sea which is beautiful, but our battalion is going up north to Bong Son where the action is hot. My men and I will carry just what we can carry on our backs. I'm ready to go to a hot area—many VC and regular Army troops of North Vietnam.

Sgt Stoddard had been through World War II, Korea, and this was his fourth tour in Vietnam—or so I was told. He was drunk when I met him at a small firebase on a mountaintop. We shared a muddy bunker, sleeping on ammo boxes, and he was pleading with me not to take his platoon away from him. He cared about the troops, was normally a good NCO, but he drank too much. I told him I'd rely on his judgment to help me run the platoon. I was aware of the age-old tension between officers and enlisted men, but I thought I had a little more going for me than the average "90-day wonder" that may have been made an "officer."

Although I was an ROTC graduate and not a former enlisted man who went to Officer Candidate School (OCS) and not a West Point graduate, I was a Distinguished Military Graduate (DMG) from the University of Arizona—one of the best and largest ROTC programs in the country at the time. DMGs were offered Regular Army Commissions—the same as West Point graduates. I refused mine to attend law school. I had also been an athlete in high school and college, and this experience helped me as a leader of a combat infantry platoon.

> 1520 hrs. Dear Mom and Dad,
> Another quick note to let you know where I am and what I'm doing. I got in Phan Thiet yesterday, but the whole battalion is going up north near Bong Son where the action is. I met my platoon last night and today we're getting ready to move out on Saturday. We will wear our combat gear in the cargo transport plane and carry our duffel bags. Once we hit LZ English, we'll be put out into the field to conduct long-range patrols. The area has regiment-size regular Army North Vietnamese so it won't be a picnic.
>
> I'm writing now because I don't know when I'll be able to write again. It's raining and cold up north and we will be out in the field for at least two-thirds of the month. We will carry all our gear but choppers may drop us sleeping bags at night. My platoon sgt., Sgt. Stoddard, has 23 years of service, is very capable, but drinks literally all the time. He was high when I met him last night. He somewhat resents a new platoon leader taking over (I've been told), but we get along okay. I think things will be fine. I like my men; they're the best platoon of the company. I'm looking forward to leading them in combat; I just hope all goes well for us. I still haven't

received any letters from home in case you've written and the delay may be longer because now I'm moving again.

    Tell Bob, in case you don't hear from me in a while, that I'll be in the field for a while and probably won't get to a PX to get him a present for his birthday. I'll try to get something to him later. This is not going to be a picnic or ROTC play exercise. This is the real thing, and it's rough out here. It's a great experience. I wish I bought an "Instamatic" camera earlier, but I'll get one later. I'm keeping a diary you gave me, Dad, and some of the entries coincide with the info in some of these letters. Well, Mom and Dad, I'll write when next I can. Mom, if you want to pray for me, go ahead; I think my men and I will need it. But don't worry because I've got a great group of men and the faster I learn, we'll be all right.

    Love, Joe

Friday, January 19

0925 hrs. I cleaned my M-16 this morning. We're supposed to get new weapons up north but I'm counting on this one at present. The officers and NCOs got drunk last night. Lieut. Gaylord and I each put in $10 to buy beer, as we'll both make first lieut. in the field—he will about two weeks before me. It's scary listening to all these war stories of these guys' men getting wounded and killed. About two-thirds of my platoon is new, going to a new area, with a new platoon leader so it will be a challenge to all of us. I'm going to shave now.

Saturday, January 20

> 0835 hrs. D Company is sitting around on duffle bags waiting to get on the C-130s. The planes won't come in until 1600 today so we'll sit on our butts all morning and part of the afternoon. Sgt. Stoddard got drunk again last night and he's sleeping on his duffel bag. The rest of the platoon is standing around eating their C-rations. We should be at LZ English sometime this evening. Capt. Rapper, who was wounded by a punji stake, is back with the company, and I met him yesterday. Lieut. Linsey and I slept outside on some plywood sheets last night.

Captain Rapper was D Company commander, my commanding officer—CO. He had stepped on a punji stake and went to the hospital for the wound. The VC (Vietcong) dug little pits big enough for a man to step into with his foot. The pits had sharpened bamboo stakes (often smeared with human feces to promote infection) planted into the base of these pits. Rapper was from California and looked like a muscular, chiseled-body, tan surfer from the West Coast. He was a UCLA graduate, a wrestler, and had a ROTC commission, too. He and I got along well. I got the impression that some of the officers didn't like him because he had a college degree. I sensed I had that problem later on, too.

> 1630 hrs. Well, we've been waiting all day sitting around in the hot sun. I have a headache and my forearms are sunburned. I've been talking to my men at various times to try to get to know them. I'm afraid I'm going to get too close to them and feel it when I lose some of them. Sgt. Stoddard is sober now and is more serious. He got a battalion article 15 from the Sergeant Major for being drunk and I told him I'd help him out if I could if he can't talk himself out of it. I wish we'd get to LZ English soon.

When I took over my platoon, I had only about 20 men or less. An Army infantry platoon normally has around 40 men, but attrition due to casualties had diminished the size of mine. Most rifle (infantry) platoons had four squads of about 10 men each. Due to the circumstances, I divided my platoon into three squads. My platoon used to be part of a recon company with Jeeps with radios in them. Some rifle companies (each composed of four platoons) had only two PRC-25 radios for the whole company, but I kept all the radios (originally allocated to the previous recon organization) for my platoon so that my platoon had five PRC-25 radios.

Each one of the three squads of my platoon had its own radio for commo, and I had two RTOs (radio-telephone operators or radiomen) in my platoon headquarters or "CP"—Command Post. This gave us greater capabilities and a sense of security. So, I had three squads which eventually grew in size as replacements came in. Each squad had a PRC-25 radio; two of the squads had M-60 machine guns; one squad had a 90 mm recoilless rifle (like a giant Bazooka); each squad had a man who carried an M-79 grenade launcher and a .45 cal. pistol; every other man carried an M-72 light antitank weapon (LAW); and every man, except the grenadiers and the RR man, carried an M-16 rifle, plenty of ammo, and fragmentation and colored smoke grenades.

My job was to "lead" my platoon. I had the map and got the orders for our missions. I directed the formations we used while moving; I called in artillery or mortar fire when needed; I sent out LPOPs or ambushes; I led and controlled my platoon's actions. Our overall mission as an infantry unit was to close with and kill or capture the enemy by means of fire and maneuver. I carried an M-16 rifle, a bandolier of ammo, smoke, and "frags." We all wore jungle fatigues and steel pots (helmets). Some of us carried our "bug juice (mosquito repellant) in a little white plastic bottle tucked under the helmet-cover elastic band. Our web gear consisted of a pistol belt, harness, ammo pouches, first-aid kit, bayonet and scabbard, entrenching tool (folding shovel), canteen with cup and cover, poncho, poncho liners, and butt pack. We were supposed to wear our flak vests, but we often traveled light—no vest and not even the butt pack. I put C-rations or a sweater or my socks in the butt pack if I used it. Because we could go out on patrols from a base camp or conduct air assault, I would carry just what I needed in my thigh pockets of the jungle fatigues. That's why people today call them "cargo" pants. Sometimes, on short patrols, to avoid having to take the butt pack, I'd put my Cs in socks and tie them to my harness. I'd tie a string around my poncho liner and tie that to the back of my harness. We were "Air Cavalry"—we often were transported by helicopter and we often traveled light—confident of helicopter support when we needed it. We were a formidable unit.

Sunday, January 21

1250 hrs. Last night we got to LZ English. We spent the night sleeping on the ground in the open. It rained and the whole company was drenched. I slept on an air mattress under a poncho liner and poncho, and all of us were muddy and wet just like in a war movie. Today we took Chinooks (choppers) to LZ Two Bits where we are now. My platoon has six bunkers to occupy. Right now I'm in a wood "hooch" drying off while everyone else is doing the same.

I distinctly remember the miserable experience of that night. I blew up my air mattress, placed it on the dry ground, and went to sleep. Then it rained, and to make matters worse, we had picked a low spot to place our air mattresses. The water drained into the low spot where we were sleeping, and to make matters even more "worse," my air mattress deflated. I was flat on the ground in two or three inches of water. This was part of the life of an infantryman.

```
Monday, January 22
1135 hrs. Dear Mom and Dad,
    Well, we are here at LZ Two Bits which is near
the city of Bong Son. We got to LZ English day
before yesterday in the evening and we slept out
in the open ground where it rained and became
muddy. I slept on an air mattress with a poncho
and poncho liner over me as it rained. I woke up
at about 2 in the morning sleeping in a gigantic
mud puddle.
    Right now I'm in a hooch (a little house)
made out of empty 105 mm artillery round boxes
filled with dirt. The rest of my platoon is
occupying 7 bunkers made of sandbags. We are on
a mountaintop overlooking the valley and rice
```

paddies and mountains off in the distance. Last night as usual there was a lot of firing off in the distance with occasional artillery fire and illumination flares. It is very interesting up here, but we are supposedly in a bad area for VC and NVA (North Vietnamese Army) troops. This LZ is being abandoned because the rest of the division is going up north to Hue which is almost on the DMZ where most of the action is. We expect to be up there soon but we don't know when. We eventually will be patrolling the area around here looking for mortar positions. I've already told my men that I don't want anybody to win any purple hearts in my platoon. We'll just do our job as safely as we can.

    The sun is shining now and the view off in the distance is very pretty. I let some of my men go to Bon Son to buy ice and Coke but I told them to wear their "pots" (helmets) and take their M-16s.

    Yesterday some Vietnamese children came up in front of one of my bunkers where I had mines set up near the barb wire, but I "shooed" them off so they wouldn't get hurt.

    The ARVNs (Republic of Vietnam) will take over the LZ when we leave and they brought a couple of tanks up about an hour ago. We've got a lot of firepower here--tanks, artillery, and our armed helicopters. At night I worry about being mortared or an attack of some kind, but things have been quiet so far. Maybe when we go out on patrols we'll see some VC.

    I've got some real characters in my platoon. Pee Wee (small guy) and Sneed are my two RTOs (radio-telephone operators), and "Doc" is my medic. Sgt. Ross works with me in this platoon headquarters as well as does Sgt. Stoddard. As I wrote before, Sgt. Stoddard drinks a lot but he's okay in the field here so far. I like him and he's a good NCO.

Well, I thought I'd write from here as I had time. I'll go to the company HQ now to see if any new info concerns my platoon.

Oh! Don't worry about my contacts. I have been wearing just my glasses because of the dust and night movement. The living here is very austere, wearing the same clothes for a week or more and not showering for just as long. It's just like in the movies and books about combat soldiers, but I can honestly say it's an interesting experience. I just hope everything turns out okay for my men and me.

I haven't received word from you people. What's happening at home? Remember, I'm in the Air Cavalry Division, not the 199th. I'll write later if something new happens, such as our company going back to LZ English or to the Bong Son bridges, which we may.

Love, Joe

Monday, January 22, (cont.)

2324 hrs. I fixed my hooch up today at my platoon CP. My bunkers are well secured and I hope we don't have any trouble. Sneed is playing his harmonica in the room next door. Today I took a nine-man patrol about 75 m outside our perimeter to check for breaches in the protective wire in front of my platoon's seven bunkers. There were breaks where kids would come up, but we fixed them all except one which we'll use as an exit through the wire for patrols. There is a machine gun and Claymore mine on it so there is no problem. I got a letter from home today. I'm sleeping on the floor in a sleeping bag which my RTO found. My M-16 is right by my side.

The previous entry (2324 hrs.) is 11:24 p.m.—nighttime. I wrote by flashlight late at night as I often slept very little. I had two radios at my platoon CP (command post), which was wherever I set up in a perimeter defense. My CP was Sgt Stoddard, Pee Wee, Sneed, "Doc" Henderson (my medic), and me. We all took turns monitoring the radios, getting "sitreps" (situation reports) from the squads' various locations on the perimeter. I was lucky to get three hours of sleep a night. Each night, when I went to sleep, I turned my steel pot upside down, put my glasses in it, and rested my M-16's barrel on the helmet to keep it out of mud or dirt.

Tuesday, January 23

1410 hrs. Last night third platoon saw two VC in the wire in front of their bunker 48. I went out to my bunker 43 and sat radio watch awhile. I didn't get much sleep last night. Today the CO told us three platoon leaders that there is a division of NVA in the area. I sleep with my M-16 right beside me. Today, we policed up extra ammo from our bunkers. We stored it all in a room next to mine. There are M-16 rounds by the boxes, M-60 rounds by the cases, a case of M-79 grenade launcher rounds, and .50 caliber machine gun rounds there. If a mortar round lands nearby or if spontaneous combustion starts a fire, the ammo will go off like an ammo dump.

Wednesday, January 24

0815 hrs. It's nice and cool outside my hooch. The scenery off this mountain is beautiful, as I can see the green rice paddies, jungles, and mountains off in the distance. The ground is damp but my platoon headquarters and I are very comfortable in our hooches. Nothing much happened last night.

1920 hrs. Ross, Sneed, Pee Wee, and I went to the outskirts of Bong Son today. All four of us got a woman and got satisfaction. We have to be careful here, as the VD rate is very high. Bulldozers started leveling the area around my bunkers so that just bunkers and my CP are left. Tomorrow we'll move to the middle, giving up the bunkers to be destroyed. We'll probably leave this area in a couple days. I haven't had a shower or a change of clothes in about five days. I'm sitting in my CP (command post) hooch writing by candlelight.

[We were shrinking the defensive perimeter little by little, destroying the bunkers and base camp structure before we moved on.]

2331 hrs. Bunker 48 (third platoon) saw through the starlight scope four VC on the other side of the wire walking along with children. The third platoon leader said it looks as though the kids had hand grenades. I hope we don't have any problems tonight.

[A starlight scope was a night vision device like a big telescope. It was probably one of the first generations of night vision devices that we pretty much take for granted now. With all the equipment I had in my platoon (clothing, equipment, weapons), the starlight scope was the only item I had to sign a hand receipt for. I was told that if we lost it, I was responsible for about $3,000.]

Thursday, January 25

2120 hrs. I am in a fortification—sandbags, 50-gallon drums, and wooden rocket ammo boxes filled with dirt. I'm writing by candlelight. I only have four bunkers, 38, 40, 41, and 43, manned. We moved across the airstrip and I'm with my two RTOs. I got on the radio and called the CO and he said that we could fire only when we checked in first at the CP. He says the VC must be inside the wire before we can fire. This war stinks with rules like that. We were told today that the NVA are planning a major attack on one of five major LZs before *their lunar new year. Because we are not well defended, it could be us.*

There were restrictions on firing at "targets." Some areas were "free fire zones," but usually around the more populated areas, they were "no free fire zones." I remember one time we were sniped at from a village, and I wanted to level the area (call in artillery)—and Captain Rapper emphasized that we were to engage identifiable targets. I resented these restrictions at first and then grew to understand the reasoning behind the restrictions. I understood the reasoning, but I still didn't like it, especially when my men and I were being shot at.

> Friday, January 27
> 1350 hrs. Dear Mom and Dad,
> This is a quick note to let you know I'm okay. We are destroying this LZ at Two Bits (near Bong Son). I got a letter today, Ma, about Candice --don't worry. Also I got my lenses and cases. Thanks. But I have been wearing my glasses all the time. The dust and lack of sleep aren't conducive to wearing my lenses. Today we got some clean fatigues after a week. I still haven't had a bath in a week. Each day a logistic ship (supply chopper) brings us food, water, mail, toilet supplies, etc. So, we're pretty much okay. We are still destroying this LZ. By the time you get this letter, we may be gone on an operation out in the boonies somewhere or to guard Bong Son bridges. I still have some bunkers (4 of them) on the perimeter here, but most of the company has moved to the center of the LZ off the perimeter. I slept in bunker 43 last night and

Glasses I wore in Vietnam.

32 | JOE ABODEELY

called artillery illuminating fire on our area so we could see if people were moving toward our position. It's scary at night. An Khe got hit by 60 some NVA (North Vietnamese Army) troops the other day. I'm still afraid we're due for an attack because we're pulling people off this LZ, leaving ourselves with less defense. Oh, well. Things are all right. I'm in a little barricade affair made of oil drums, ammo boxes, and sandbags. I have two plastic ponchos for a roof to keep rain out. My RTO, Pee Wee (nickname), is here. I'm going to walk about 600 m to check bunker 38 because they've had radio trouble and civilians keep coming up to their position destroying the wire barricades, and we can't shoot them. In fact we had orders not to shoot unless fired on which puts us on the defense. What a screwed up war! Well, I'll write later.

    Love, Joe

    P. S. Handle the contact lens deal as you want.

[I think the reference to the contact lens deal was that I originally ordered a new set, but I didn't need them now. My dad was to cancel the order.]

1410 hrs. Last night (26 January) I went about 250 m forward to bunker 43. It was scary. Beginning at about 2400, I called Lieut. Stoneman, our artillery FO, and he called to the guns on LZ English to fire illuminating rounds. I didn't get much sleep last night. Today I just cleaned my M-16 and now I think I'll sleep after I read some mail I just got.

[I sometimes would check my defensive positions at night by actually going to them. I was careful, but that was a good way to get shot in the pitch-black night. It also ensured that my guys weren't sleeping during their watch shift.]

1545 hrs. Pee Wee, my RTO, got me some clean fatigues. Log ships (supply choppers) bring us water, food, and other items as we need them. Even though I haven't showered in a week, I feel clean with clean fatigues which I haven't had in a week.

Sunday, January 28

Maintained perimeter. We are still shrinking the perimeter. I had a discipline problem with Sgt. Stoddard, and the CO backed me 100%. I think it will be all right now. I know that my brother has a birthday, but I haven't been anywhere to get him something.

[I don't remember if it was a drinking problem or an insubordination or efficiency issue with Sgt. Stoddard.]

Monday, January 29

0740 hrs. We have shrunk the perimeter. There is only our company and an ARVN company in the compound on this LZ. The dozers have destroyed most of the bunkers. All of my platoon is on the east side of the runway, and we have three bunkers on the other side of the ARVN compound. We still have problems chasing the civilians off the old perimeter because they are such scavengers. I checked my perimeter (which is almost a straight line of defense) 0630 this morning.

Tuesday, January 30

1155 hrs. Last night we had an intelligence report of 500 NVA forming around Bong Son. It was a cloudy dark night last night. The Vietnamese celebrated their lunar new year last night at midnight by shooting off flares and rifles and automatic weapons. I moved my RTO and myself right next to the concertina wire of the ARVN compound. One of my bunkers said they received incoming fire. It could've been just the ARVN s celebrating. At about 0100 or 0130 all positions on our company perimeter were put on 100% alert. I was up all night. At LZ English, a bunker was hit by a rocket. Anyway, the truce we were on yesterday is broken. Today we get brand-new newly modified M-16s.

1950 hrs. Another sleepless night coming up. We got a report that an NVA company was spotted about 1000 m from here. Tomorrow, the company goes on an operation. We'll walk from here for about 7000 m. There are NVA all over. I hope all goes well tomorrow on my first combat operation. I've only slept 45 minutes today with almost no sleep last night.

Wednesday, January 31

1215 hrs. We moved out on company operation. Right now I'm sitting on a 2-foot wide trail. The jungle is so thick that the whole company is moving in a single file. We stopped about 45 minutes ago to eat C-rations. We've already crossed a couple of rice paddies. We all got new M-16s yesterday; I haven't fired mine yet.

The Tet Offensive had begun. Tet is the Chinese Lunar New Year's celebration, but the Communists intended their multiple attacks at various cities, towns, and military installations would prompt a popular uprising against the Republic of Vietnam (South Vietnam) and U.S. forces. It was an abysmal failure for the Communist forces of the Vietcong and the North Vietnamese Army, but the American media and others with their political agendas misinformed the American people and portrayed Tet as a Communist victory. This day had the distinction of having the most casualties of any day in the war.

Walter Cronkite reported:

"To say that we are closer to victory today is to believe, in the face of the evidence, the optimists who have been wrong in the past. To suggest we are on the edge of defeat is to yield to unreasonable pessimism. To say that we are mired in stalemate seems the only realistic, yet unsatisfactory, conclusion. On the off chance that military and political analysts are right, in the next few months we must test the enemy's intentions, in case this is indeed his last big gasp before negotiations. But it is increasingly clear to this reporter that the only rational way out then will be to negotiate, not as victors, but as an honorable people who lived up to their pledge to defend democracy, and did the best they could."

His editorial misrepresented that the US and ARVN forces were overwhelmed by Communist forces at Tet when the truth was the exact opposite. Even President Johnson realized that when the war lost the support of Cronkite, it lost the support of the American public.

February, 1968

Thursday, February 1

1605 hrs. Yesterday, we moved over some hills after we went through the thick stuff. We returned to our position by way of a large village. The people seemed wealthier than most with more cattle, water buffalo, and chickens. The edge of the village was along the river. We got a few sniper rounds but nothing of any consequence. At 0600 this morning, the whole company walked through the town of Bong Son to where we are now—the Bong Son bridges. These bridges are of very high strategic value as they link a vital supply line. I'm in my CP bunker at the south end of one of the bridges. I took a bath in the river after 13 days no bath.

Sometimes, we'd see a water buffalo being managed by a young boy. I heard stories about how it took many hits from U.S. weapons to put one down if it went berserk. We tried to stay clear of the animals if we could. Walking through the jungle and villages, my senses were heightened. It was as though I could see, hear, and smell as I never could before. My eyes scanned and panned trails or open fields or the tree line for suspected enemy positions. I listened intently for the thoomp of mortars or metallic sounds or the rattling of brush, but I sometimes heard a rooster crowing in the distance. I often smelled the smoke of burning wood from camp fires or betel nut which darkened its chewer's teeth.

Friday, February 2

1950 hrs. I'll lead a nine-man patrol almost 1000 m from the bridge today. I'll take eight of us to set up an LPOP on a sand bar to observe any VC crossing the river. I'm very scared and everyone says the job is dangerous, but I think it's important and to use the cliché—it's a challenge.

Saturday, February 3

1330 hrs. My eight-man patrol left after dark last night. We walked to the river close to the bank for cover and silent movement. At one point, part of the bank fell on my RTO knocking him down into the river. The radio got wet and we had no radio contact back to the company CP. We could hear them but we couldn't talk to them. We had to break squelch on the radio to signal them. We made positions along the bank with our backs to the river, but we got sniped at from the other side. We slept in a garden between the irrigation furrows. I thought for sure we had it.

This eight-man patrol (plus me) taught me many lessons. The Bong Son bridges spanned a wide river and were the only passage for vehicles and the rail lines on the bridges. We had an M-42 "duster" (tank chassis and two .40 mm pom-pom guns) near our bunker at our end of the bridge. It fired H&I (harassing and interdicting) missions into the jungles, "messing" with the VC, but a patrol needed to see what was out there. When I got the order to send out a patrol about 1 click (a thousand meters) from our bunker at the bridge to recon for VC, I had never led a combat patrol by myself before. I thought Sgt. Stoddard or his buddy, Sgt Ross, would take out the LPOP (listening post-observation post), but both Stoddard and Ross had their reasons why they couldn't lead a patrol along the river.

There were no other NCOs in the platoon at the time—only PFCs and Specialists—no "hard striper" sergeants. I looked at the guys and told them that I would take out the patrol. I sensed an "Are you shitting me?" response from some of the young men who knew I was a relatively new platoon leader in country. I had no choice as I had my orders to send a patrol along the river. I had previously been told that the bridge was so important that if the VC ever blew it up, I'd better be on it. There was a starlight scope and a 90 mm RR rifle with beehive rounds on the top of the bunker at our end of the bridge. These rounds had thousands of little darts (looked like miniature arrows) and were devastating antipersonnel ammunition.

The patrol would travel light—no packs, no food—only water, weapons, ammo, and the PRC-25 radio. Pee Wee carried the radio. At dark, we left our perimeter and bunker area, crossed the road and tracks and stepped down the steep riverbank into the water. The riverbank was 10 feet high and we walked at the base in the water sometimes up to our chests. As we traveled along, we had commo with the bunker, and we were being observed through the starlight scope. Some ARVNs or somebody was shooting from across the river. We were about halfway to our objective when Pee Wee touched the side of the riverbank and a large chunk of dirt came down on top of him knocking him and the radio into the river water. A PRC-25 radio has a handset like a telephone with a small circle at the mouth piece covered with a membrane that you speak into. When it gets wet, it doesn't work. The bunker could no longer see or hear us.

We traveled about a click from the bunker, got out of the river, and made a small perimeter on a furrowed field facing the jungle with the river to our backs. The bunker personnel tried to contact us; we could hear their calls, but they could not hear us. The handset was wet. When the radio is on, it makes a *shissss* sound. When you squeeze the hand set to talk, it stops the *shissss*. My call sign was "Heavy Bones 2-6." The bunker was "Heavy Bones 2-6 Alpha." We figured out a way to communicate. "Heavy Bones 2-6; this is Heavy bones 2-6 Alpha. If you are having radio trouble, break squelch twice. Over." We replied *schissss...schissss*. "Heavy Bones 2-6, if you are at your objective, break squelch once. Over." Schissss. "If you are all right, break squelch three times. Over." *Schisss...schissss...schissss...* And so it was.

We all tried to stay awake lying in a circle with our feet touching another's foot to kick the other guy awake. But we were wet and cold—no cover, no jackets, no blankets. The jungle was maybe 30 or 40 meters to our front and one good hand grenade toss could have killed all of us. We lasted the night, and with dawn we moved into the jungle and made our way back to the bunker. We crossed some streams and I distinctly remember getting a several inches-long leech on my leg. I borrowed a lit cigarette (I never smoked) and burned the leech off.

Lessons learned: A leader must lead. He must lead by example, not by just giving orders. Take care of your people. Take care of all critical equipment, including radios. Radio communication is important for coordination, resupply, fire support, or help. Never ask your subordinates to do anything that YOU wouldn't do. From then on, I never had a problem with my men going out on a patrol or LPOP (listening post-observation post).

> Sunday, February 4
> 0950 hrs. Dear Mom and Dad,
> We're here at the Bong Son bridges. We walked from LZ Two Bits a couple of days ago. These bridges (2) are extremely important as a supply link. We are to defend these bridges at all costs. My platoon guards the south end of one of them and I've got two-M-60 machine guns on two of my bunkers. Night before last I took an 8-man patrol along the river (in the water) about 600 m to set up an ambush and observation post. My RTO (radio man) fell in the water and the radio got wet and wouldn't work all night. The whole company was worried. We got sniped at by some VC on the other side of the river. I got my men to a garden where we stayed all night crouched between little irrigation furrows for cover. I was really scared, but I was surprised that I could stay fairly calm. It's scary when you hear bullets *twang* over you especially when the only cover you have is nothing except darkness to conceal you. We'll be at these bridges for a couple of days and then go out on an operation. In about a week, we'll probably go to Hue near the DMZ.
> I wonder what the States' newspapers are saying, but we're on a big push. So are the VC. Don't worry; I plan on being very careful. I've got a CO that I like. He's ROTC (from UCLA) and he was an athlete, too. He used to wrestle, also.

He's from Santa Monica, California. He sent me on that patrol because I guess he figured I could handle it best even though I'm the newest lieut. in the company. Also it's unusual to go out with less than a platoon but I did all right with only 8 men.

    I still haven't been to a PX since I was at An Khe so I haven't got Bob a present, yet. I'll still get him one, but I don't know when I'll get back to civilization. I lost Bob's flashlight, but I still have mine. I sure miss that red bulb for night, but I'll fix mine up. Around the bridges, near my gate on the bridge, are some huts. The kids sell Cokes and shine our boots. I always take a couple of my men with me and we have our M-16s wherever we go. I have found out by quizzing the kids that there are a lot of VC in the area. One of the problems of this war is that the VC harasses us at night and we can't shoot unless we're sure it's them because we might be shooting at some farmer or kids standing by the fence.

    Well, I just got a call on the radio. I've got to go to the company CP. I'll write later. I'm fine.

    Love, Joe

2110 hrs. Nothing exciting happened today. I fired about 3 M-72 LAWs (light antitank weapons) off the bridge. It's dark now and Sgt. Stoddard, Pee Wee, Sneed, and I are listening to my transistor. I got a letter from Lieut. Lindsey (first platoon leader) this evening. We'll probably go on an operation Tuesday.

Monday, February 5
1120 hrs. Dear Mom and Dad,
   I wrote a letter yesterday but I'm writing today because we'll probably go out in the boonies for a couple of days beginning tomorrow. I see the colonel's chopper from my bunker up here on the bridge so he's probably telling my CO what our operation will be. Anyway enclosed you'll find a pay voucher. What I'll do is send them home for you to save as they'll get wet if I keep them in my field pack or on my person. I still haven't got paid my $50 norm pay but it will probably come this February 15 or maybe it was included in the money sent to you. All my check except $50 pay each 15th of the month to me will go home to you.
   I'm going to carry my transistor with me once we get to Hue so would you please send me some transistor radio batteries? The best I can describe them are that they are nine volt with the snap on connection. The battery I have now is a Novel, 006P, nine volt. Send me about 3 of them as I owe one of the other platoon leaders a battery and they are virtually impossible to get where we are and where we've been.
   Nothing else much is new. We've been guarding the bridge and taking it easy. Some of the villagers came up to one of 3rd platoon's positions saying there were VC in the village, and these people wanted protection; but we couldn't do anything because if we shot into the huts, we'd kill some innocent people. Meanwhile, we can only shoot when fired upon and when the target is positively identified. This war is really lousy. I'll write later.
   Love, Joe

1635 hrs. I played touch football on the sand in the riverbed for the last 1½ hours. I found out that we'll go on an operation Thursday. Sneed told me that two men in C Company got killed while walking point.

[The point man was the first person in the order of movement. He moved out ahead of the unit, whether squad, platoon, company, etc., and was a likely first target for the enemy. A good point man could detect booby traps or ambushes ahead of time and keep the rest of the unit out of trouble. A not-so-good point man or an unlucky one could get killed.]

Tuesday, February 6

1655 hrs. I went to one of the huts outside my bunker perimeter and I got a haircut. The barber used hand clippers. He also shaved the hair on my forehead and ears. Then he cleaned the inside of my ears. He also shaved my face and gave me a hand, neck, shoulders, and forearm massage. I gave him $2.30 American money which was too much, but I felt it was worth it. I bathed in the river today. It's cool and windy now.

[Normally when we bought goods or services, we used MPC (military pay certificate) rather than U.S. currency. U.S. money could be converted to MPC to avoid U.S. money from getting into the Vietnamese economy.]

Wednesday, February 7

2043 hrs. Tomorrow, we'll air assault at 0900. We'll go about 4000 m from here on a search and destroy mission. We may not go to Hue for a while because of guarding these bridges and the need to operate around this area. Tomorrow will be my first air assault. I'm ready to go to bed now on these wooden boards.

I wonder if I'll ever be able to sleep in a bed again. Sneed and Powell (first squad) are sitting here bullshitting right now. We should be on this operation for 10 days or so. We got another starlight scope for the platoon. I took the grenadiers and one machine gunner down the road to fire their .45 pistols which they carry along with their main weapons. I coached them on their firing and they shoot pretty well.

Thursday, February 8

1910 hrs. We walked from the bridges instead of being air assaulted. We're now in an open field with two platoons in a perimeter defense. We are in VC Valley. How appropriate. We did a lot of walking today.

I remember searching lots of VC bunkers and "spider holes" (foxholes with camouflaged covers from which a VC can spring and fire) in VC Valley. They had been abandoned, but we used thermite and concussion grenades to destroy what we could to deny their use in the future. I sometimes felt bad about going through a village with about 30 heavily armed soldiers searching homes and possessions of the people, but we had to do that.

Friday, February 9

1910 hrs. It's just getting dark now so I'll make my entry. I had lead platoon today for the company, and we moved through many huts and villages. We checked them out as we moved. We have a perimeter in a graveyard. It's dangerous here because of mountains nearby where VC can sneak up and fire down on us. I'm going to sleep on the ground near a big mound (grave). We have a mortar tube set up about 20 m away and it just fired a couple of spotting rounds in a nearby mountain. I hope we don't get hit tonight as we are vulnerable. I already checked my positions.

Our company had four platoons—three rifle or infantry platoons and one 81 mm mortar platoon. Sometimes as in this case we moved out in company-size operations; sometimes in platoon-size operations; or as previously described in the Bong Son bridge patrol—squad-size or less. The "spotting rounds" fired by our mortars was basically a "sighting in" action for the tubes. The Vietnamese buried their dead above ground in this area because if they dug too deep they'd hit water. The graves were large round mounds which provided us cover as we slept near them. We also felt confident that the VC would not mortar the graves of their ancestors.

Saturday, February 10

1300 hrs. We're just relaxing right now. We'll move out, each platoon in a different area, to set up "goats" (ambushes). We'll leave at 1400. We (second platoon) already went on a patrol this morning. We got on a hill where I could see for miles. I can even see the South China Sea about 4500 m away. My RTO heard a call on the radio last night that two VC battalions are formed in the area. In the past few days I've done a lot of walking and searching of villages but no VC. We may hit some soon. I'm not so scared anymore, but I still try to be cautious.

We were patrolling and trying to get to a designated location when we came to this cliff on our direction of movement, rising straight up in front of us. My recollection is 20 feet or more. We had our packs, other web gear, weapons, and ammo; but we grabbed vines and other vegetation and climbed to the top of this hill where I could see for miles. I started singing the lyrics to the song "I Can See for Miles." The U.S.S. New Jersey was off the coast conducting a fire mission. I saw the fire, the smoke, and then heard the report from the battleship's big guns firing. I could actually follow a shell traverse many clicks away and crash into the jungle off in the distance. Trees and earth flew on impact. Naval gunfire, especially battleship naval gunfire, is very impressive.

USS New Jersey firing off the coast of Vietnam (Wikipedia).

Sunday, February 11

1540 hrs. Nothing happened last night. We did a lot of walking straight up about to the V of a box canyon where we set up an ambush site. Today we walked over 4500 m and we are now near the South China Sea which is to the east over a small mountain about one click (1000 m) away. Tonight my platoon is to set up an ambush across the rice paddies on a graveyard area about 300 m away. The chopper should pick us up tomorrow. I let my platoon burn an old shot-up house today.

Monday, February 12

1620 hrs. We set up our ambush perimeter site at a graveyard in the middle of the rice paddies. We walked to the site on dikes so we didn't get wet. The graveyard was a grassy area with mounds for graves. We positioned ourselves behind the mounds. Nothing happened last night except it rained early in the morning, and my whole platoon and I got soaked. We walked back to where the company CP was, and we were picked up by Chinook helicopters (carries a whole platoon) and brought here—LZ Mustang. We'll be running patrols from here. I'm still drying off as my clothes and gear are wet. I haven't slept on a bed in a long time and I miss it.

Tuesday, February 13

2030 hrs. As can be seen, the pages are wet. I went on a patrol today and we waded several streams and forded a river. A year ago today, I entered active duty in the Army. I should be a 1st Lieutenant today, but apparently the paperwork hasn't gone through yet. My feet are still cold from being wet.

Wednesday, February 14

1435 hrs. The battalion cmdr. just left and since the CO was at LZ English and Lieut. Gaylord was on a mission, I was ranking man and I greeted the battalion cmdr. He asked what we were doing and I said we were just taking it easy which is the wrong thing to say. Anyway, I corrected it by saying we were doing certain tasks. I took a chopper to LZ English today and picked up my goodies that Mike, Roberta, and Kathleen sent. I wrote them thank-you letters.

2310 hrs. I just checked the map for a patrol tomorrow. I'm writing by flashlight light as it is dark in this bunker. I already hear the mosquitoes buzzing around.

Thursday, February 15

2100 hrs. We really traveled today. We spotted many old bunkers and fighting positions, and we destroyed them with concussion grenades. We blew the hell out of them. About 15 minutes ago we had a 100% alert. A grenade exploded inside the perimeter. We fired flares and the quad .50 caliber machine gun and mortars and artillery, but we couldn't see the VC who threw the grenade.

Friday, February 16
1515 hrs. Dear Mom and Dad,
 I believe the last time I wrote I was at the Bong Son bridges. We were to make an air assault (platoon carried by choppers) but we walked out on an operation because nonavailability of choppers. We set up ambushes, platoon- and squad-size, and we slept in graveyards while out in the boonies. We were airlifted by Chinook choppers to LZ Mustang farther north in the An Lao Valley where I am now. We'll be here for a few more days and then we'll go out in the boonies again or maybe back to the bridges. Tomorrow I go on my 1st air assault. About 7 choppers will take my platoon and drop us off somewhere.
 I got my hair cut today. A Vietnamese with hand clippers did the cutting. We're near another river so I bathe once in a while. I haven't been near a PX or any Americanized area since An Khe. I still haven't had a chance to get Bob anything for his birthday because I have been out in the jungle and rice paddies the whole time. As soon as I get back to civilization, I'll send him something. I got paid my $50 norm pay for February and enclosed is the receipt. How is my money-saving doing? Mom, I got a letter from

a Sister Maria who said she met you. It was a nice informal acquaintance letter so I guess I'd best answer. What's new in Tucson? Everything here is pretty much the same, but at the same time there's always excitement and adventure. Yesterday on a patrol, I had my men blow up old bunkers we found which the VC had built and used. A friend of mine, 1st Lieut. Stoneman, is an artillery forward observer (FO) and he goes out with my platoon a lot. I'm glad of that because if we run into anything we can't handle, we can back off or get behind good cover and he can call artillery in to cover us. Dad, how is the practice teaching going? Also, how is my car running? That reminds me that I've ruined my driver's license crossing a stream. The water came up to my neck but I held my M-16 out of the water. We got the new M-16s which don't jam and my weapon works beautifully. We're still waiting to go to Hue. I don't know if the States get the same info we do but there's a lot of action going on at Hue and Saigon. I just as soon hang around here even though there are NVA, just not as many. Today, I hopped a ride with a bubble chopper (two-seater, small) and I reconned the area where we'll go tomorrow. The pilot and I saw a gigantic buck on a hill (looked like an elk) and I said, "Let's get it." We swooped down on the deer and I threw a hand grenade at it, but it was already hidden in the foliage. I threw grenades two more separate times, but we couldn't see the deer. Oh, well, the C-rations aren't that bad. Well, Mom and Dad, say "hi" to everyone for me and don't worry about me anymore; I've got the hang of things a bit better so I know more what's going on. I'm still cautious though. I'll write later.

    Love Joe

Friday, February 16, (cont.)

1635 hrs. Today is Friday—it's TGIF and I wouldn't have known it was Friday unless I'd have opened this book. Tomorrow my platoon is to go on air assault. Today I hopped a ride on a bubble chopper and reconned the area. They fly treetop level. The pilot and I saw a deer (big buck) and I tried to get it three times with a hand grenade but it hid in the foliage. I just took a cold dip in the river. Cold running water surely wakes one up.

I was helping my platoon fix some fighting positions, and I had my shirt off. A "bubble chopper" landed and my CO showed me a map where my platoon was to air assault the next day. He told me to jump in the chopper and recon the LZ. I grabbed my shirt and no other equipment—helmet, web gear, or rifle—and we took off. The pilot loved to zigzag and climb and dip, and we went above a forest. Suddenly, I saw a big buck in an open area among the trees. The helicopter is a two-seater and between the pilot and me was an ammo can filled with fragmentation hand grenades. I grabbed three of them and we made a couple of passes so I could throw them out at the deer. We had been eating C-rations for a while, and venison would have been great; but I never hit the deer. War is hell.

Saturday, February 17

1700 hrs. Dear Mom and Dad,
I got your last letter dated 10 February. This letter will be short and fast. We're moving tomorrow from here--LZ Mustang (An Lao Valley) to LZ English tomorrow. Then up north near Hue. We've been expecting to go there all along and now I guess it's here. That's where the hottest action is so I guess I'll be even more cautious.
Ma, I wrote Sister Maria in Cleveland. Also, Charlene (Uncle Joe's wife) wrote me and I wish you'd write her for me and thank her for writing. I'm just writing this letter now to you and I won't have time to write to her as I have to get

my gear ready for tomorrow and also check on my men. I'll probably have to send a squad out on an ambush tonight, too, so I have many things to do. I'm glad Bob finally got on the ball. I knew he could do it if he wanted to but he just didn't have any constructive or realistic values set for him.

Well, I'll cut it short. Say "hi" to everyone for me. Don't worry, I'll be careful. Oh! The CO told me the paperwork for my promotion to 1st Lieut. is in, but the col. hasn't received it yet and when he does he'll come out to wherever we are and pin the silver bar on me. Remember, Mom, when you pinned my gold bar on and Dad took the pictures of it? Well, I'll write when I can if it's dry or if I'm under shelter. I keep letter-writing material in my pack in a plastic bag. It should be okay.

Love, Joe

2037 hrs. We didn't go on an air assault after all as it was third platoon's turn to go out. We got the news today that we are moving north to Hue or close to it. There's a lot of action there. I've packed for tomorrow. First platoon set off hand poppers from LZ Tate just one click away. We are firing .50 caliber ammo to get rid of it as we're moving. The CO said the paperwork is in for my being first lieut. When it reaches the col., he'll come out and pin the silver bar on me—so I'm told.

Sunday, February 18

2045 hrs. We're here are at LZ English again all bunched up on the ground to sleep. We flew by Hueys (choppers). I love to fly in helicopters—it's almost like really flying. The CO is at a meeting now.

Monday, February 19

2110 hrs. I'm sitting in foxhole at Quang Tri. Doc, Pee Wee, Sneed, and I are huddled together. Sgt. Stoddard and one other man from my platoon were on the other plane from LZ English and they haven't come in yet. In fact, only first and second platoon are here. It's drizzling, but we put ponchos over us. We are nearer to Hue and this whole area is bad. We're listening to my portable radio. We have a little light bulb hooked up to a PRC-25 battery. Sneed and I are playing Crazy Eights (cards).

Tuesday, February 20

2210 hrs. I'm writing by my pocket flashlight. We left Quang Tri by convoy today and came here to Camp Evans. It was wet, cold, and miserable last night. We're going out on an operation tomorrow. I believe it will drizzle all the time here. We are now north of Hue about 4 miles. I'm afraid we'll see a lot of action here. I'm going to sleep on top of my duffel bag, as the floor of this bunker is wet and muddy.

Wednesday, February 21

1909 hrs. At 0600 this morning we "saddled up" to move to where we are now. Along with our full field gear, we have been wearing flak vests as VC and NVA here have artillery. Today we flew from Camp Evans to where we are now which is between Hue and the DMZ. The choppers buzzed very low over the rice paddies and it's almost like flying without a machine as I sit next to the door (open). We landed here near a bridge and a village. Just our company and some ARVNs on the bridge are defending two artillery batteries—six 155 mm guns and six 8-inch guns. My platoon made bunkers all day from scraps of this old French compound. Today another building was dynamited to clear for artillery fire. Sgt. Stoddard went to see a doctor today about a swollen leg. Sgt. Blanko from third platoon is with me now. He's a fine NCO.

[The "old French compound" was a series of masonry buildings previously a convent or monastery, but it had suffered the ravages of war. Our company was providing security for the artillery batteries that were providing fire support for action around Hue. We used scraps of the damaged buildings for our bunkers. The tin from the damaged building's roof I used really vibrated from the concussion of the artillery blasts. I decided to move my position.]

Thursday, February 22

2140 hrs. I moved into one of the old French buildings where the company CP is because one of the 175 mm guns is blasting away right outside my bunker, and the shockwave is too great. We got sniper rounds last night and some already tonight.

Friday, February 23

1015 hrs. My third squad built this latrine where I'm sitting now. My platoon has built some outstanding bunkers. In fact some of the people started bunkers and tore them down again to improve them, and I didn't tell them to do so. Sgt. Stoddard came back on a log ship this morning. The howitzer just fired and shook the hell out of this shit house. Sgt. Blanko went in today as he cut his shin on an engineer stake. Today we'll probably repair our defensive wire.

1200 hrs. Dear Mom and Dad,
Here I am again at a different place. The last time I wrote I was at LZ Mustang in the An Lao Valley area and since then I've flown to an

airbase at Quang Tri and then took the truck convoy to Camp Evans about 5 miles away and then flew by chopper to where I am now which is less than 10 miles north of Hue. The choppers picked us up at Camp Evans and buzzed real low along the rice paddies, villages, and fields before we landed by this old French compound near a bridge on a river. I really enjoy flying in helicopters. That's why the 1st Cavalry Division here is such an outstanding unit. We have much logistical support and air support and transport by choppers.

Air Cavalry Huey at Camp Evans.

Flying crane

Right now D Company (my company) is at this old French compound. The artillery has two batteries (comparable to an infantry company) here which just my company is defending. The howitzers are right next to us. In fact one of the guns was 20 m from my bunker and when it fired I had to move out because the muzzle blast shook my bunker and it caused too much concussion. These guns are firing on Hue. I wonder if the news in the States is talking about all the fighting going on at Hue. If we take the city or level it, I'll probably move even farther north. As it is now we're almost on the DMZ. My people have been building bunkers for the past few days we've been here because besides VC, there are NVA (North Vietnamese Army--regular troops, not just guerrillas) here with all the weapons--

artillery and antitank weapons and automatic weapons that we have. Night before last we got a couple of mortar rounds and three people from 1st platoon got wounded by shrapnel. One of my bunkers had two grenades thrown right in front of it. Whenever we receive sniper fire or grenades, I leave my bunker and move along the perimeter to check my people and make sure they are all right. Also, I try to assess what's happening to act accordingly.

    Our CO doesn't like us to fire indiscriminately into adjacent villages because of innocent people, but the goddamned VC and NVA shoot from the same village which is 50 m from our perimeter, and we can only fire when we have a definite target instead of leveling the whole village, which we can do. Right now I'm in one of the old French buildings where the company CP is. CP means command post or headquarters. I left my platoon CP to sleep here last night because of the artillery firing. This building here has shingles on the roof half blown off by fire, and every time one of the howitzers fires, shingles fall. We all try to dodge the bits and pieces as they fall. I hope our company pulls security for these guns for a while because we're dug in here.

    It's drizzled every day since we've been here except for day before yesterday. We are always wet and muddy and it's cold up here. I have just a sweater under my jungle fatigues to keep me warm. Also, we got issued flak vests which we wear. They have a nylon (pressed) fiber inside to help stop shrapnel and other bursting shell fragments.

    Well, I'm running out of info. I just thought I'd write to let you know I'm still okay. If we go any farther north, though, we'll be heading for Hanoi. Ma, I got your letter postmarked 16 February. Also speaking of batteries, I could use some flashlight batteries size AA for a penlight. Many times my penlight came in handy. I'm sorry I lost Bob's penlight though.

    Everything else is pretty much the same. We're in a perimeter defense here and I send out and takeout patrols occasionally. I always keep my people alert so if we get hit hard, we'll come out okay. Also if we look alert, maybe the VC and NVA won't mess with us; and that's equally fine with me as long as we get our jobs done. I've got a good platoon and even though I'm frequently uncomfortable and the area is dangerous, I'm living through some experience. I'll write in the next few days or if we have to leave suddenly.

    Love Joe

    P.S. I darkened in my yellow bar on my fatigues, as I'm a 1st Lieut.

We were at this old French compound providing security for 8-inch guns (8-inch diameter shells) and 175 mm artillery batteries. The guns gave fire support to the Marines and some 1st Cav units at the battle of Hue, the ancient Imperial Capital of Vietnam. The NVA had captured portions of Hue Citadel, and their intent was to "liberate" the entire city as part of a countrywide popular uprising to sweep the Communist insurgents into power. They failed. The people of Hue turned their backs on the Communists as did people in other parts of Vietnam during the Tet offensive, and the ensuing 26-day effort by the U.S. Marines, U.S. Army, and ARVN to recapture the Citadel produced a stunning military defeat for the invaders. Yet the strategic victory ultimately went to the Communists because the media led by Walter Cronkite misinformed the American public about the U.S. success at Hue. The scenes of bloody fighting in Hue, Saigon, and other cities in Vietnam during the Tet offensive really shocked the American people who experienced a war for the first time up close on their television sets, so that the pressure to withdraw from the war became overwhelming.

The postscript about darkening my yellow bar referred to the rank insignia on my jungle fatigues. A second lieutenant insignia was a subdued yellow bar, and the first lieutenant was a black bar; hence, I darkened the yellow bar with a pen.

Saturday, February 24

1040 hrs. At about 0600 we received mortar fire on the bridge. Three ARVNs were wounded, one mortally. I got out of this one-man hole which my men built for me and checked two bunkers where we were firing M-79s for searching fire. It's drizzling again and everything is muddy and slushy and wet. Right now my people are repairing the wire which they didn't do yesterday.

Late entry—1044 hrs. The battalion cmdr. flew in by chopper and pinned my first lieut. bar on me.

My battalion commander was LTC Roscoe (Robbie) Robinson. He was a Black man, or as we said in those days, Negro. He was an excellent officer and later became a four-star general. LTC Robinson was one of the first and few Blacks to attain general officer rank after the Vietnam War. Another prominent Black general officer who served in Vietnam was Colin Powell. Many people do not know that in WWII, military units were segregated. President Truman integrated the services during the Korean War.

Sunday, February 25

1636 hrs. This morning the company HQ, first platoon, and second platoon (mine) swept the area. My platoon was sniped at about four times. I'm wet and muddy and cold and miserable. My feet are shriveled up from being wet.

When we conducted "sweeps," we walked through jungles, on the sands along the coastal area, crossed streams and rice paddies, searched villages—the houses, hooches, or huts. We looked for VC, NVA, weapons, or rice caches, which were their food supply. In the more vegetated areas, I moved my platoon along in a column, or single file, or a modified column, which was more of an oval-looking formation, if the terrain allowed enough space. Our weapons were always "at the ready." Many of us who carried an M-16 would take a hand grenade ring from the pin and attach it to the front rifle sight. Then we'd take a nylon cord or shoelace and fasten it to the ring at the front of the rifle and to the stock at the rear. We slung our improvised sling over the shoulder and had the shooting hand on the pistol grip of the rifle and the thumb on the selector switch of the rifle ready to flick it from "safety" to "semi" to "auto," if necessary. But my main job was to lead and direct my platoon, not fire my gun. When we crossed open areas, like rice paddies or along the sands or if we were in an assault phase, I put my platoon "on line"—a straight lateral line with weapons forward for maximum firepower. I believe our "ready for action" image may have prevented some hostile contacts by the "bad guys."

> 1645 hrs. Dear Mom and Dad,
> Well, it's still rainy and drizzling outside and the sun hasn't shown since I've been at this place (the old French compound about 7 to 10 miles northwest of Hue). I just got back in from a sweep made by the company HQ (headquarters--CO and his radioman and artillery forward observer), the 1st platoon, and the 2nd platoon (mine). We moved on line through the villages looking for VC and NVA (North Vietnamese Army) troops. My platoon, which led, was fired on at least 4 times today. The sniper shots came close to my men and me because we can hear the crack of the bullet as it breaks the sound barrier and then the *twang* as it goes by. All of my platoon and I hit the dirt (mud) whenever we come under fire. Then I get on the radio and tell the CO and the 1st platoon wherever they are what's happening.
> None of my people were injured--just "pissed off" about the mud and slush and all-day drizzling. This monsoon season is supposed to

last for about 3 weeks more. Right now I'm sitting in a rectangular foxhole about 8' x 4' and about 3 feet high. My clothes and boots are covered with mud. My shirt and pants are wet-- the pants are soaked from crossing streams and ponds. My feet are shriveled and cold. I'm very uncomfortable but believe it or not I feel as though I'm doing something worthwhile. Hue is pretty well controlled on the outside by our troops but scattered units of VC and NVA are still inside.

Mom, I got your letter with the letters from the schoolchildren. Thank them for me. Also I am in the 1st Air Cavalry Division. Then there are other units under it. I'm in the 2nd of the 7th Cav under the 1st Air Cavalry Division.
The 2nd of the 7th is Gen. Custer's old outfit. Don't worry; we're not planning any last stand anywhere. Yesterday, the battalion commander pinned on my silver bar for 1st Lieut. I made 1st Lieut. the 13th of February and I get paid from that date. Well, I guess I'll heat my C-rations and eat now. I'm fine except for being a little uncomfortable.

Love Joe

Monday, February 26

1705 hrs. I'm sitting on the "shit can" that third squad made. I moved from my gravelike foxhole to one of the old buildings. There is tin on the roof and I made a secondary roof of tin. The CO and I took a bath in the river. It was freezing but I felt better afterwards. My platoon HQ is making a bunker. It's going to be a good one. It's still overcast and drizzling. I hope the monsoon season ends soon. I got radio batteries from home and a lecture from Carol McKune in Louisiana. Third platoon brought in a VC suspect. My new hooch is good except no adequate overhead cover from mortar fire.

[My recollection is that the "lecture" was about being safe and not to try to be a "hero."]

Tuesday, February 27

1735 hrs. I haven't much time. We just got back from an operation. My platoon went on a patrol north along the river. We were pinned down and surrounded by sniper fire by what seemed to be a company, possibly battalion. The CO brought the rest of the platoons. Five of my men were wounded. I thought several times today that I was going to die. Thank God we're back. Now we have to move by 1815 to somewhere else.

On February 27, Capt. Rapper (my CO) called me over to his CP and said, "Skeeter," (as he used to call me and as we looked at a map) "I want you to take your platoon and go north along the river." We were hoping to make contact with the enemy. I got my platoon ready—we checked our weapons, ammo, smoke and fragmentation grenades, gear, radios and SOI (signal operating instructions), and C-rations. We walked out of the perimeter at the French compound and proceeded on our mission. Occasionally, we heard the artillery at the base pound away on fire missions directed in support of units at the ancient city of Hue. The Marines and a couple of units of the 1st Cav saw hell in the battle of Hue. And these big guns had supported them.

It had been raining for days, but the sun was out this day. My platoon moved out in relatively open areas in a modified squad column for ease of movement, control, and security. I formed the platoon into three squads—each with a PRC-25 radio, and I had two RTOs with PRC-25s at my side for constant communication. When we got into the jungle, we went into single file with troops posted as flank security, and I positioned my RTOs and me behind the lead squad for the best command and control and reaction capability.

We came to a village, which was deserted except for an old man who had his nose cut off. His face had the triangle scar of where his nose should be (like the triangle cut in a Halloween pumpkin). He told us that there was no VC (Vietcong) in the area. Sgt. Duk (pronounced Duke), an ARVN interpreter along with us, did the questioning; neither Duk nor I believed this guy. We left him and moved through the empty village. It was ominous that no one else was around.

As we moved along on our patrol, we were still moving in a platoon column formation with my RTOs and me positioned behind the lead squad. I heard small arms fire up in front of my lead squad. Since we all had stopped to eat lunch (our Cs), I checked to see what was happening up front. Specialist 4 Sands (the point man) told me that he saw what appeared to be an ARVN (Army of the Republic of Viet Nam soldier) fire at him. The ARVNs were the soldiers of the Republic of South Vietnam—the people we were there to protect from the Communist NVA (who invaded from the north) and the Vietcong who were insurgents and "terrorists" to the people and government of South Vietnam.

Sands said he shot the "ARVN," and he thought he hit him. He said he thought the guy was an ARVN because he was wearing green fatigues. Whoever this guy was, he wasn't friendly. We moved to the area where Sand described, and we saw a small ditch. We also saw some blood, which indicated that Sands hit the "ARVN." At about the time we found the blood, a small "bubble" chopper flew overhead nearby and we heard automatic weapons fire apparently directed at the chopper. I did not want to pursue the "ARVN" who we thought did the firing at the chopper because it looked like he was leading us away from our objective—which was to proceed along the river heading north. We ignored his firing as we continued along the river.

Finally, we got to a road, which went over a small wooden bridge, which traversed the small stream. There were trees and other thick foliage around the bridge and stream. The platoon carefully and quickly crossed the bridge and assembled behind and around an abandoned stone house surrounded with trees and other vegetation. On the side of the house to our front was a rice paddy clearing with the tree line and stone buildings approximately a couple hundred meters away. Sands came back to my location and said, "2-6, I just saw about 12 or 13 NVA moving along in a trench" off to our left front. "2-6" was my call sign and nickname. The "2" meant second platoon and the "6" meant leader. He assured me they were NVA because of their khaki uniforms and pith helmets.

I immediately tried to get everyone assembled in a good defensive position around the house because we weren't dug in and were extremely vulnerable. All of a sudden all hell broke loose! RPG (rocket-propelled grenade) rounds started coming in, exploding on the other side of the stone house. Automatic weapons fire seemed to come continuously from our left front, front, and right front. Bullets were popping by us no matter where we moved. Bullets make a *pop* or *crack* sound as they break the sound barrier when coming very close to you.

I saw Sands lying in a prone position popping out a lot of rounds from his M-16. I saw a bullet hit his steel pot (helmet) and throw sparks as it glanced off. Sgt. Villa, Sands backup point man, stood up behind Sands and fired several rounds. All of a sudden he got hit in the arm and in the torso. Some of us were able to get into one of the NVA trenches near our position for cover. Bullets were coming from everywhere, and we expended a lot of ammo in return fire. A blond kid we called "Smitty" was firing his M-60 machine gun from an old leafless tree. He was standing up behind the tree making the machine gun spew forth its rain of steel as fast as the metal links of the ammunition belt would allow without jamming the gun. Since he was not behind cover, he took a round clean through his arm.

We got him into our location in the trench, gave him morphine; and he slept throughout the rest of the firefight. When Sgt. Villa got hit, Dr. Henderson (my medic) and I crawled out of the trench under heavy enemy fire and dragged Villa back to the trench. Villa was gurgling; he had been shot in the arm, spun around, and shot in the lung. I found out later that he had transported to Tokyo and lived. I now had five men wounded (three with the first incoming RPGs), then Villa and Smitty.

Lieut. Stoneman, the artillery forward observer who came along with us, was trying desperately to get some artillery support for us. He kept calling on his radio for artillery, but all the guns were trained on Hue because there was a lot of action going on there, so we couldn't get artillery. I saw Sgt. Ross take out a C-ration can of apricots, open it, and start to eat. I asked him what the hell he was doing, and he said, "Sir, we're surrounded; we can't go anywhere; so why not eat the apricots?" There was some logic to his thinking. But I had a firefight to contend with. We were completely surrounded by a much larger and entrenched force; I had wounded men; and we could not get artillery support. Things were not good.

At one point, we tried to see if we could get back across the bridge. I asked a young sgt. to take a few men to see if they could get back over the bridge. He said, "Sir, we'll all get killed if we go out there." As scared as I was, I knew I was going to have to lead a few men to check out the withdrawal route. I took my RTO and a few other men and we slowly eased out of the NVA trench and low crawled to a plowed field. Bullets were still flying everywhere as we hugged the earth for dear life. As our mini "patrol" inched back toward the little wooden bridge, two snipers in trees at the bridge started firing at us. They pinned us down and we couldn't move. Lieut. Stoneman was able to get an ARA (aerial rocket artillery gunship). It was a Huey armed with rocket pods and two M-60 door gunners. The ARA's call sign was "Blue Max."

As we inched toward the bridge, the snipers kept us pinned down, so we lay flat in the furrows of the field. I could hear the snap of the bullets breaking the sound barrier as they passed by. We hugged those furrows for dear life. We directed the ARA to fire on the trees with the snipers. The helicopter made a couple of passes firing rockets. The screaming hiss of the rockets seemed to go right over our heads and convinced me we would be hit by "friendly fire." I just knew they would hit us—but they didn't. The gunship did a good job of hitting where we told him, but the snipers were still there. We crawled back to the trench after the unsuccessful attempt to get back across the bridge.

The firefight continued; at one point, we called in a couple of Medevac choppers for our wounded. Prior to their arrival, Sgt. Blanko, my platoon sergeant, and I used machetes to try to clear a LZ (landing zone) so they could land. We hacked at saplings and brush and made a suitable LZ to pick up our wounded. For some mysterious reason, the NVA firing lightened up as we were clearing the area. As the Medevac helicopters began their descent and then landed, the NVA quit firing. We loaded the five wounded troopers onto the choppers, and they took off. After the Medevac choppers were in the air, out of the fighting, and on their way to save lives, the firing started up again. To this day I don't know why the NVA stopped shooting when they did, but I'd like to think they recognized the big Red Cross on the front of the Medevac ships and honored the Geneva Conventions.

While all of these events were occurring, we of course notified Heavy Bones 6 (my CO), and he was bringing the first and third and mortar platoons up to give us some support. It seemed to take forever for them to get to our location. Prior to their arrival, we were able to get some "4-Deuce" fire support. I never really appreciated the effectiveness of the 4.2-inch mortar until that day. When those 4.2-inch mortar rounds were called in, they came crashing down in the open rice paddy entry and tree line in front of us. The explosions were tremendous—trees were flying, smoke was rising—the *thoomp—thoomp, thoomp—thoomp* had rhythm. One has to remember that the 4.2-inch round is like a 105 mm howitzer round; in fact, it's bigger; it's 107 mm; so we finally got artillery after all.

As Capt. Rapper got closer to our location, he tried to pinpoint where we were. We guided him to our location over the radio, but it was difficult for the rest of the company to know where we were because we had traveled through some jungle; and now, we were taking cover in NVA trenches. To make matters even worse, first platoon was "reconning by fire" (shooting randomly into the jungle to secure their path of approach) as they came to us from our right rear. We were worried about getting hit by our own guys now. We stayed low, and eventually, Delta Company got to the tree line to the right of the NVA as we observed them.

My platoon laid down a base of fire as the "company-minus" (the other two rifle platoons and the mortar platoon) acted as the maneuver force. We let loose with our M-16s, M-60s, and M-79s. After the company swept through the enemy positions, we regrouped south of the wooden bridge. The company had run into what was estimated to be an NVA company or regimental headquarters. It was right on the direct supply line to Hue. Some of the guys told me that there was commo wire all over the place, indicating a major headquarters. The Cav troopers killed an NVA officer, and one of them got his 9 mm pistol as a souvenir.

We called in an air strike to level the whole area, but we had to get a good distance from the target area. I think we moved about a click away, and a jet roared in and dropped its thunderous payload. We were in a prone position on the ground when the explosion occurred. The ground shook; it was extremely loud. After the blast, I heard this whirling, buzzing sound coming my way—then a plop. About two feet from my leg was a 6" x 5" chunk of metal fragment from the bomb, still smoldering in the dirt.

Capt. Rapper and Lieut. Gaylord, the mortar platoon leader, said I did a really great job that day. I had five guys wounded; none killed. It was that day that I made up my mind I would not lose any of my men if I could help it. By the end of my tour, I had kept my promise. I put Sands in for the Silver Star, and he got it. Other decorations were also awarded—none to me.

I got the satisfaction that I led my men the way an infantry officer is supposed to lead, but more importantly, I kept them alive. The survival instinct in my training as a combat infantry unit commander served me well. The day had been terrifying, exhilarating, challenging, ultrastressful, and emotionally draining; but I learned a lot about the meaning of life, infantry tactics, and myself from that experience. After Lieut. Gaylord complimented me, I went over behind a big tree so nobody could see me and cried.

Wednesday, February 28

We came by chopper yesterday evening to Camp Evans where I am now. We walked to an area which we were supposed to man but it was the wrong place so we walked to another area. After we got settled, my CO and two other captains came by to show me another sector of the perimeter which I am manning now with 15 men until a company comes in to replace us. Sneed is fixing his PRC-25 (radio). I'm tired.

Thursday, February 29
Dear Mom and Dad,
   I'm in the boonies now on an operation. We left that bridge, flew (choppers) to Camp Evans, then flew (choppers) to here--somewhere north of Hue. Day before yesterday, my platoon ran into a VC company headquarters and we were pinned down. I called the CO on the radio and he brought the other two platoons to help us. An artillery forward observer with me called in artillery and mortars and we blew the hell out of the VC. As a result of my platoon making contact we destroyed the VC headquarters. My men were outstanding and I was surprised I can operate under fire. Ma, if you've been praying, please keep it up. Five of my men were wounded, and I was almost hit several times. I'm scared but with luck, I can make it. I'm still careful. I know this worries you a little but I'm just being honest. We're north of Hue and the NVA are tough. Just keep praying that the war ends soon and that my men and I stay

safe. Luckily, I got my men out of an almost surely fatal predicament with no mortal wounds. Well, the monsoon seems to be ending and it's going to be hot. I'll write a longer letter when I get a chance.

    Love Joe

[Although I referred to the enemy as VC in my letter home, the February 27 action pitted my platoon against an NVA company or regiment. As Specialist 4 Sands even noted, they were NVA. I often referred to the enemy as VC even if they were NVA.]

Thursday, February 29, (cont.)

1935 hrs. It's dark and I can hardly see. We are set up in the boonies on an operation. I took a combat patrol out last night. I slept in a foxhole with no blanket for cover and lay there as it rained on me.

March, 1968

Friday, March 1

1420 hrs. We moved out from last night's position across a river due west. The mortar platoon and my platoon are in perimeter defense while first and third platoons are on patrols. I put my men in position and then ate my C-rations.

1500 hrs. I'm lying in the grass on my poncho looking at the pale blue sky. Rain clouds overhead. The temperature is nice. A jet just flew overhead. Doc and Sneed are cutting bamboo to make tents with our ponchos for tonight.

Saturday, March 2

0935 hrs. Sneed and Pee Wee (my RTOs) are in a tent made of two ponchos with me. It's raining like a son of a bitch outside. My men are on the perimeter getting drenched. My platoon is supposed to go on an ambush patrol today but I hope we don't. Yesterday third platoon ambushed some rice carriers but their machine gun jammed after the first shot and the gooks dropped the rice and fled. I hope we go back to Camp Evans today.

I learned the pejorative term "gook" to refer to the enemy Vietnamese—the VC and NVA. Some soldiers referred to all Vietnamese as "gooks," "slopes," or "dinks." Not only were these terms derogatory, they were incorrect as they were used to refer to the North Koreans in the Korean War. I have learned to love the Vietnamese people and associate with many of them today.

Saturday, March 2, (cont.)

1500 hrs. We'll be air assaulted by chopper to about 1500 m from Evans to spend the night.

Sunday, March 3

1722 hrs. I sent out two "goats" (ambushes) last night. I was miserable all day yesterday as it rained all day and we all were soaked. Today we air assaulted and now we're camped on sand (a beach) 2000 to 3000 m from the South China Sea. Thank God it hasn't rained yet today.

Monday, March 4

2100 hrs. It's dark. I'm writing by moonlight. We're on the beach again. My platoon led a drive up the coast through villages. The artillery is moving around us as we were fired on tonight. I dug a foxhole in the sand in the dark.

```
Tuesday, March 5
0840 hrs. Dear Mom and Dad,
    Well, we're on another operation. The last
letter I wrote telling about when my platoon
got pinned down--I was on an operation near
Camp Evans. Now we've been air assaulted right
along the coast of the South China Sea. In fact,
last night and the night before, we dug in our
positions and set up our company perimeter in
the sand on the beach. The beach is so big that
it is about 2000 to 3000 m to the sea. Yesterday
our company led a drive through villages looking
```

for VC. My platoon was in the middle, leading our company.

Today, our company will be in reserve just resting at this position while another company will drive through the villages ahead. Later we'll be airlifted by choppers in a leapfrog manner, constantly moving north. Last night we were mortared and we received small arms fire. I always hit the ground quickly and try to determine where it's coming from. We (the company) have an artillery forward observer whose job it is to call in artillery on the enemy. Part of this artillery is ARA (aerial rocket artillery). These are choppers with rockets on them and they are extremely effective. Tomorrow, we'll probably be a blocking force. We're sweeping the coast north of Hue near the DMZ (south of DMZ). When we get air assaulted tomorrow we'll be deeper in VC territory. This work is really interesting and exciting. I got a good platoon.

About that day my platoon got pinned down, as a result of that contact, we destroyed a VC or NVA headquarters. The artillery forward observer (FO) with me called in much fire on the enemy. My point man and lead squad killed several enemy. I was maneuvering under fire, directing my men. It was exciting and scary, but I learned how devastating firepower can be. We always move with caution. None of us are out to be heroes; we try to do our job without getting killed. The VC fear the 1st Cavalry because our choppers make us mobile and bring much firepower on them.

So much for propaganda. The weather is breaking now and it's getting hot. Before, we would be drenched and sleep in soaked clothing and poncho liners. At times things seem unbearable and little things like a dry day or no mud on the boots or a change of clothes seem like a big deal. The chaplain flew in by chopper and most everyone is attending services on the sand. Mom, I'll let you do my praying for me. I'm just not interested in conventional or formalized religion right now. I can hear the chaplain reading Scripture right now; he's only about 50 m away. All is pretty quiet except for rifle shots and artillery pounding off in the distance (it sounds like thunder).

    Well, what else is new at home? How is my car holding out? It's funny but I haven't ridden in a car or slept on a bed in such a long time. I'm so used to walking or flying by chopper if it's a long, long distance. I forgot to mention that yesterday while I was on this sweep, I had an ARVN 1st Lieut. and his platoon with me. ARVNs are the Vietnamese army (South) and they help us once in a while since we are trying to help their country. They are little people--look like pygmies. They have assorted pieces of American uniforms and equipment and our World War II weapons. They are good though. They walk in front of us, looking in tunnels and bunkers and finding booby traps long before we can detect things. They know the land and the people because it is their land and their people. The ARVN 1st Lieut. is called Chungwee. *Chungwee* means "1st Lieut." I am a Chungwee to them. We found a young man in one of the bunkers who we thought was VC. The Chungwee told me he was a deserter and took him and beat him with a stick. Then they took the deserter away. I heard a shot. These people are primitive in some ways, but highly effective.

    I guess I'm due to have my R&R in May. I think

I'll go to Bangkok. Time flies a little faster now that I've been here. I'll probably have to stay in the field only 6 months which is customary in most units, but I hear that the 1st Cav frequently keeps their officers in the field all year rather than rotate them to a staff job.

So much for here. All is fine. I am very careful. I constantly get on my platoon to be careful. Don't worry. Tell Bob he doesn't know how lucky he is to be in school. I can hardly wait to get back to law school, as I think I'm learning much about a lot of things to help me with that type of profession. Mom, see if you can get Bob or Dad to drop me a line to tell me what they're doing.

Love, Joe

Tuesday, March 5, (cont.)

1044 hrs. We're still in the same place we were in last night. We're on the beach with brush that looks like pine. I'm sitting on the sand on my poncho liner. It's slightly overcast, but it's a nice day. I can tell the sun will come out. We'll be air assaulted today or tomorrow to act as a blocking force on this battalion operation. The ARVNs who worked with us yesterday moved on. They are good at searching and finding booby traps and the VC.

2025 hrs. We're set up for tonight. We can hear another company in the distance firing on VC.

Wednesday, March 6

1200 hrs. We walked about three clicks (3000 m) to an old Catholic church. My platoon is in line on the trail waiting to ambush about 25 NVA seen moving this way. Artillery is about to fire behind the NVA to flush them this way. The sun is shining brightly.

[We were a "blocking force," which meant we were to be in a fixed position while other units (in this case, artillery fire) drove the enemy to us.]

Wednesday, March 6, (cont.)

1353 hrs. Artillery fell near us. We couldn't see the NVA, so we headed back to the church. I didn't even get to eat lunch when we had to saddle up ASAP and move to where we are now—on the hot white sand waiting for NVA to come out of the tree line.

```
   1507 hrs. Dear folks,
   We are on an operation waiting on the sand
behind bushes for VC. I thought I'd write a
postcard on a C-ration box lid. We are allowed to
write on them if we want to. It's hot right now
and we walked a long way. This operation should
end soon unless it's extended. We are still north
of Hue and south of the DMZ sweeping the coast
parallel to the South China Sea about 3000 m
from the water. All is well as best as can be
expected.
   Love, Joe
```

[Written on a C-ration box lid—"Meal, Combat, Individual, Turkey loaf, B-1 A Unit"]

Thursday, March 7

1437 hrs. My platoon is waiting on the sand in seven-man groups for the choppers to pick us up. We are air assaulting into a new AO (area of operations). Today we wrote up people for awards for action on 27 February.

The way the Cav operated in conducting air assaults was that units to be air lifted would assemble in small groups or "lifts" so as each chopper came in, a group was ready to board. On this day we had seven-man lifts, but when we went into the A Shau Valley, we had five-man lifts because of the altitude the helicopters had to achieve and because we took more ammunition with us—I had five men and mortar ammo on my lift. The size of the ARVNs allowed more men per lift. We put members of our platoon in for awards for the February 27 action. I was put in for the Silver Star. I heard that the acting company commander for Captain Rapper nixed the recommendation for my award. Awards were very political and depended on who was nominated, who did the nomination, the philosophy of the unit about giving awards, and the actual merits of the basis of the nomination for the award.

Friday, March 8

0945 hrs. We air assaulted yesterday on rice paddies. Last night we set up on a road along the river. At about 2100 last night, one of my positions opened up on a boat sneaking across the river. We killed three women, captured one man, and captured two weapons and one grenade. We feel bad about killing women but they snuck up on us. One of the women had her brains hanging out of her head. They all were VC.

1921 hrs. We air assaulted back to the sandy beach again. We are right out in the open. Flying here, we were sniped at in the air. We will sweep the beach tomorrow.

Saturday, March 9

1055 hrs. We moved off the sand into the village. My second squad found a great deal of stored rice which choppers came in and picked up. We are resting and checking the immediate area.

Lieut. Stoneman is hacked off about something and he laughed as I recounted old experiences in my diary.

[The reason why we had choppers come in and pick up the rice was to deny it to the enemy.]

Sunday, March 10

0740 hrs. We went out on a platoon-size ambush last night. We are here at the site now at the schoolhouse where two paths intersect. We moved about one click at night and we were very quiet. Children and women crossed the path but no men with weapons. We'll be walking back to the sand and company perimeter soon. We are in the middle of the village now. We set up the ambush site in the middle of the VC village. We found lots of rice yesterday.

I was pretty pleased and proud of this action because it showed some special capabilities of my platoon. We left our defensive perimeter on the sands and moved into a village after dark. We traveled extremely light with only weapons, ammo, water, and radios. My platoon had grown and we had about 30 men sneaking into a Vietnamese village at night. Even our dog tags were taped so as not to jangle.

We moved single file into the village, passing huts where people were cooking around fires, and we could hear them talking. They did not know of our presence— or at least they acted like they didn't know. We set up in a schoolhouse made of concrete—no furniture inside. We could observe the intersection of two paths, and we placed Claymore mines and trip flares on the paths to be alerted if VC or NVA traveled on them. There was a general curfew that people were not to be roaming around at night, but how could this be enforced in each village?

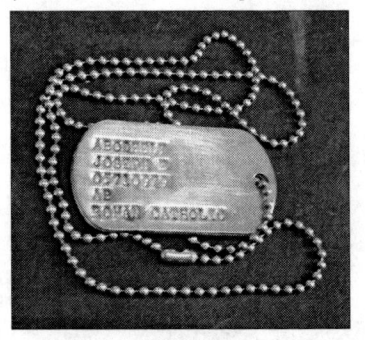

My dog tags.

Often, the Vietcong would infiltrate the

villages at night and terrorize the people who were basically farmers and peasants who didn't care about politics—Communism or Capitalism, Vietcong or the Americans. We waited in the schoolhouse for enemy troops of any stripe, and all of a sudden trip flares lit up. We had the Claymores and the M-60 ready to zap bad guys, but we saw it was a group of children playing at night who set off the flares. It seemed nobody knew we were there in the village. We had no contact with the enemy, and we didn't kill any innocent people. I took an abacus, a green Buddhist peace flag with a white Lotus flower on it, and a 1' x 2' Republic of Vietnam flag as souvenirs.

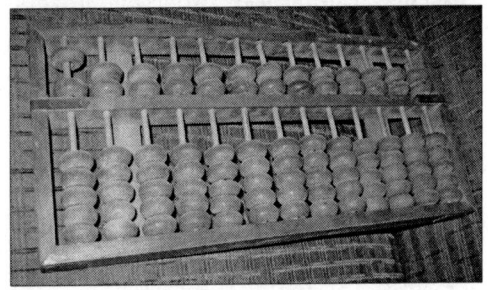

Buddhist peace flag and abacus.

Monday, March 11

1325 hrs. Right now I'm sitting along the river on the grass and sand while I am stark naked. We're on patrol and we stopped to wash ourselves and our clothes. A bunch of children were around me but I "shooed" them away.

2215 hrs. It's nighttime and I'm writing by moonlight through the hazy sky. I'm sitting on the sand. There are supposed to be about 40 VC in the area. Artillery is hitting off in the distance to our south. Otherwise, all is quiet except for crickets and frogs and mosquitoes which I hear buzzing. Last night we received four mortar rounds in the perimeter. Shrapnel zinged through my poncho tent. We'll probably be mortared tonight.

If the circumstances permitted, each night when we established our perimeter, my RTOs and I dug a foxhole and put two ponchos together to make a "tent" roof. Ponchos are a plastic cover with an opening and attached plastic "hoodie" which the soldier wears to keep dry from the rain. They have snaps and grommets which allows them to be fastened together and to be tied down. We used saplings as uprights on the ends and got a longer branch for a crossmember to place on the saplings.

We used our bayonets as tent stakes. I always believed that if we needed the bayonets for hand-to-hand combat, we were already in very deep shit. The apex of our makeshift tent might be two feet above ground, and we dug a shallow foxhole. I distinctly remember this incident of the mortaring and the shrapnel going through the tent because it was inches above us. The nice-sized hole from the shrapnel in the poncho verified that. This was another reminder of my mortality.

Tuesday, March 12

1350 hrs. The whole company walked about 2½ clicks from yesterday's site. Today, first and second platoons searched a village. First platoon killed two "gooks"—VC. Right now we are waiting to be extracted and possibly carried to Camp Evans. We may later go farther north right near the DMZ. Last night we were mortared.

```
Wednesday, March 13
0900 hrs. Dear Mom and Dad,
    Here I am again at Camp Evans. We were
extracted from the boonies yesterday after about
13 straight days in the field. We ate hot chow
last night and slept bunched up on the
ground near a chopper pad. The big 8-inch guns
(howitzers) on the perimeter fired all night,
making the ground shake. About 1 a.m., we got
rocketed. I didn't see any of them yet but the
other side of Camp Evans was being hit. Today
we're supposed to be air assaulted to some
bridges farther north between here and Quang Tri.
    Lately, I've been getting replacements which
```

I needed badly. At times I had as few as 6 men per squad when I should have 11. Now I'm almost at full strength. The operation we just came off of was a sweep in various areas along the coast between Hue and Quang Tri. Our company was successful in finding thousands of pounds of rice bagged for VC. Also, my platoon killed 3 VC and captured one when we set up along the river and ambushed them as they came on the bank. We captured 2 weapons and a grenade. There is rumor that we may move farther north near the DMZ.

There's a place called Khe Sanh which is near the DMZ, and the Communist fire artillery and rockets there constantly. Wherever we go, I know we'll clear the area out because the VC respect the 1st Cavalry. We fly in and give them hell and then we fly out to another place and do the same. This airmobile concept of war is really effective.

Well, the weather seems to be clearing for a while. It makes us a little more comfortable and the skies are clear for air strikes and chopper (ARA) assaults. Actually, I must admit that being in the field where we were wasn't too bad because we did a lot of walking in the sand. The sand is white (like New Mexico's White Sands) with scattered bushes here and there. We're out in the open but so are the VC and we have the advantage because we have choppers and he doesn't. We've been careful on our sweeps through villages.

(10-minute break)

I just went up the hill here as the CO wanted me. My platoon just got issued a demolition kit. In it are fuses, blasting caps, detonation cord, and C-4 which is a puttylike explosive. We'll use this stuff to blow booby traps we find. Well, they

are issuing clean clothes now so I'll go change.
I got my radio batteries. All is well. I just
wish I could take a bath once in a while.
   Love Joe

Wednesday, March 13, (cont.)

0940 hrs. Yesterday evening we were air assaulted to Camp Evans. We ate hot chow last night and this morning. We all got a good night's sleep last night except for when we were rocketed. I got several new men which helps a lot. Today we are supposed to go to some more bridges.

1530 hrs. We were picked up by Chinooks and half the company went to one bridge while the other half went to another bridge. Then we walked toward each other along Highway 1, leaving some men at each bridge. We're on a grassy hill with Highway 1 just to our front (200 m) and a river just to our rear (150 m). We all dug in and now we're fixing tents and relaxing.

My recollection is that I had some men from my platoon at both bridges. I remember going to one of the locations, and "Doc" Henderson said there was a wounded Vietnamese baby in the nearby village. In order to avoid a confrontation in the village or intimidate villagers, I walked down a path through the jungle by myself to personally assess the situation. I came to a hut, or hooch (their houses), and saw a group of people standing around. I walked up and in broken Vietnamese told them I was an American 1st Lieutenant, and asked where the injured baby was. I had my trusty little Vietnamese phrase manual to refer to and I think the best I could come up with was "sick" rather than "injured."

An old man and old woman came forward with a baby with a foot wrapped in bloody bandages. I told them we could go to the village to see a doctor. There was a young man in an OD green uniform without unit markings who seemed very hostile to me. After he and the "old ones" argued in Vietnamese, the elderly couple, the baby, and I walked out of the village back to where part of my platoon was; and we called for an ambulance. Phong Dien, the district headquarters and largest nearby town located right near Camp Evans, sent an ambulance with one medical person/driver.

He pulled up to the Vietnamese couple, baby, and me and asked, "Where is the wounded American GI?" Doc Henderson must have told them that story or they would not have come out. When I explained and showed the baby's condition, the Vietnamese medic started slapping the old folks around. I stopped that and told him to take the three to the hospital. They went down the road, and I don't know if they ever made it; but I tried. It was stupid of me to walk into a Vietnamese village by myself.

Thursday, March 14

1855 hrs. Today my platoon walked about 10 clicks (total) on a road-clearing operation. We were security guards for some engineers on a minesweeping operation on Highway 1. When we got to the end of our sweep, I let my men rest and relax in a village. They bought Cokes and got haircuts. Now we're resting at our company perimeter. Tomorrow we'll sweep along the road again in the other direction, but we'll go off the road to look for VC who threw rockets in Camp Evans today. Last night, a squad I sent out on an ambush saw some VC in the distance. We may catch them tomorrow. I got a letter from Aunt Lorraine today. I better write her and Mary.

Friday, March 15

1503 hrs. The second and third platoons and CO and his HQ are waiting for extraction to Camp Evans. We're all lying on the grass in our seven-man groups for each chopper as it comes in. Today, my platoon swept Highway 1 toward Camp Evans for about one click and then we cut across the rice paddies to the top of the hill where we could see for miles in all directions. I sent two squads to two different hills, and we "cooled it" until called back here to be picked up.

That's what we did. We patrolled in various-sized units. We had been operating in a company-size search and destroy mission. A squad normally had about 10 men; a platoon normally had four squads (about 40 men); and a company normally had four platoons—one of them being a mortar platoon while the other three platoons were infantry. When the lift ships (helicopters) came to pick us up, we gathered in small groups to board the choppers.

> 1915 hrs. Dear Mom and Dad,
> Well, here I am back at Camp Evans again after two days clearing Hwy. 1 between Quang Tri and Camp Evans (4 miles north of Hue). On road clearing--my platoon and I walked along the road while an engineer unit used mine detectors on the road to see if the VC were going to blow up any convoys. Mom, thanks for the map. It is accurate. Also, thanks for the flashlight batteries. I noticed the return address was Box 5196, so if you mailed them, Dad, thanks.
> Last night in our company perimeter out in the boonies, a sniper opened up on us. My RTOs and I dug a shallow square hole about 1 foot deep and about 6' x 6' square. We had our ponchos in a tent fashion over it, so since we slept in the hole, the bullets just whizzed overhead. About that time I was pinned down; thank God we all got out alive.
> My platoon was instrumental in destroying a company-size VC headquarters. Almost all of my platoon and I are up for various medals. It was really close that day and I learned a lot about my platoon and myself that day (27 February). It was amazing about one thing--5 of my men were wounded; several of my men maneuvered under fire to help them, and when the Medevac choppers came in to pick the wounded up--the VC didn't fire at the ships or the wounded. To this day I don't

know why. Also, another exciting incident--I maneuvered one of my squads out of the trench to cross a bridge and we were pinned down by sniper fire. We lay in a plowed field as the bullets cracked and zinged right over our heads. Lieut. Stoneman, artillery FO, called in ARA ships (rocket choppers) and they blew up the building where the snipers were. The rockets fell within 50 m of us--to give an idea of how close they were shot in.

Well, we'll probably go out in the boonies again tomorrow to search villages for VC or rice caches. I'm sending two payroll vouchers. Save them for me. It's too dark to write now so I'll close. Aunt Lorraine wrote and I'll try and write her. Give my regards to everyone.

Love, Joe

Saturday, March 16

2000 hrs. We took it easy today here at Camp Evans. I just checked the perimeter as we had to fill in for first platoon who was on air assault about 2½ clicks away to set up a "goat." We got a new platoon leader for third platoon. We still don't have a replacement for Lieut. Lindsey, who was first platoon leader and was wounded. It's dark and I'm writing by my penlight. I hope we don't get rocketed tonight.

[The NVA and VC like to routinely send some 122 millimeter rockets into Camp Evans. To help put it in perspective, our main artillery fire support was 105 millimeter. We often used 4.2-inch mortars for indirect fire support. The "four-deuce" as it was called was 107 millimeter. The incoming rockets were 122 millimeter. They were big and destructive.]

Sunday, March 17

0827 hrs. My platoon is waiting along the road at the entrance to Camp Evans to go on a road-clearing operation. We're waiting for the engineers. This morning my platoon (second) and third platoon were getting C-rations at the CP when two mortar rounds dropped in on us. This happened at 0615.

[The NVA or VC often used the 60 millimeter mortar simply to harass us. It was a small, light mortar, and the ammo was small and light enough for one or two "bad guys" to setup, pop off a few rounds, and then get out of the area. Mortar fire was very psychologically intimidating. You just didn't know if the round was going to land right on top of you.]

Monday, March 18

0730 hrs. Two times last night at 2000 and 0300 we got mortars or rockets fired in the large perimeter here at Camp Evans. We also received small arms fire from outside the perimeter. Today my platoon is on 15-minute standby, which means we must be ready for anything today in 15 minutes. Sgt. Brown, our old first sergeant, is now with my platoon because he got a new first sgt. who outranks him.

Tuesday, March 19

0923 hrs. Last night my platoon went out on a goat about two clicks away. We had to cross a couple of wide streams. We got into position after dark. All was quiet last night. Tonight I'll send out an LPOP. I just got done shaving.

1510 hrs. Sgt. Brown, Sgt. Blanko, and I walked to the water point and swam and washed our clothes. It felt great, as it is extremely hot.

Wednesday, March 20

1333 hrs. My platoon and I are on the northwest sector of Camp Evans perimeter. My men are laying concertina wire with the engineers. We're expanding the perimeter. I'm sitting on a grassy hill overlooking the hills and mountains and streams. It is very hot. Today I borrowed a three-quarter ton truck to go get water for my platoon. It rained last night. Second platoon will probably have to go out on goat tonight when we get back.

1700 hrs. I got use of another truck and found a way to buy four cases of beer for my platoon. They really enjoyed it. As I suspected, we do have a platoon-sized goat tonight. The sky is very cloudy.

[The beer we got in Vietnam, if and when we got it, was 3.2% alcohol. We called it "near beer," and I think there was an authorized ration of two beers per a certain period which I don't remember. It was a very small perk and a morale booster, but it never presented a problem like "drunk and disorderly conduct." We didn't get beer that often.]

Thursday, March 21

0845 hrs. My platoon went out on a goat last night. We left a little before dark on a 180° azimuth. Only one stream showed on my map, but we crossed two so I stopped on a hill and set up. I had artillery shoot two white phosphorus aerial bursts so I could locate our position. I slept well last night. Nobody saw anything. I got a letter from Mom and one from Dad.

1440 hrs. Dear Mom and Dad,
This time it is a legitimate greeting as I received both letters (from both of you) yesterday. Thank you both for writing. Today is

the 1st day of spring and it's very hot. It's been getting hotter (both day and night) and we still get occasional showers in the evenings. I'm sitting on an air mattress on the ground. I rigged up a little sun shelter composed of 4 stakes in the ground to which I tied my poncho liner (quiltlike cover). At night 6 of us (my headquarters) sleep in a 3-sided sandbagged fortification because the VC frequently rocket and mortar Camp Evans. In case you're wondering what Camp Evans is--it's going to be the 1st Cav's HQ up north as An Khe used to be. My back is to the perimeter wire now so I'm looking into the center where there are many tent structures. There are loads of trucks and Jeeps and, of course, choppers. There are underground fueling points where the choppers refuel and can be airborne immediately. My company, D Company, is manning the southern sector of the camp's perimeter. If we go to the field on an operation (sweep of villages or search and destroy), then other units are substituted to cover the perimeter.

So far we've been here a few days now. Each night and sometimes during the day, the company sends out patrols. Last night, my platoon went one way and 3rd platoon went another. We've been receiving our missions pretty late in the evening so last night we moved out just before dark. We moved about 1000 m to a hill where I put my platoon in a perimeter defense. Because it was dark and I could not see the surrounding hills to shoot an azimuth on my compass, I called for artillery to shoot two air bursts of white phosphorus from which I took readings in the dark and knew exactly where my platoon was located on the map. When we set up night "goats" (ambushes), we dig in (usually on trails or well-traveled paths) and set up trip flares and Claymore mines to give us warning of enemy approaching. Last night nothing happened and we walked back to this perimeter this morning.

One night when we were sweeping villages along the coast, my platoon set up right on a river to catch any escaping VC moving down the river. I was sitting in my foxhole with bamboo thickets between the river and me when I heard a lot of automatic weapons fire about 30 m away. I jumped down and got my weapon and then I checked the situation out as I discovered I wasn't being shot at. One of my positions, about 30 m away along the river, opened up on people getting out of a sampan (boat). They were VC. One man got away; we captured one man and woman, and killed two women. I had no remorse about seeing the wounded man and woman or the two dead women as we found a Chinese-Communist grenade and two rifles in the boat. One of the dead women had a VC insignia on her clothing. As I stared at her head, split open by an M-16 bullet, and saw her brains hanging out, I felt no remorse at all. Five of my men were wounded on 27 February and my men and I have been shot at too damn many times for me to feel sorry if a young boy or woman dies who sides with or personally participates with those trying to kill my men or me. This incident is just to give some insight into the horror of this war; but, nonetheless, it is war.

I read the articles you both sent me and I want the war to end, too; but I believe we have commitments--to ourselves and to others. We're fighting a worthwhile war, but we're not going all out. I believe the government (U.S.) and the people should go all out--send troops, gear the economy, etc.--to win the war rather than prolong it. People who want to pull out, or stay half-ass, either don't realize the military and the political repercussions, which are bad, or they have other interests which they are putting first. No one is brainwashing me on this stuff; I just hate to see these times exist. I must admit though, there are some light moments and good times.

I have a good platoon, as you would expect because I constantly check on them. There is a waterhole right outside the perimeter where the camp purifies water, and some of my men and I went swimming bare-assed in the waterhole. We also washed our fatigues there as there is no laundry set up yet. I wear the same clothes weeks at a time. I haven't had a good bath in months, except in waterholes, or even some murky waterholes filled with leeches.

Yesterday, my platoon was on a wire-laying detail on the other side of the perimeter. It was hot and the men were tired. Because I am the platoon leader, I didn't lay wire so I bummed a truck and went to the PX. Beer and Coke can only be bought at battalion level, but I talked a sgt. into selling me four cases of beer for my platoon. I took it back to the perimeter where they were laying wire and we drank beer until we had to come back to our sector of the perimeter. We've been getting a lot of replacements lately so now I have 38 people in my platoon. I was down to 27 at one time.

I don't know how long I'll be here at Evans (between Quang Tri and Hue). We may just work out of Evans for a while and conduct patrols nearby or maybe they'll send me back along the coast to sweep villages there. There is rumor that we may go to Khe Sanh where the Marines are getting rocketed and mortared just about every day. I suspect that if we don't go there, we'll stay here just in case the VC and NVA make another bid for Hue. We're close enough that we can support a defense there.

    Ma, I believe I told you before that I got the radio and flashlight batteries. Thanks, I use both. I have my radio in this bunker. We listen to it at night when reception is best. Dad, thanks for the letter and the statistics money wise, etc. I'm not worried about my money. Don't you worry about me--hang on to what you get through liquidation. I'll have the G.I. Bill when I get out. I still want to finish law school, but I'm seriously considering extending in the Army for 6 months, only if I get the job I want. That way I'd make capt., get more money, and enjoy myself if I get a job like officer in charge of an R&R center. I'll have to wait and see what happens. Meanwhile I live day-to-day hoping I get through it to the next day. I just hope everything turns out all right. I'm glad to hear Bob is doing well in school. I think he'll like teaching. It'll give him the time he needs for his extracurricular activities, such as hunting and scuba diving. Tell Bob I could show him a few tricks about living in the boonies under very adverse conditions.

    Well, I'll close for now. All is well. Give my regards to everyone--Aunt T, Aunt Emily, Grandma, Uncle Kenny, Rose G, and anyone else who asks about me.

    Love Joe

Friday, March 22

1507 hrs. It's hot. I'm sitting under a poncho liner tied to four stakes for a sun shelter. Tonight my platoon is to go out to set up a goat on Highway 1 to catch any VC setting up mines on the road. We're supposed to be air assaulted but we could go by truck or walk. We turned in one of our M-60 machine guns today to get a new one. Rumor still is that we'll go to Khe Sanh. During the evenings, it's been raining.

[Highway 1 was a main highway which ran along the east side of the country from Hue (and points farther south) all the way up north to Dong Ha which was the last major city before the DMZ. When we went out with the engineers, they used mine sweepers to make sure the road was safe for travel.]

Saturday, March 23

0637 hrs. My platoon and I are sitting on top of a hill overlooking Highway 1. It's dawn now and I just went to my positions to check if the men were awake. As we moved in last night, three of my men saw two people across the highway on the other side. I thought for sure we'd be sniped at but we weren't. Today we'll probably act as a blocking force.

["Air cavalry" substituted helicopters for horses to do traditional cavalry tactics, such as reconnaissance, raids, flanking actions, and acting as a blocking force. Instead of being transported by helicopters for this operation, we walked to our "blocking" location, set up, and waited for the company commander and 1st platoon to drive the enemy into us— we were the "blocking force" to block the enemy's advance. We waited until we got a radio call from the CO, Captain Swenson, who replaced Rapper, to hurry to his and 1st platoon's position about 200 meters away.]

2310 hrs. We hit some NVA today. Several of the first platoon got wounded; one medic killed. My platoon and I moved under fire to get the wounded out. Tomorrow we will go to recover the dead body.

We had to hustle to that location with all of our equipment. When we got there, a firefight was going on. There was a stream, not too deep, between the CO's and my position and where the firing was about 50 meters away. The CO, Captain Swenson, ordered me to take a few men, cross the stream under fire, and help out 1st platoon who were under fire. Captain Swenson was new to the company, had just come from being the S-4 (battalion supply officer), and had walked his unit into an ambush. I took an RTO and a few other men, and we forded the stream quickly as bullets whizzed past.

We got behind a huge dike which gave us good cover. There was a dry rice paddy to our front and some hooches with enemy firing at us. The 1st platoon leader and his medic got hit. Osterman, one of my grenadiers, yelled out he actually hit a VC with the 40 mm round, which did not detonate from his grenade launcher. While my other guys were firing from behind the dike, my RTO and I crawled out a few yards in the dry rice paddy (like tall grass). We had no cover, but we hid in the dry vegetation. We started getting sniped at. We couldn't move—the bullets kept popping by us, signifying that the shooter was barely missing us each time.

There was a lull in the sniping at us, and a medical service officer came to our position and was standing up and looking around as though nothing had been happening. He moved on without incident, although I heard that he took four rounds in the chest later on and still survived. The sniping started up again and we called in an ARA gunship to spray the area.

Since we were hidden in the rice paddy, I was concerned that the gunner couldn't see us. We lay down a base of fire to our front, and my RTO and I were able to get back behind the dike. That ended the action that day. We went back to base camp, but we air assaulted to this firefight location the next day to find the medic's body. The 1st platoon leader who was hit survived, but the medic didn't.

Sunday, March 24

1635 hrs. We air assaulted to find the body. My platoon found the body. The medic was shot in the eye. Tonight we go out on a goat not far from Camp Evans.

My platoon found the young medic's body. He had only been in country for about a week. He was brand-new, and he was shot in the eye. We put him in a body bag and searched the area. When my RTO and I were pinned down in the rice paddy the previous day, I noticed a mound of dirt with a lot of vegetation on it sitting in the center of the rice paddy. We checked it out and found the vegetation was matted down where the sniper had been lying prone shooting M-1 carbine rounds. We found numerous shell casings. That sniper almost killed me. He probably killed the medic and wounded the medical service officer.

Monday, March 25

1700 hrs. Last night on a goat it rained. VC started mortaring Camp Evans but I called artillery in on the mortar positions in the dark. Today my platoon found the mortar site and brought back mortar rounds and other equipment. The battalion commander, S-2, and CO were all pleased. Now we're at a bridge in an old French bunker. An ARVN Sgt. is in here; we made friends as I talked to him from my translation book.

We got our orders late in the day to go out about a click just as it was getting dark. We moved out for our night ambush mission, and after several hundred meters, we came to an open area like a field or dry rice paddy. Beyond that was a tree line. The sky was overcast, the sun was going down, and I did not like the idea of crossing an open area heading into a tree line. My recollection is that we were supposed to go into that tree line.

There was a hill to our right about a couple of hundred meters away, so I took my platoon there and lied when reporting back by saying we were at or near the tree line. We got on top of the hill and made a defensive perimeter among some bushes that remind me of jojoba bushes. We couldn't dig in because the ground was too hard. It started raining. I had my poncho draped over me to try to stay somewhat dry and went to sleep. All of a sudden, I heard *thoomp, thoomp, thoomp, thoompa, thoompa, thoompa*—it was the sound of several mortars firing simultaneously. I thought, *Oh, shit! They know we're here, and we have no cover. We're gonna die!*

As I waited for the rounds to land on us, I heard and then saw explosions behind us at Camp Evans. I saw the silhouette of a watchtower at Camp Evans when one of the explosions lit up the area around it. A couple of my men came to my position and said they heard the mortar tubes shooting in the tree line where we were supposed to have gone. It was still raining, so I was still under my poncho with my military flashlight with red lenses looking at my map. I called "Guide on 8," our artillery fire support, told them I knew where the mortar fire was coming from, and that we wanted a "fire mission" on the location where the sound was coming from. We got it.

We heard our "big guns" pump out those artillery rounds and we heard the impacts in the tree line. The next day we were ordered to recon the impact area. Some of the rounds we called in by sound in the dark in the rain hit within 15 meters of the mortar pits where they fired the mortar tubes. The killing radius of a 105 howitzer round is 50 meters. We found aiming stakes and some mortar rounds—but they took the tubes. It was a good thing we did not go into the tree line because the mortar firing positions (five mortar pits with aiming stakes) were just inside the vegetation of the tree line. A few meters behind that was a stream with a couple dozen fighting positions dug into the bank.

Tuesday, March 26

1655 hrs. Today I coordinated with the major at the ARVN compound down the road. On the way back, Sgt. Blanko, Private Osterman, and I stopped and had a beer in the village. We got in trouble with some MPs who passed by and said we were "off limits." A "mama-san" who sells stuff nearby came to the bunker. I got laid today. My men are filling sandbags now. Some ARVNs are helping them. We're setting Claymores and trip flares all around our positions—more than usual. Last night a VC turned two Claymores around. It was good we did not set them off.

[A Claymore mine is a plastic container about 10" x 8" by 3" deep packed with composition 4 (C-4), a puttylike explosive behind a metal plate which breaks into shrapnel fragments when the mine is detonated. Usually there are blasting caps wired to a hand detonator which when squeezed three times (for safety reasons) detonates the mine. The container rests on four little metal "legs," and the key is to remember to point the explosive direction toward the enemy. Sometimes, the enemy would sneak up and turn the mines to face inward toward U.S. troops who, if prompted to explode the mine, got a huge surprise. It was a very effective antipersonnel weapon.]

Wednesday, March 27

1115 hrs. Last night we spotted some VC moving around and shot at them. I called in some artillery illuminations. "Mamasan" came today and we bought 14 more hats. She left some "pot" with me for safekeeping because the ARVNs will kill her if they find out she has it. I'm going to the ARVN compound to coordinate further.

[Although it was the 1960s, I never smoked "pot." "Mamasan" was concerned about her safety, and I did not want to get prosecuted for possession of drugs—so I buried the marijuana in the dirt at the base of the tower bunker.]

1900 hrs. Dear Mom and Dad,
It'll be dark in a few minutes so I'll write fast. I'm sitting on top of an old French tower so I can adjust artillery fire tonight. The other night my platoon was on a "goat" and I woke up at night (2:00 a.m.) and heard VC mortar tubes popping rounds into Camp Evans. I got to the radio and called artillery fire in the dark without seeing the enemy who were about 700

m away behind the tree line. The next day my platoon was ordered to look for the enemy mortar site which we found. I had called artillery fire right in on their positions (some artillery fell as close as 15 m from their dug-in positions). I saw the battalion commander and gave a report the next day and he was pleased.

Enclosed is a confidential report put out by battalion of what happens by each unit. Our CO underlined the section about my platoon and he wrote the comment on the side. The 06 KIA (killed in action) and 26 WIA (wounded in action) were at Camp Evans. The report shows what we found and turned in. It was my very first artillery fire mission and I was right on target. Beginner's luck.

Enclosed is a picture of some of my men and me. I have the sunglasses on. We bought these hats from the Vietnamese. Normally, we wear our metal helmets, but we were goofing around that day. None of us smiled for the pose.

Well, we'll be at this bridge for a day or so

My third squad. I'm wearing the hat and sunglasses.

more. Then we go back to Camp Evans and then to LZ Thor just southeast of Khe Sanh. This is the last NVA stronghold south of the DMZ. We've been hitting the hot spots and this is the place where VC will run or fight. They have everything there. We'll push them out and occupy Khe Sanh without getting hit like we have been.

Well, I'll probably be moving for the next several days to come so be patient if I don't write. I'll be careful. I'm going to call in some illumination rounds so I'll close now.

Love Joe

The Battalion confidential report dated 26 March 68 said:

"Headquarters, 2nd Battalion, 7th Cavalry, APO San Francisco, California 96490 2600308H March 68
Summary of Enemy Activity: Opn Jeb Stuart w/no significant contact.
Ground Activity: Co D 2-7: I D547294, 250050 H 2nd plat obs mortars being launched against LZ Evans. Initiated early warning and adjusted effective artillery fire on to mortar locations. Results 06 US KIA, 26 US WIA, 250925 H search area fnd 05 mortar firing psns, 08 - 82 mm rounds, 10 fuses, powder charges, aiming stakes (homemade-wood), 01 knife, and 01 entrenching tool (VC)..."

Thursday, March 28

1130 hrs. Some of my men and I are here at the river. I'm sitting nude on the grassy bank. Some Vietnamese children are washing my pants and socks. We got the word yesterday—we move north. Some of the children are sitting next to me. My men are swimming. We will probably leave the bridge today or tomorrow.

[The children were cute and must have thought we were unusual. The kids liked to run their hands over my arms to feel the hair. The Vietnamese were not a very "hairy" people.]

Friday, March 29

0940 hrs. The sun is getting bright now. I'm in the tower bunker. There are a lot of flies. The ARVNs got in a firefight this morning to our south. We could hear the shooting. I've been practicing speaking Vietnamese and I can get by okay now. One of the ARVNs told me this morning that four VC slept in the village last night and left in the early morning. My company will probably go back to Camp Evans today.

The Vietcong were Communists who were recruited, trained, and armed by Communists. They often slept in the villages at night and conducted military operations in the daytime. They had some sympathizers who supported them, and they also terrorized people for support. Those who did not cooperate or who were a threat to the Communist cause were treated very harshly. Consider the thousands who were executed, discovered in mass graves after the battle at Hue.

Saturday, March 30

1235 hrs. It's cloudy and we're still at the bridge. We should be moving to Camp Evans soon.

1435 hrs. My half of the platoon moved to the company site along the road between the bridges. It was relaxing being at the bridge. The kids who sold the Cokes and beer were cute. Now we'll go to Camp Evans to move north near Khe Sanh.

Sunday, March 31

1440 hrs. We are here at LZ Pedro. There is artillery and infantry on these grassy, gently sloping hills. The sun is hot, but there is a breeze. We are to go to LZ Thor tomorrow. We dug in today.

April, 1968

Monday, April 1

0817 hrs. We are waiting to be picked up to go to LZ Calu. From there we go to LZ Thor. Thor hasn't been decided definitely yet. The terrain there is thick and mountainous.

LZ Calu (Stud) was the main staging area for Operation Pegasus. (Wikipedia)

B-52 bombing around Khe Sanh. (Wikipedia)

Tuesday, April 2

Late entry—0645 hrs. We air assaulted to the top of this mountain. It's jungle and grassy. I jumped from the chopper and hurt my arm. At 2100, I could see bomb strikes off in the distance as the sky lit up and the ground shook.

[I landed on my left forearm, cut it, and had a scar for years afterwards. The bomb strikes were "Arc Lights"—B-52 carpet bombing of NVA troops and materiel.]

1000 hrs. The sun is out. We're on a high mountaintop surrounded by a river on three sides. Today, D Company (mine) is to air assault to a new location to set up there. We just got a log ship with food and water. It was nice sleeping last night.

[My comment about the "nice sleeping" referred to the weather. Our sleeping gear was a poncho liner and maybe an air mattress, if a trooper wanted to carry it.]

1720 hrs. D Company led the air assault to where we are now. My platoon led a ground movement. We found a site for .50 caliber antiaircraft gun. Also, some of my platoon found some ammo and grenades (NVA). Now we're waiting to see where we will set up. We are hot and tired.

When we were in the air, I recall seeing what looked like a downed jet in a ravine below. I remember thinking that if the NVA could shoot down jets they sure as hell could shoot down helicopters. When we dismounted the helicopters, we took cover in gigantic craters left by massive bombing, and then I gathered up my platoon, put them in a modified column formation, and moved out to recon the area. We were point platoon. We did not carry our "butt packs," but we had web gear, C-rations, fragmentation and smoke grenades, ammunition, M-16s, M-60s, LAWs (light anti-tank weapons), PRC-25s (radios), and a 90 millimeter recoilless rifle. My M-79 grenadiers traded in their M-79s for 12 gauge pump shotguns with buckshot or flechette shotgun shells because the jungle was going to be very thick where we were going. Some wore flak vests, but we avoided doing so whenever we could. My point man that day was a guy we called "Hippy." He was a lanky guy and had a peace symbol on his helmet, but he was an excellent point man—the first guy in order of movement as we moved through "Indian country." He found the machine gun site and an NVA helmet and a bag of raw opium. The NVA used opium for medicinal purposes and perhaps to prepare themselves for sapper (suicide) attacks. I told Hippy to take the bag back to turn it in. I never checked to see if he did.

Wednesday, April 3

0953 hrs. We are sitting in the jungle right now. Third platoon hit some NVA a little while ago. They got one of their men KIA. The S-3 carried him back on his shoulders and then three of my men took the KIA to the rear. We are waiting for artillery to come in. There are huge bomb craters all around. I can hear the choppers circling the area now. There are trees, high grass, and ferns all around.

Our company was moving through dense jungle, and 3rd platoon was the point platoon on this advance. Our whole company was moving through the jungle and we all were strung out over a long distance. The 3rd platoon made contact with the NVA, and we could hear the firefight up ahead of us through the jungle. The vegetation was thick and the soft, rich dirt had been upturned by the bomb explosions. The gigantic craters made great predug foxholes.

In a firefight, you did not see a person shooting at you—bushes shot at you. The NVA had a special knack of dragging away their casualties immediately so that, although you knew you hit someone, as soon as you got to their location, if the situation permitted, they were gone. It was ominous. It was as though the NVA were ghosts.

I recall that the person killed in action was a popular young NCO in his platoon. The story was that he went to retrieve an enemy RPD (light machine gun) and was killed. The S-3 (operations officer) brought him back and placed him on the ground near my position. Before he set the dead soldier down on the ground, the body started regurgitating—the involuntary action of the body after death.

I had never seen that before. This was another reminder of my mortality. I often had bouts with internal terror, but I could not show fear as I was leading about 40 men and trying to keep them alive while at the same time accomplishing whatever mission we were given.

The NVA were great fighters. They fought the Japanese, later the French, and now the Americans. But we were better. It is a truism that we won almost 100% of the actions in combat. We were able to control the area we chose to control.

Wednesday, April 3, (cont.)

1808 hrs. We moved to this Hill-242. NVA mortared us; we had 10 or 11 WIA. NVA have us surrounded now. One platoon from another company tried to bring us food and water but got pinned down. I hope we make it through the night. We dug in and made overhead cover.

Hill 242 was thick jungle not far from Route 9. We set up a company-size perimeter, and because we wanted to get resupplies from log ships, we started clearing a LZ. We were in a combination of jungle and forest, so we had to clear trees. We wrapped "det cord" (detonation cord, which burns at thousands of feet per second) around some of the smaller trees and blew them in two, but there were too many trees. We were unsuccessful in the LZ construction. The NVA surrounded us in the jungle but apparently did not have the force or will to attack us directly.

One of the other units took a mule (small flatbed utility vehicle) and tried to bring us supplies along the road. They were ambushed—some KIA. We didn't get the food or water except for rain water we gathered on our ponchos. We got mortared that day, and we made fortifications with trees and overhead cover. About 10 or 11 of my men got minor wounds from shrapnel, and they were extracted from our perimeter by a jungle penetrator—it's like a heavy plumb bob, dropped through heavy jungle canopy, that a person can sit on and be lifted to the helicopter.

The platoon sergeant and I were checking our section of the perimeter when we heard that distinctive clank of the bolt of an AK-47 being pulled back from outside our perimeter. I yelled, "Get down," and we pancaked to the ground as the automatic weapons fire started chopping the leaves above which fell down on us. Prior to our mission to go to Khe Sanh, the platoon got two brand new M-60 machine guns for gunners. One young Black trooper took great care of his M-60, as they could sometimes jam when you most needed them. When that AK opened up, the trooper started pumping M-60 fire into the jungle in the area of the sound of the enemy fire, and that M-60 just kept spewing fire for what seemed like an inordinate amount of time and never jammed once. He probably saved my life.

Thursday, April 4

1540 hrs. Last night we received more mortar and artillery fire. We're back at the guns.

[My platoon had five PRC-25 radios. Some entire companies had only two, but I wanted my five radios. Two RTOs were near me constantly, and that night I heard the company commander get on the radio and state that it appeared that there were artillery rounds which landed in our perimeter but did not explode. He said that they could be "duds" or chemical agents. I stayed awake all night thinking I might die from a nerve agent, but it didn't happen. We moved back to a position where the 105 howitzers had been brought in by Chinooks.]

1800 hrs. I have my platoon in position on the perimeter. As we came back today, we picked up a couple of the dead and wounded who tried to get us supplies yesterday. When we got back here, we saw more dead and wounded. The second platoon leader of C Company was killed. One Medevac chopper was shot up. The NVA here are dangerous. I don't like this area. I hope we all get out alive. I got a card from Kathleen today which cheered me up. We didn't have any food or water all day yesterday and for most of today. Everyone is tired.

After a while, I got almost numb to the idea that I was mortal and could be killed at any time. I had been scared before but always did my best to hide it, as I was the platoon "leader." In my view, if anyone has ever been in real combat and he tells you he never was scared—he's simply a liar. My mind could keep me somewhat detached when I saw the dead and wounded; but when I saw the 2nd Platoon leader of C Company dead, I personalized this, as I was the 2nd Platoon leader of D Company. It bothered me, and my sense of invincibility deteriorated.

Friday, April 5

1550 hrs. I got the word today that our battalion will make the walk to Khe Sanh tomorrow. This could be disastrous. We've incurred a lot of dead and wounded since we've been here. I hope to God we make it alive. I've had a lot of close calls and I'm getting scared again. Everyone is scared of this area. The NVA are numerous and good fighters. We're digging in again for tonight.

1720 hrs. Jets keep circling this hill. There are a lot of choppers in the air. Artillery kept pounding the surrounding areas also. I hope that the NVA move out. They ambush a lot here.

Saturday, April 6

1400 hrs. Well, we tried to walk from this LZ to Khe Sanh, but we had to come back as the two forward companies received effective fire. Now our company is supposed to air assault to 500 m east of Khe Sanh. This is a glory wish to see who can be the first to walk into Khe Sanh. I hope we make it; we have many reporters with us.

General John J. Tolson, the 1st Cavalry's Division commander, wrote on "Airmobility 1961-1971" in *Vietnam Studies* that the heaviest contact on April 6 occurred in the 3d Brigade's area of operation as the 2d Battalion, 7th Cavalry, continued its drive west on Highway Nine. In a daylong battle which ended when the enemy summarily abandoned his position and fled, the battalion had 83 NVA killed, one POW captured, and 121 individual and ten crew-served weapons captured. The 1st Cavalry Division troops were airlifted to Hill 471, relieving the Marines at this position. This was the first relief of the defenders of Khe Sanh. Two companies of troopers remained on the hill while two other companies attacked to the south toward the Khe Sanh hamlet. The 1st Cavalry forces on landing zone Snapper were attacked by an enemy force using mortars, hand grenades, and rocket launchers. The attack was a disaster for the enemy and twenty were killed. At 1320, the 84th Company of the Vietnamese 8th Airborne Battalion was airlifted by 1st Cavalry Division aircraft into the Khe Sanh Combat Base and linked up with elements of the 37th Ranger Battalion. The lift was conducted without incident and was marked as the official link-up of forces at Khe Sanh.

One of the aspects of the mission of Operation Pegasus yet to be accomplished was to clear Route 9 from Ca Lu to Khe Sanh, and my platoon became the tip of the spear to do that. Although 1st Cavalry units relieved Marines at Hill 471 and airlifted Vietnamese Airborne into KSCB (Khe Sanh Combat Base), Route 9 still had to be cleared. It was common practice for commanders to rotate personnel or units as point elements, and on this day it was other units' turn to be ahead of D Company. We were last in order of movement on this day, and we thought we got a break. But the forward companies made contact with the NVA, and we were ordered to reverse our movement to go back to the road to be picked up by chopper to leapfrog over

1st Cavalry troops in Operation Pegasus. (Lutz)

the two companies in contact to continue the mission to clear Route 9. Now my platoon was the lead unit again.

Sunday, April 7

1045 hrs. We air assaulted to an open area on a mountaintop and received light sniper fire. We found a complex (NVA) with rockets, mortars—tubes, and ammo—AK-47s, and all sorts of materiel. I have a sharp AK-47 which I hope to keep. We are to go to Khe Sanh.

We air assaulted near the top of a mountain that seemed to be solid rock. As we were moving toward the crest, I heard bullets whistle overhead and noticed that the ground had no cover and was just too hard to dig in if we had to. We just kept moving toward the crest. The point squad radioed that they saw bunkers as they approached, so I had the platoon get in a line formation so all firepower would be to the front. The lead squad got to the bunkers and radioed that there were no NVA. My platoon and the rest of the company secured and occupied this area at a location near the intersection of Route 9 and the road which lead to Lang Vei. It had been a regimental-size NVA complex with all kinds of weapons—mortars, machine guns, antiaircraft guns,

Captured NVA mortar rounds and arms. (Lutz)

NVA bugle that I sounded "charge" on entering Khe Sanh.

ZPU-4, AKs, RPDs, RPKs, RPGs, and commo wire linking bunkers surrounding the whole area. We found dead NVA soldiers in bunkers with blood coming out of their ears.

One of my guys found an old French bugle and put parachute cord on it to make a tassel. His nickname was "Turtle." He told me he found the bugle in a trench, and while putting the cord on it, a cobra snake rose up, puffed out, and he shot it with a .38 snub-nosed pistol he carried. It was his personal weapon and was unauthorized, but it came in handy that day. Turtle brought the cobra to show us stuck on an SKS rifle bayonet. It was a beautiful bluish- and silver-colored creature, pretty much shot up. Turtle must have put all six rounds in the snake. I got an AK-47 and a NVA bayonet and ammo pouch as souvenirs. I still have all the items except the AK, which became an issue for me later on. The area was pockmarked with bomb craters courtesy of the U.S. Air Force. The bombing was probably the result of Arc Lights. The jet jocks can brag about how sexy their "fighters" are, but I love B-52s.

We were about two miles outside of Khe Sanh, and although this NVA bunker complex was abandoned, Route 9 to Khe Sanh still had to be cleared. My platoon was tasked to lead the clearing action. We had to avoid the "toe poppers" (bomblets dropped by the Air Force) and other potential booby traps, and we still did not know the status of the NVA. We proceeded along the road, and I had some of my men straddle the road by 30 to 40 meters or so to act as flank security. As I did with my troop movements, I kept my RTOs nearby for commo with whomever I needed to have contact with, especially my squads. Of course, our weapons were "at the ready" as we did not know what awaited us.

I was constantly aware that we could be ambushed at any moment because the Marines could not move up and down Route 9 for over two months. My senses of sight, sound, and smell all seemed to be enhanced. I seemed to have a prescience or sixth sense when in my "combat mode." Captain Rapper recognized my prescience in tactical operations when he wrote in my Officer Efficiency Report that:

"Lieutenant Abodeely has unerring knowledge of basic infantry tactics. In addition to his basic exceptional knowledge, Lieutenant Abodeely has illustrated uncanny ability in land navigation and map orientation. This unique bit of perception appeared to give him an unusual ability at times to diagnose the enemy's intentions before they fully materialized."

When Lang Vei Special Forces camp was attacked by NVA with tanks, the Marine contingency plan for two Marine companies to exit Khe Sanh to go down Route 9 as a relief force could not be implemented because the NVA controlled the area. This was the same road we were on. There were bunkers strategically placed lining the road all the way to the wire at Khe Sanh to ambush anyone going down the road. We found "gook packs" (backpacks), opium, weapons, etc.—but the NVA had vanished. We led the movement for two miles to the Marine base and were ordered to stay outside the wire. There was no enemy contact.

Sunday, April 7, (cont.)

1700 hrs. We are at Khe Sanh camped outside the east entrance on Highway 9.

My parents sent me newspaper clippings about the Marines at Khe Sanh, and I thought that if there were a place on earth that was close to being HELL—it was Khe Sanh. General Westmoreland and the Marines who manned Khe Sanh carried out a campaign to block North Vietnamese infiltration into South Vietnam by way of the Demilitarized Zone that divided the two Vietnams. They also built up a base area which would serve as a jumping-off point for a proposed American advance (that was never authorized) into the panhandle region of Laos in order to cut off the Ho Chi Minh Trail.

The Khe Sanh base was located about fifteen miles south of the Demilitarized Zone and barely seven miles from the eastern frontier of Laos. It was almost completely surrounded by towering ridges, and it stood in the center of four valley corridors leading through the mountains to the north and northwest of the base. To the south Khe Sanh overlooked Highway 9, the only east-west road in the Northern Province to join Laos and the coastal regions. The base itself was laid out on a flat laterite plateau. It was shaped somewhat like an irregular rectangle and covered an area approximately one mile long and one-half mile wide. A key feature of the base was a 3,900-foot aluminum mat runway which during favorable weather conditions could accommodate fixed-wing aircraft up to C-130 transports.

The North Vietnamese built up forces in the area to confront the Americans in order to tie them down while their Tet Offensive in 1968 was carried out throughout South Vietnam in their ill-fated attempt to win the war with one knockout punch. President Johnson and his advisors were terrified for weeks that the siege of Khe Sanh would be the prelude to a full-scale assault on the Marine Combat Base at Khe Sanh, comparable to General Giap's 1954 Viet Minh victory over the French at a similar base at Dien Bien Phu. President Johnson had a table mock-up of Khe Sanh and he obsessed over the fate of the firebase.

Although the feared full-scale assault never materialized, largely due to the extremely intensive American bombing of the NVA positions around Khe Sanh and its satellite bases, American casualties were high; the Special Forces Camp at

President Johnson and advisors analyzing Khe Sanh mock-up table. (Wikipedia)

Lang Vei was overrun; and aerial resupply of the Combat Base was endangered by intense shelling, which forced the Air Force to devise methods of dropping pallets with supplies from the cargo aircraft which were skimming the runway without landing (LAPE—Low Altitude Parachute Extraction).

In early 1968, press correspondents dramatized the situation by repeatedly telling the public that Khe Sanh was likely to be a "very rough business with heartbreaking American casualties." The impending battle was viewed as a major test of strength between the U. S. and North Vietnam, with heavy political and psychological overtones. General Tolson, Commander of the 1st Cavalry Division (Airmobile), devised a plan for the relief of Khe Sanh.

The mission of Operation Pegasus was three-fold: one, to relieve the Khe Sanh Combat Base; two, to open Highway 9 from Ca Lu to Khe Sanh; and, three, to destroy the enemy forces within the area of operations. To accomplish the mission, the 1st Cavalry Division would be augmented by these nondivisional units: 1st Marine Regiment, 26th Marine Regiment, III Army of the Republic of Vietnam Airborne Task Force, and the 37th Army of the Republic of Vietnam operational control. The basic concept of Operation Pegasus was: The 1st Marine Regiment with two battalions would launch a ground attack west toward Khe Sanh while the 3d Brigade would lead the 1st Cavalry air assault.

On D+1 and D+2 all elements would continue to attack west toward Khe Sanh; and, on the following day, the 2d Brigade of the Cavalry would land three battalions southeast of Khe Sanh and attack northwest. The 26th Marine Regiment, which was holding Khe Sanh, would attack south to secure Hill 471. On D+4, the 1st Brigade would air assault just south of Khe Sanh and attack north. The following day the 3d Army of the Republic of Vietnam Airborne Task Force would air assault southwest of Khe Sanh and attack toward Lang Vei Special Forces Camp. Linkup was planned at the end of seven days. Of course, I did not know the "big picture" at the time as I was only the platoon leader.

Monday, April 8

1130 hrs. Today, D Company was the first to walk into Khe Sanh on Highway 9 in two months. The Marines have been pinned in but now they can move. My platoon was the first in. This place is bunkers and trenches. The incoming artillery is deadly. I sent my AK-47 in with Specialist 4 Sands who I hope will take care of it for me. My men sent in their captured weapons yesterday and they've been distributed out as training materials. This pisses me off, but I talked to the CO and maybe we can do something about it.

1445 hrs. Dear Mom and Dad,

Right now I'm sitting in a shit-house at Khe Sanh. Everything here is in bunkers beneath the ground as the NVA continually shoot artillery here. My company--D, 2nd of the 7th Cav--was the first unit to walk into Khe Sanh. My platoon walked in first. Newsmen, etc., were all around as we probably did something significant. You're probably reading about the Cav being in Khe Sanh now--we freed the Marines to get off their asses and go chase the NVA. This could be a turning point in the war. I hope all goes well. Anyway, we walked in on Highway 9, where no one before could travel because of ambushes. We cleared it. We are on the Khe Sanh perimeter now and tomorrow will go to a nearby LZ to walk out of there. I got the March 28 letter and I'm writing while I'm shitting. It's hot and the flies are unbelievable.

Well, I'll write later. I'm in a hurry. All is well. I'm still careful.

Love, Joe

[My unit pride got the best of me with the comment about the Marines getting off their asses to go chase NVA. The Marines were outnumbered, surrounded, and NVA artillery had the base zeroed in. My personal observation and reflection now tell me that movement down Route 9 before the 1st Cav cleared the road would have been catastrophic. The fact that we met little resistance from the enemy was a testament to the B-52 bombing and the "air cavalry" tactics of maneuverability and air mobility. The NVA came and went as they chose as Laos and the DMZ were not that far away. And we did not send large concentrations of forces to either area.]

Monday, April 8, (cont.)

2345 hrs. I'm writing by moonlight. I'm sitting on guard at a bunker. I can see to the west (Laos) where flares are shot over the mountain. A plane is shooting red streams of tracer bullets into the mountains.

My platoon was the first platoon to walk into Khe Sanh. It was the lead platoon, as it usually was on most actions, when we entered the wire perimeter at Khe Sanh, single file. My company commander asked me if I could play the bugle I had, and I told him I thought I could; I used to play trumpet and cornet in high school. He said to play the cavalry charge, and I blew the cavalry charge on the bugle. I was probably a sight as I led the 1st Cavalry troopers into Khe Sanh, with my equipment, M-16, and AK-47, and blowing "charge" on a bugle. We all knew this was a big deal at the time because Khe Sanh was all over the press, and apparently a couple of guys from another platoon wanted a photo op. They shook hands through the wire, and I think I did, too, since my platoon led the relief. The Marine captain I reported to directed me to where my platoon was to provide security that night. *The Los Angeles Herald Examiner* dated Monday, April 8, 1968, reported the event:

> SAIGON (UPI)--Blowing "Charge!" on a captured Communist Bugle, American ground forces linked up with the long-surrounded Marine fort of Khe Sanh and then fanned out and killed at least 103 North Vietnamese in the hills on South Vietnam's northern frontier, U.S. spokesmen said today…
> At Khe Sanh, where round-the-clock Communist artillery fire had driven 6000 Marine defenders underground, the Leathernecks Sunday whooped it

GIs Link Up at Khe Sanh, But Fight On

SAIGON (UPI) — Blowing "Charge!" on a captured Communist bugle, American ground forces linked up with the long-surrounded Marine fort of Khe Sanh and then fanned out and killed at least 103 North Vietnamese in the hills on South Vietnam's northern frontier, U.S. spokesmen said today.

A two-mile victorious march by the Army 1st Air Cavalry Division formally ended the 76-day Communist siege of the fort Hanoi vowed it would take and American generals pledged would never be lost.

The siege was over. But the battle for control of South Vietnam's Communist-infested northern frontier roared on. Besides the fighting in the hills near the fort, Leathernecks 25 miles southwest of the coastal city of Da Nang killed at least 68 Communists in a Sunday battle that cost no American casualties.

At Khe Sanh, where round-the-clock Communist artillery fire had driven 6000 Marine defenders underground, the Leathernecks Sunday whooped it up as Army 1st Lt. Joe Abodeely's unit walked the last two miles into the camp.

Abodeely, 24, of Tucson, Ariz., and his platoon formed the 1st Air Cavalry s p e a r h e a d of the 20,000-man Operation Pegasus drive that broke the Communist grip around Khe Sanh in a week-long drive that covered 12 miles of jungle, hills and minefields.

The lieutenant triumphantly blew on the bugle he found in a captured arms dump. Its notes echoed across the red dirt plateau. Abodeely's unit had landed by helicopter two miles from Khe Sanh and met no resistance the rest of the way. The helicopter leapfrog technique, plus a Marine road-clearing drive, formed the backbone of Pegasus.

The payoff came when the lieutenant's men reached the barbed wire around the camp. "Hey! We're here!" shouted Pfc. Juan Fordondi of Bay Amon, Puerto Rico. Marine Lance Cpl. James Hellebuick of Mount Clemens, Mich., whooped and from inside shoved a hand over the wire. GI Fordondi clasped it.

"We're really glad to see you guys," Hellebuick said, speaking for the defenders that for two days had seen relief only on the green hills of the horizon or on the landing strip where a token force of South Vietnamese paratroopers arrived Saturday.

The sudden collapse of Hanoi's might around Khe Sanh was seen in the trenches North Vietnamese troops had dug up to the fort's barbed wire defenses and then abandoned the past few days. In the trenches Abodeely's men found dozens of fresh field packs complete with Communist identification tags and clean uniforms.

Newspaper clipping about ending the siege at Khe Sanh.

up as Army 1st Lt. Joe Abodeely's unit walked the last two miles into the camp…

Abodeely, 24, of Tucson, Arizona, and his platoon formed the 1st Air Cavalry spearhead of the 20,000-man Operation Pegasus drive that broke the Communist grip around Khe Sanh in a weeklong drive that covered 12 miles of jungle, hills, and minefields.

The lieutenant triumphantly blew on the bugle he found in a captured arms dump. Its notes echoed across the red dirt plateau. Abodeely's unit had landed by helicopter two miles from Khe Sanh and met no resistance the rest of the way. The helicopter leapfrog technique, plus a Marine road-clearing drive, formed the backbone of Pegasus…

Sun Tzu, a famous Chinese warlord 2500 years ago is reputed to have said:

"Hence to fight and conquer in all your battles is not supreme excellence; supreme excellence consists in breaking the enemy's resistance without fighting."

That's what we did.

General Tolson wrote on "Airmobility 1961-1971" in *Vietnam Studies*:

"…it became increasingly evident, through lack of contact and the large amounts of new equipment being found indiscriminately abandoned on the battlefield, that the enemy had fled the area rather than face certain defeat. He was totally confused by the swift, bold, many-pronged attacks. Operations continued to the west…"

He also reported that on April 8, at 0800, the relief of Khe Sanh was effected, and the 1st Cavalry Division became the new landlord. The 3d Brigade airlifted its command post into Khe Sanh, and 2d Battalion, 7th Cavalry (my battalion, my company, and my platoon), successfully cleared Highway 9 to the base and linked up with the 26th Marine Regiment. The 3d Brigade elements occupied high ground to the east and northeast of the base with no enemy contact.

Nardi and Lutz with sign. (Lutz)

Tuesday, April 9

1055 hrs. Our company is waiting along the airstrip to get air assaulted back to LZ Mark (named after CO's son—also called LZ Thor). We'll secure the firebase there. I've still got a VC bugle that I blow for the company. I blew it when we came to Khe Sanh. There is rumor we'll go back to Evans soon. I hope so.

1515 hrs. Dear Mom and Dad,
Yesterday I wrote a letter from Khe Sanh. By the time you receive that letter and this one, you'll have already heard that the 1st Cavalry walked into Khe Sanh. Today, we airlifted to the artillery firebase we made near Khe Sanh. We are relaxing and gloating as we rescued the "glorious" Marines. Khe Sanh was noted for constant artillery bombardment and last night we did not receive one round. The NVA don't like to

mess with us. My platoon found many enemy weapons on the way into Khe Sanh, and I got a beautiful automatic weapon I'm going to try to keep. I also got a bugle which I blew as we walked into Khe Sanh. My platoon was the first to walk into the perimeter and take over part of the Marines' sector. I was interviewed and photographed by various press people, but I don't know if anything will come of it. One interviewer taped our conversation.

Well, I'm glad to hear Bob likes his real estate course. What kind of car is he driving now? I surely am homesick. I hope I can go on R&R soon as I need a break. Enclosed is another receipt for pay. Dad, find out for me what I have to do for income tax.

Well, I guess we'll still be securing this road to Khe Sanh for a while. I believe the NVA are clearing out as the Cav is here, but I'm still careful. Well, I've things to do. I'm going to clean my weapon, change socks, and check our bunkers.

Love, Joe

[That was more of my sophomoric hubris. The Marines put up with hell at Khe Sanh, and nobody can take that away from them. They did their job in untenable circumstances. They were in a static defense at Khe Sanh and did not have the helicopter assets the 1st Cav had.]

Wednesday, April 10

1200 hrs. We are here at LZ Thor (Mark). The first and third platoons are with the dozer repairing the road while my platoon is defending the whole company perimeter. My men and I made poncho liner sun shelters. It's hot already. We're sitting by our bunkers. I guess by now everyone knows the Cav rescued the Marines at Khe Sanh. I hope I can keep my AK-47. I have a bugle I play, but the CO wants it for the company. My M-16 is dirty again so I guess I'll clean it.

Thursday, April 11

0730 hrs. Yesterday afternoon my platoon took a bulldozer west down Hwy. 9 to fill in bomb holes and clear away trees. We found two dead NVA. They smelled, and flies and maggots covered the distorted bodies. Today we go to some bridges to secure them.

[The bodies were bloated and appeared to be larger than the normal Vietnamese stature. Someone made a comment about them possibly being Chinese. The bodies were bloated and "blackened" from a possible napalm strike. The odor of a dead burned body can best be described as a sweet stench—the sweet, cooked smell of burned fatty meat.]

1800 hrs. Today we move from LZ Thor to a mountaintop overlooking a bridge below. The rest of the company is at another bridge. I'm pissed off because we didn't get food and water because we weren't on the right radio frequency to call the log ship in. The CO didn't even act concerned.

I don't think this CO particularly liked me. I was the senior platoon leader in the field, was a little older than most of the troops, and had a college degree and a year of law school. I don't think he had a degree. There was often resentment between ROTC college graduates and the OCS commissioned officers. I think he was trying to prove himself. Most of my platoon went down to the river to swim—the platoon sergeant told them it was okay. This pissed me off, too. We were supposed to go to the top of this hill to provide security. I went up by myself and I saw a bird. I just whipped up my M-16 and killed it. I just felt like killing something.

I am kneeling (left front) kneeling with my platoon.

Friday, April 12

1405 hrs. Today my platoon hitched a ride with a Marine convoy (trucks and tanks) to LZ Thor. We're waiting here to go to Khe Sanh and later to Camp Evans. It appears that our work is done here. I hope so. Last night was cold on the mountaintop. The sky looks like rain.

Saturday, April 13

0810 hrs. I'm at Khe Sanh now. The sky is cloudy; it's windy and cold. I'm sitting in a shit house built by the Marines. The bunker my CP slept in last night was big; we could even stand up in it. Yesterday I had to go to brigade to see about one of my men who shot a hand popper. This morning I had a problem about one of my men sleeping on guard. Today we are to go to Camp Evans.

[A "hand popper" was a flare in an aluminum cylinder. You took off the cap and affixed it to the bottom of the cylinder, about a foot long and an inch in diameter. You held the cylinder in one hand and struck the cap that had a firing pin at the bottom with the other hand. The nail-type "firing pin" set off an explosive charge to send up a flare—hence, "hand popper." They provided illumination in a confined area—not as much as the artillery illumination rounds did, but they had their use. They also could light up your own unit's positions. I had to go explain to brigade and tell them it wouldn't happen again.]

Saturday, April 13, (cont.)

1416 hrs. We are still waiting to go. A C-130 landed about 15 minutes ago and crashed. Its wing is on fire about 250-300 m down the runway.

Sunday, April 14

1102 hrs. My platoon and first platoon got here to Camp Evans yesterday. The rest of the company isn't here yet. Today I went to PMO to see about getting captured weapons home.

[The PMO was the Provost Marshal Office. I wanted to send the AK-47 (paratrooper style) home legally, per regulations.]

Plane crash at Khe Sanh. (Lutz)

1107 hrs. Dear Mom and Dad,

I'm back here to Camp Evans. I don't know what we'll do next. There is talk of the A Shau Valley which is west of Camp Evans and South of Khe Sanh. This valley is supposed to be an important NVA supply route. If we go there, it will be more rough stuff. We've been through all the hotspots.

By the way, Mom, that picture was another 1st Cavalry unit. I don't know how it was written up back home, but we (D Company--mine) walked down and cleared the impassable Highway 9 into Khe Sanh. My platoon led the column walking in the perimeter of Khe Sanh. There is rumor that we may later go back to An Khe. I hope so.

About the meter--it's 39.7 inches long. We use it to measure distances.

More choppers are landing nearby so maybe the rest of the company will come in today. Those pictures of Khe Sanh in *Life* were the place. I walked on that runway at night to coordinate with ARVNs and I thought I was going to get shot by someone.

I'm going to take one of my squad leaders with me to get a haircut. Tomorrow's payday. Big deal.

I am standing (far left) with my platoon back at Camp Evans.

> I can't spend any money anyway. I just save my $50 and waste it on booze or other garbage when I can.
>   I'll write later. All is the same. Give my regards to everyone.
>   Love, Joe

Monday, April 15

1405 hrs. The HQ and mortar (fourth platoon) came in today. We're supposed to have an awards presentation sometime today. I'm afraid we may go into the A Shau Valley. Today I wrote several letters. I also got paid today and lowered my $50 norm pay to $30 as I won't need so much.

I remember going to an awards presentation, and seeing Captain Rapper, my former CO who was now the S-4 (battalion supply officer), at that meeting. Some of the other companies awarded Silver Stars and Bronze Stars with "Vs" for valor, but Rapper wasn't that generous with awards. Interestingly, he wrote in my Officer Efficiency Report:

"I have observed, on numerous occasions, Lieutenant Abodeely's exceptional ability to react with equanimity and force under conditions of duress. He is a fearless leader and an inspiration to those who follow him. His primary concern, secondary to the mission, is the welfare and protection of his men. Case in point, I watched him move into an open area, under heavy fire, to pull two wounded men to safety."

That could have been a Silver Star citation. Rapper looked at me as we left the awards presentation, and I distinctly remember him saying, "We missed the boat on that," referring to not making more recommendations for awards as did the other units.

Tuesday, April 16

1100 hrs. Today the other three companies in the battalion are air assaulting about six clicks southwest of here (Evans). D Company (mine) is in reserve. We'll go out soon. I think we're

> working our way into the A Shau Valley. Lieut. Lutstein and I had a spat about my AK-50. I'm not going to turn it in as he wants. The CO sides with me. My old medic moved to mortars and I got a new one. I hope I get out of the field soon.

When we secured that large NVA headquarters two miles outside of Khe Sanh, my men and I took a lot of souvenirs—primarily weapons. Army regulations allowed for captured weapons to be sent back to the U.S., and many of us wanted to do so. Lutstein distributed my men's weapons as training material without their consent. I had kept mine, and Lutstein wanted me to turn it in. We didn't like each other, and I think he disapproved a recommendation for me to receive a Silver Star for the February 27 action. I sent the AK-47 home later in a footlocker, due to a rapid, unexpected redeployment of my unit from I Corps to III Corps. I wanted it to be on display at the Tucson VFW building, which my grandfather raised the money to build. The AK was discovered by customs, and this became a problem for me. I referred to the AK-47 as an AK-50 in my diary because I was told that the folding paratrooper stock made it an AK-50. Actually, it was an AK-47 with a folding paratrooper stock.

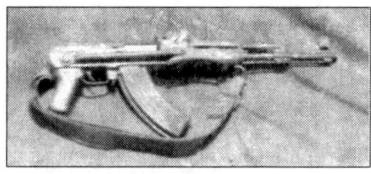

AK-47 captured at Khe Sanh.

> 1500 hrs. We got the word we are to air assault in 15 minutes. We are to set up somewhere for the night near a road and river. I believe we're working toward the infamous A Shau Valley.
>
> 1640 hrs. The air assault was canceled.

Wednesday, April 17

> 0900 hrs. Again we're sitting around waiting to make an air assault. I found out that where we were to go yesterday there were secondary explosions from the artillery prep, and ARA ships spotted bunkers. Today we may go into this area. Last night I scrounged some steaks and my men got everything else

and we had a good time. Now we're "saddling up" to move out. We're going near the A Shau Valley.

The campaign into the A Shau Valley was another major campaign like Operation Pegasus. During Operation Pegasus, the Cav sent out recon missions to determine locations of LZs and air defense artillery (ADA). During Operation Delaware (A Shau campaign) the Cav's artillery preps must have hit some ammo, and the ARA (aerial rocket artillery) and their scout ships (LOHs—light observation helicopters) must have spotted enemy bunkers. This set the Cav apart from other units—its ability to use its helicopter assets to recon the objective area before committing helicopters and troops. The 1972 Operation Lam Son 719 (campaign into Laos), which was NOT conducted by the 1st Air Cavalry Division, did NOT perform the necessary recon prior to inserting ARVN troops into Laos. One hundred helicopters were lost and 400 were damaged.

Wednesday, April 17, (cont.)

1815 hrs. We air assaulted about six clicks west of Camp Evans. We moved out today—company minus (first and second platoons)—and now we'll set up here for the night. Third platoon is going out on a goat about 200 m away. Another log "bird" (chopper) is coming in now.

Thursday, April 18

1100 hrs. I took my platoon on a patrol down to the river this morning. There were three destroyed houses, some old punji pits and spider holes, and some old trails. A chopper just brought some water in. It's hot already. We're supposed to be air assaulted sometime after 1200 to an area near A Shau.

Friday, April 19

0700 hrs. We air assaulted to a large assembly area for the battalion near a river. Many of us went swimming yesterday.

Today we have one of two missions—secure radio relay station or create a battalion firebase—both missions in the A Shau Valley. Last night one of our platoons air assaulted in the dark. It's weird to see the choppers fly in the dark.

Saturday, April 20

0930 hrs. The mission was canceled again to go to A Shau, but now it's on again. We're still at this battalion assembly area about six clicks outside of Evans. We're getting all kinds of extra supplies we have to carry as we may have supply problems. I heard four ships were shot down in the A Shau area. This will be the worst area yet. We're going to the top of the mountain to set up a firebase.

[We got extra food (C-rations) and ammo because we didn't know if we could get routine resupply where we were going.]

1115 hrs. I'm listening to the radio; the first ship of one of our companies is on the mountain at A Shau; another ship hit a tree and is burning. We'll go in later.

[Going into the A Shau Valley was sounding very scary as we monitored the radio.]

1470 hrs. The weather is getting bad so we'll abort the mission until tomorrow. The choppers can't fly.

Sunday, April 21

1520 hrs. Choppers just landed 150 m away to pick up one of the companies, but I think the weather is still too bad to complete the mission.

Monday, April 22

0710 hrs. Here we go again. We are going to try to get to that mountaintop. One company has been stranded there without food and water for three days. The B–52 strike on the mountain missed and there is no artillery support, and the forest is thick so everything is bad. Also, the weather doesn't permit much chopper flying. NVA have mortared the company at the mountain already—2 KIA, 1 WIA.

1450 hrs. My troops are playing poker and blackjack while I'm monitoring the battalion push. Most of the other two companies got to the mountain (LZ Pepper), but the weather is bad again. Our company may be stuck here tonight if the cloud cover doesn't break.

[Because helicopters were an integral part of our operations, the weather was a crucial factor. Operation Delaware, or the A Shau campaign, was difficult due to the weather and the terrain—high, steep, heavily vegetated mountains.]

Tuesday, April 23

0755 hrs. Part of another company and our first and second platoons are on the PZ (pickup zone) waiting to go to LZ Pepper. The sky is still a little cloudy, but we may make it today. The terrain there is supposed to be very thick. Some flying cranes with bulldozers were shot down a couple of days ago.

[LZ (landing zone) Pepper was to be the battalion's headquarters area.]

1145 hrs. We finally made it. We flew high above the mountains and clouds. Two helicopters which crashed burned here. The terrain is thick except for a few bomb craters. We're trying

Crashed helicopter at LZ Pepper. (Lutz)

> to clear the area. Not 300 m away we can hear a firefight. There's a lot of automatic weapons fire. I don't like this place.

Our "lift" was only five men and some mortar ammo. We heard that we would fly over some high triple-canopy jungles and mountains to get to the A Shau Valley. We were monitoring the radios and heard about the flying crane (gigantic helicopter) carrying a bulldozer being shot down. We were assembled in our lift groups when the choppers arrived. I had my jungle fatigues' sleeves rolled up because it was hot waiting in the sun to be picked up. On my lift, I had a grenadier, an M-60 man, a rifleman, an RTO, and me. We got picked up and the helicopter kept climbing and climbing. I remember rolling my sleeves down as it was getting colder. We flew over triple-canopied jungle with winding rivers. It looked like a scene where a brontosaurus might emerge from the river; it was primeval. The pilot spoke over the headset which I wore when conducting air assaults and let me know we were approaching the LZ. It was all steep mountaintops with bomb craters, broken and burned trees; and I could see a downed helicopter partially burned in an open area right where we were to land. In

Chinook hovering at LZ Pepper. (Lutz)

fact, its crash site was the only open area for us to "un-ass" the chopper. Our helicopter did not even land; it couldn't, so we jumped as it hovered over the ground. There were steep ridges on this mountaintop (called LZ Pepper), and we were ordered to take "point" from where firing was coming. As usual, we took the lead again. I moved my platoon to a narrow area which was the "point" of the battalion units. We dug foxholes and put timbers of downed trees in place to make fortified fighting positions. I remember it hailing on us, and all I had was a sweater and my jungle fatigues. It was very cold.

Wednesday, April 24

1025 hrs. Yesterday, we worked on clearing an LZ. A Chinook crash-landed right over our company location. Several of our people were hurt. One of my men was injured badly. A man in third platoon had a leg severed. The Chinook kept exploding near my platoon's positions as it had fuel and artillery and 90 mm ammo. I had to move my platoon to a different location in the woods in a ravine and set up in the dark. It was somewhat of a problem. I pulled a muscle or something in my left leg.

A Chinook is a large turbine-powered cargo helicopter with two large, horizontally mounted rotors, front and back, which can carry 30 infantry troops or a lot of cargo. We were at our defensive position when we heard the extremely loud screeching of the Chinook's turbine engines fast approaching right overhead. I could tell it was coming in too fast and was not going to land correctly. It crashed into a ravine, and we were told it carried a lot of 90 mm ammo, much of it beehive rounds—the kind of ammo we had at the Bong Son bridges—thousands of little metal inch-long "arrows" or darts per round. A couple bystanders were seriously injured when the Chinook crashed. Two men each lost a leg from flying debris. Ammunition was exploding, and we had to move our position in the dark, traversing very rough terrain. I had pulled a tendon in my leg, making it difficult to move around or check positions or go to meetings with the CO.

Thursday, April 25

1055 hrs. We've continued to improve the LZ. The artillery has four guns on this Hill. We're still set up in the woods. My men built outstanding positions with overhead cover and camouflage. The battalion HQ and brigade HQ will set up behind my platoon HQ. I went to the field aid station and the doctor said I pulled a tendon. Eventually, we'll probably operate off this mountain. The forest is amazingly thick and difficult to move through. The area around here is high and mountainous and heavily vegetated. It's very cold at night. We're only about three clicks from Laos.

[Four guns referred to four 105 millimeter howitzers. Perhaps the battalion and brigade headquarters felt most secure near my HQ, or perhaps it was the simply the best location.]

Friday, April 26

1345 hrs. I'm sitting by some log bunkers my men made overlooking the valley far below. It's almost eerie as the fog roles in through the forest and the skeleton trees with the limbs and leaves blown off from Bangalore torpedoes. The Catholic chaplain gave mass which I attended. I had a dream last night that my mother and father got killed in a car accident. It happened when my dad missed a turn on the freeway. I hope nothing like that happens. The fog has rolled in again where I can't see the valley below. There is rumor that we'll air assault to the valley tomorrow if the weather is good.

[Bangalore torpedoes were "pipes" filled with composition 4 (C-4), a puttylike explosive. You fit the pipes together end to end to extend 30, 40, maybe 50 feet, depending on the terrain and circumstances. You slid them under concertina wire barricades or into mine fields or into thick brush and detonated the "torpedoes" to clear a path. They were very effective.]

Saturday, April 27

0945 hrs. We're supposed to air assault to the valley today for a three-day operation. It's still foggy. We'll probably walk off the mountain which will be a real hike.

1310 hrs. It's still foggy. Choppers won't be able to get in and it looks like we won't have to walk down to the valley today.

    1312 hrs. Dear Mom and Dad,
    I haven't written in a while so I thought
I'd write to let you know I'm still alive.
Our battalion is set up high on a mountain
overlooking the A Shau Valley, which runs into
Laos and is an NVA stronghold. Two of our

companies are on two adjacent mountaintops and another company and ours are pulling perimeter guard around four artillery 105 howitzers and the battalion and brigade headquarters. This operation is to rid the valley of NVA building up to possibly attack Hue. Some of our other units have found tanks and vehicles provided by the Russians to the NVA. My platoon is presently set up in a very thick forest. My men cut down small trees and vegetation with machetes to clear fields of fire and make log bunkers. Army engineers used explosives to blow down large trees for us. The weather has been raining. We haven't been able to get very many resupplies by chopper because the mountains are constantly in clouds. When the first choppers tried to land troops in here, two of the choppers crashed. Their blades hit trees and caused the ships to crash. After our company got here, a big Chinook chopper was bringing supplies and it crash-landed less than 30 m from one of my men's positions. One of my men got some broken ribs from flying trees and debris. Two men in the 3rd platoon each lost a leg as flying pieces from the chopper severed their legs. Right now we're having a logistic problem. We've had no water brought to us in two days. We've been catching rainwater for drinking. I hope this operation ends soon because the monsoon will set in and they'll never be able to get choppers in to get us out. I pulled a tendon in my knee, but I can't let up as there's nothing that can be done for it. Please tell the Barcelos thanks for writing me and that I'll write when I can borrow some more stationery and when I get the time. Ma, if you get the chance could you send some goodies like cans of peanuts and some candies and maybe some cans of sardines or fruit? I'm tired of just

C-rations 3 times a day. I hope we get through this area okay. It's another "hot" one, but we should be all right.
    Love, Joe
    P. S. The article was given to me. I blew the bugle. Also another pay voucher is enclosed.

Sunday, April 28

0810 hrs. Music to the ears—choppers are coming in landing on both log pads with food and water. Because we weren't resupplied before, we couldn't move out, but with food and water we are supposed to walk to the valley floor. The mountain we are on has a 45° slope and is very thickly wooded. It will be a challenge to get off this mountain.

1105 hrs. We are taking a five-minute break as we move off this mountain. I got mail with clippings today.

[We actually were walking off of this very high mountain to go down to the valley floor.]

Monday, April 29

0715 hrs. Our whole company climbed out of a ravine last night to the top of this hill. We stayed here as we had reached the valley. One of the other companies was in heavy contact on the adjacent ridge. We all slept on the hill's slanted slope. Today we should reach the valley. I don't like the area. The NVA have too much here.

[I slept between saplings so I wouldn't roll down the mountain. It was unbelievably steep.]

2025 hrs. My platoon led today. We got off the ridge we were on; got to a hill; went down to the valley; and we're now on another hill. It's pitch-black out with fog in the sky and on the mountains. This hill was bombed before, so the trees are without leaves and the place looks desolate and spooky. Our company's mission is to walk around to the northwest over a lot of mountains to the A Shau Valley side. It's an impossible task. I'm sitting on the ground near a big tree writing by my flashlight with the red lens.

As we approached the hill in the dark of night, I remember seeing the moon behind the hill silhouetting trees without leaves. It was very eerie. In light of all I had experienced in Vietnam so far, this still actually frightened me. I wrote in my diary that the trees were leafless due to bombing, but Agent Orange may have also contributed to the trees' appearance.

Tuesday, April 30

0735 hrs. It rained last night and I'm soaked this morning. We're moving out up the mountain now. We had an artillery prep already. Our platoon will be last in order of movement today.

1515 hrs. We're waiting for a log ship.

1922 hrs. It's dark again. The company is set up on a small, narrow ridge. It's only 5 m wide with cliff drops on each side. We are set up in the bamboo and other vegetation. We never did get a supply of food and water. The choppers couldn't make it. Today I disagreed with the CO and FO on the company's location on the map. I was right. We've been doing a lot of hiking lately.

Cutting through the elephant grass was an exhausting and slow process. A couple of soldiers with machetes would lead the company column moving in single file at only the speed the cut vegetation would allow. It was hot and humid, and we were perspiring profusely. The insects, like land leeches and ants, were annoying. We missed a routine logistic supply of food and water, but we carried enough with us to survive until the next resupply. Reading the map of the terrain in this area was extremely difficult. There were many deviations of elevation—hills, mountains, ravines, saddles, etc. The commanding officer (Capt. Swenson), the forward observer, and I weren't sure where we were, but I thought I knew. We verified with artillery marking rounds, and I was right. This was not an ego issue—it was a security and safety issue. Lieutenant Stoneman, my old artillery forward observer, taught me the importance of knowing where you are on the ground.

May, 1968

Wednesday, May 1

1230 hrs. We got a change of mission. We are to go around this high ridge. We got resupplied today which improved our morale. I believe that this company is doing all the hiking out of harassment. It's very hot. I'm sitting on the trail cut in bamboo 20 feet high. The land leeches and ants are numerous. I had a disciplinary problem with a new guy. He didn't pull guard and I'm going to court-martial him. I hope we don't run into any contact. We're the only company in our battalion who has walked off this mountain.

[The problem soldier was transferred to another unit, so I didn't have to deal with him. He happened to be a Black soldier, and I don't know how he was treated before I got him. I think he was a problem in his previous unit and I inherited him. Everyone did guard duty, but he simply refused. He was moved to another unit.]

Thursday, May 2

0900 hrs. We set up on this hill yesterday evening. It's all bamboo and we had to cut our way through everything. Today my platoon will be point platoon. The CO wants us to move about one click today. There are old bunkers and a trail where we are.

I think we'll follow this trail and hope we don't get ambushed. We're supposed to hit another trail in about 400 m, which could be an NVA supply route.

Friday, May 3

0920 hrs. We're moving out again. Yesterday we got completely soaked in rain. We are still on our same mission. We can't move too far at any time because the terrain is so mountainous and heavily vegetated. Fortunately, we've had no contact yet, but we're due.

1945 hrs. It's dark now. We're camped at the base of Hill 900 and we'll be going around to the north. First platoon saw two gooks today. I hope we don't hit the shit tomorrow. Today ends our sixth day in the boonies. We've been humping a lot of mountains. Right now we are only a click and a half from Laos.

[The A Shau Valley and Laos were where the NVA main supply route was. We were trying to interdict that supply process, but we were not to send troops into Laos. The NVA could just go hide across the border.]

Saturday, May 4

0945 hrs. We got an early start today. We are rounding Hill 900 and heading north by northeast. We all have heavy beards. The sky is cloudy. We are all up high in the jungle forest. I can see ants walking on leaves, and I can hear the jungle birds and insects making noises.

[I got stung by a bee on my hand that day. My hand slowly began to swell up.]

Sunday, May 5

0835 hrs. We are on the "road" again. My platoon is point (lead) today. Yesterday I got stung by a bee on my left hand forefinger. My finger and hand are swollen but I don't dare go in as my "shamming" platoon sgt. hasn't come back from Camp Evans. Last night I fired artillery on a hill where my men saw tracers being fired from. I got a large secondary explosion which means I got an ammo dump or POL location. My men helped me adjust—Sgt. Ross and Spec 4 Jasper.

This was an eventful day for me. I had two men with machetes cutting through elephant grass faster than the other platoons had done. As we got out of the elephant grass into the jungle forest, I had a squad ahead of me in order of movement. *Boom!* A gigantic explosion concussion knocked us down. At first, I thought it was an incoming RPG round. It hit about 10 meters (33 feet) away on the other side of a big tree.

My company commander, Capt. Swenson, called on the radio: "All Heavy Bones elements, be advised that we are firing friendly redlegs (artillery) about 200 mikes (meters) in front of the lead element." I grabbed the handset from my RTO's still-shaking hand and told the CO his "damned" friendly "redleg" almost took out my lead element. A 105 mm howitzer round impact has a killing radius of 50 meters.

He admonished me to observe proper radio discipline. The company commander couldn't believe we moved so far so fast. Remember, he and the artillery forward observer who called in the artillery were wrong before about our unit's position on the map when I was correct. This is another time I was reminded of my mortality and the potentially fatal hubris and incompetence of others. So-called "friendly fire" almost killed my men and me.

It was pitch-black that night. I couldn't see my hand in front of my face, but I could see the tracers shooting up from the darkness at a helicopter patrolling in the dark. I called in artillery at what I thought was the location of the source of the tracer rounds. Ross and Jasper helped me adjust, and we saw a secondary explosion—a fireball explosion from impact of our artillery. We hit something in Laos.

Monday, May 6

0735 hrs. We are moving out again. We won't go too far right away as we'll make an LZ for resupply. I'll go in today to have my hand checked as it is swollen. Sgt. Ross will go in today, too. This operation should end soon.

1915 hrs. Here I am back at LZ Pepper. The company comes in tomorrow. I came in today because of my swollen hand. We'll be here for a few days. I finally shaved today after nine days in the field.

Tuesday, May 7
0900 hrs. Dear Mom and Dad,
I've been really busy lately. We stayed up here at LZ Pepper south of A Shau Valley and then D company (ours) had to walk off this high mountain down to the valley floor. Yesterday was the 9th day that we've been walking around the base of these mountains. The terrain is fantastic. There are thick forests, bamboo 20 feet high, and loads of all kinds of insects--especially leeches. Yesterday, I came back here to LZ Pepper, as I got stung by a bee 3 days ago and my hand was still swollen. Today the company will be airlifted here to Pepper. We'll man the perimeter here for a while. Other units of the Cavalry have found enemy weapons and supplies, but we haven't seen much. This operation should end soon and we'll go back to LZ Evans.

I haven't had much time lately so I'm going to try to catch up on my letter writing. When I get a chance, I think I'll try to get my toe checked in the rear area. Tell Bob that I got a letter from Jim Khan, and I'll try to write as soon as I can. All of my people are beat after 10 days in

the boonies with little food and water (sometimes
none until a chopper can land at an LZ we may
cut in a bamboo area). I'm okay. Just tired and
somewhat disgusted with this operation because
we walked so far needlessly. Well, say hello to
everyone for me, and I'll write later.
   Joe

[The comment about getting my toe checked referred to an old football injury I got in high school. A player stepped on my second toe, left foot, and I've had a calcium deposit there ever since. I go to a myopractor now and have the calcium rubbed out. I thought maybe the Army could take care of the problem, but now I am glad I never had it operated on.]

1050 hrs. The company came in today and we are manning this perimeter.

Wednesday, May 8

0855 hrs. It rained heavily yesterday. The wind blew the monsoon rains all around. It hailed, too. We are still manning this perimeter. LZ Goodman got rocketed and mortared last night. I got packages from Kathleen.

1405 hrs. Dear Mom and Dad,
   I'm sending back a clipping you sent me, but this one was sent to me by Jim Khan. Also enclosed is a clipping sent to me by some woman in Georgia who is sending my platoon packages of goodies. Well, we're on this perimeter (a mountaintop overlooking the A Shau Valley). This operation should be done in a week; I just hope we don't go out into the boonies again before then. Many of our choppers have been shot up,

but we are cutting off the main supply route and
retreat route of the NVA between Laos and Hue. I
hear that Paris Peace Talks are due about 10 May.
I hope all turns out well. Not too much more to
add. I'm going to try to work on getting a staff
job again. I'm tired of being shot at, but the
adventure is exciting.

   Joe

Thursday, May 9

1240 hrs. It's hot today. We're all just sitting around. Last night one of the other companies accidentally shot an artillery round into our perimeter. Nobody was injured. A Company, who took our places, ran into some NVA. We were lucky we didn't stay out one day longer. They had three KIA and several WIA. There's an estimated NVA battalion where we were. Air strikes have been called in. Luckily the artillery round hurt no one, but on 5 May our FO was shooting and he actually landed a "105" round only 10 m from my platoon and me. It's a miracle nobody was hurt as its killing radius is 50 m.

[Obviously, that near miss of "friendly fire" by the 105 artillery round left a huge impression on me.]

Friday, May 10

1300 hrs. The sun is shining bright today. It's hot now. A Chinook chopper landed by the artillery about 70 m away to pick up backlog. It's hovering now throwing dust and loose items all over. Yesterday, my old CO—Capt. Rapper, now the S-4—asked if I'd like to work with the S-4 section. I told him yes, but I want to check on other things to see if I can get a better job. This job would be good as I'd handle the battalion supply.

Saturday, May 11

0637 hrs. There are four Chinooks hovering this LZ like giant bugs waiting to pick up equipment. We'll be back at Camp Evans today or tomorrow.

1045 hrs. We are clearing the LZ—destroying them and backlogging equipment NVA could use. It looks like we'll be at Camp Evans today.

Sunday, May 12

0807 hrs. We got here to Camp Evans yesterday. It was exciting flying high over the A Shau Valley which was pockmarked with artillery, mortar, and bomb craters. Last night the officers had a get-together. There's a good chance I'll get a staff job soon. Later today or tomorrow, we'll go on another operation around here.

Monday, May 13

0803 hrs. The company is waiting here by chopper pad. The choppers are warming up as we will board them in conducting an air assault to a village area. First platoon is loading now. I hope we don't hit anything.

Tuesday, May 14

0735 hrs. It's a cloudy, overcast day. Yesterday we air assaulted on the sands again. We walked the white sands and then cut into the villages. Yesterday evening we walked from one village to this location on the sand. I knew it'd happen. We got mortared. My HQ and I were sitting around and we heard the mortar tubes go thump. We were down in holes before the rounds hit. Then Hall and Sands helped me adjust our mortar fire on the VC mortars. Last night we got sniped at several times. My men have found rice caches at this location buried in the ground.

Wednesday, May 15

1030 hrs. Well, second platoon did it again. Yesterday, we air assaulted to this spot here on the sand looking into a village in a wooded area. We got sniper fire. My platoon sgt., Sgt. Blanko, took Pfc. Brand and the 90 mm and shot a cemented building where some gooks were. The CO called in air strikes up ahead. Our mortar platoon fired at the village. Last night we set up here and found punji pits, a booby trap which 2-5 blew, and we found some more rice caches. Some of the rice was already shelled. Last night we were sniped at. Today our FO called in naval gunfire to the area ahead of us.

Punji pit. (Lutz)

[That was an important mission—to find rice caches. These were not 20- or 50- or 100-pound bags of rice—these were huge baskets 10 feet in diameter and several feet deep—tons of rice. Our job was to deny this to the enemy. The villages along the coast were often enemy infested, and we relocated the villagers to district headquarters where they were safe from intimidation or crossfire from competing military forces—US or VC or NVA. "2-5" meant second platoon sergeant.]

Thursday, May 16

1040 hrs. We're here at the same place as yesterday in the sands. We are calling in an air strike to our front on a village from which we've been receiving sniper fire. I can hear the roar of jets diving and then the blast of the exploding bombs. We'll have to check the village out later. Sgt. Ross went in yesterday. It's hot again already.

1618 hrs. We moved into the village area. It's very green and fertile. There are bombed-out hooches and pagodas. Right now we're stopped on a large, open, grassy field while the FO shoots artillery up ahead. We found booby traps, but we haven't been sniped at yet. I hear roosters off in the distance so people (VC) are around somewhere. It's overcast now and I'm so hot; just humid.

Friday, May 17

1045 hrs. We're on the open field again. First platoon is checking out some bridges from where we received sniper fire last night and this morning. Today, Spec 4 Brand fired the 90 mm into some hooches and blew the shit out of them. I've got a good all-around platoon which I'm really proud of. It's hot out.

1600 hrs. We got sniped at some more. Some of the rounds came very close. I'm tired of getting shot at. I feel like a moving target. We airlifted a little while ago to a one-company LZ firebase (105 mm) on the sand just north of Camp Evans. We have sandbagged bunkers and it's like being on the Sahara desert here. I hope we can rest here for a while.

Saturday, May 18

1050 hrs. Dear Mom and Dad,

We are at a company-size LZ on the sand just north of Camp Evans. The last 4 days we've been sniped at both day and night. I hope I get out of the field soon. I go on R&R 25 June. I'll probably want some money sent so I can buy a tape recorder and other stuff. I decided to go to Singapore. It certainly is hot here on the sand. We are operating around Camp Evans checking VC villages. Do you think you can send me another one of those little radios? The last one I had was in a combat pack which they sling out by chopper in the evenings, and the ship dropped the sling from high as we were receiving sniper rounds. The radio broke and I'm not sure I can fix it.

Well, what else is new back home? I guess the war is still not near to ending. Nobody understands that these peasants with weapons have nothing better to do than fight, and they don't care about political goals. I just hope I live through this hell to get back to school. I guess everything will turn out all right. It's so hot now that I'm sitting here naked as I write. I'll write later about money for R&R.

Joe

1245 hrs. It's very hot out. Most everyone is in his bunker. All this white sand looks like White Sands, New Mexico. This will be a good rest here for a while.

Sunday, May 19

0900 hrs. I'm back at Camp Evans at an aid station getting my toe x-rayed. I saw a wounded G.I. in great pain. He was getting a transfusion and was suffering greatly. I got a new platoon sgt.

and squad leader yesterday. I came in yesterday by chopper to check on the assistant S-4 job. It looks good.

1600 hrs. I flew here to Da Nang where I am getting my toe x-rayed and checked.

1745 hrs. I'm sitting in the sand looking at the beautiful South China Sea. I'm talking to a pretty blonde-haired, blue-eyed nurse—Susan Franko.

Monday, May 20

0845 hrs. I'm in the hospital mess hall having a cup of coffee. I'll see the doctor in about 15 minutes. Last night a couple of the doctors, the supply sergeant, some Special Forces men, and I all got drunk. Later in the night one of the Special Forces men (Groden) and I took a Jeep and drove around Da Nang at night which is off limits. The Special Forces team rented a house and kept it stocked with prostitutes. We visited them last night.

The night with the Special Forces was surrealistic. I wound up at this large house or hotel very, very drunk. Groden and I were out riding around Da Nang in a Jeep past curfew which was a great way to get killed by someone—US, ARVN, or VC. I got a girl at the Special Forces' house; we went to a room, had sex; I went to sleep or passed out. I awoke, saw she was gone, and got very worried that I could be assassinated without anyone knowing. I survived the night and finished my business at the hospital the next day.

1705 hrs. My plane to Phu Bai is to leave tomorrow. I'm with three other officers who are in transit. The dr. said I'd have to wait to get my toe operated on. Da Nang is big and well developed (military).

[Da Nang was a large city and a large military supply area.

The Marines first arrived there in 1965 when the 1st Air Cavalry arrived in Vietnam and went to An Khe in 1965. The Navy brought tons of supplies to this port city. The Army had aviation and logistical assets at Da Nang. There was a hospital there, too. Marines operated around Da Nang to provide security. Monkey Mountain overlooked the military operation located at Da Nang.]

2030 hrs. Four of us just left one of the officers' clubs which had the Tokyo Dollies for entertainment. They were great. Now we're at another club.

Tuesday, May 21

0705 hrs. I'm in an air terminal to catch a plane to Phu Bai, then to Camp Evans. I just finished the book Courtroom by Quentin Reynolds. It's about Sam Liebowitz—the famous criminal lawyer, later judge. More than ever I want to be a lawyer—probably a criminal lawyer. Meanwhile, I guess I'll just worry about staying alive. I'll probably make it back to my platoon tonight if I don't have any flight problems.

1425 hrs. Dear Mom and Dad,
I'm at the company supply room at Camp Evans waiting for a chopper to go back out to the field with the company. The past few days I've been in Da Nang checking on my toe. The doctor there said I'd probably need an operation, but they can't do anything for me until I get back to the States as the hospitals in Tokyo are filled with seriously injured patients. I understand this, but I just wanted his opinion and recommendation on my health records so I can get the Army to pay for it before I get out. We are operating around Camp Evans, and there are many VC in the villages. I hope I last, as I've been informed from reliable

sources that I should be at a staff (battalion assistant S-4) job by June 1. I'll run the supply for the battalion which is a very important and difficult task. Well, we'll see what happens.

    Mom, thanks for your letter. I'll take care and be looking forward to your package. Dad, keep in mind I need money for when I go on R&R which is about 23 June. I'll send more details later but I'll probably want close to $800 as I want to buy a tape recorder ($400-450?), some clothes ($200?), and other items. I'll give you details later. All is okay. I just hope I get this assistant S-4 job. I'm tired of getting shot at.

    Joe

Wednesday, May 22

1120 hrs. I'm with the company again. We're in a village area. Two other companies are sweeping toward us. There are NVA in the area. We found a trench which is important. I had a problem with Sgt. Blanko and Specialist 4 Bart (RTO). I got a new platoon sgt., Sgt. Links. I hope all turns out well.

Sergeant Links was a Black man with about a year left for retirement. He had been stationed in Germany and must have offended someone to get sent to Vietnam right before retirement. Maybe he got a new commanding officer from the South. Those were interesting times—the Civil Rights Movement, Black Panthers, Black Power—but Links and I got along fine. I was not brought up racially prejudiced. I went to school with Blacks, Mexicans, Indians, and all kinds of races; and I played on athletic teams with various races. I had Puerto Ricans and Blacks in my platoon, and I had some of the good Southern boys, too.

    They knew I would not put up with any racial dissention. Colonel Robinson who promoted me was Black; the M-60 machine gunner who probably saved my life outside Khe Sanh was Black; Pfc. Daws whom I consoled when his close friend was killed was Black; Major Black who got me the job at the R&R Center later was

Black; and Pfc. Gaines who I defended in a court-martial and saved his freedom later on was Black.

The year 1968 was a volatile year in Vietnam with the Tet offensive and the major operations to relieve the siege at Khe Sanh and the 1st Air Cav's incursion into the A Shau Valley. It was also volatile in the U.S. as the antiwar protests raged; the Women's Liberation Movement progressed; and the Civil Rights Movement was in full force. Martin Luther King was a great leader for his fight for justice and equality of treatment for "Negroes" in those days, but he made inaccurate comments about a disproportionate number of Negroes fighting and dying in Vietnam. His assertions fed the already vile prejudice against the "Negro" in the U.S. by many. Being of Lebanese descent, even in those days I appreciated the diversity of the American society. But racial prejudice still existed in the U.S. and even in the Army. I would not tolerate it in my unit, and I treated my platoon almost paternally—I felt that responsibility.

Thursday, May 23

1200 hrs. We are held up at this time. It's very hot. We were sniped at many times last night. As usual I got little sleep. We got about 300 meters to go to our new objective area. We saw the Air Force bring in an air strike up ahead about 20 minutes ago.

Friday, May 24

0915 hrs. The company set up a perimeter here on this road near a bombed-out village. I set a squad-size ambush on the trail and the road across the bridge last night. Last night we got a report of a VC convoy moving toward us, so 3-6 (Lieut. Ron Lawson) and I jumped into a foxhole and we were pulling guard for a while. I had Braun on the road with the 90 mm recoilless rifle. Red was in the hole with 3-6 and me with the radio and the M—60 machine gun. The convoy never came. Today my platoon is on the company perimeter while the CO took the rest of the company to check the area.

[It was unusual for two platoon leaders to be at the same location to pull guard, but we wanted to be certain if a convoy was en route to our location. We were concerned about enemy tanks so we had the 90 mm RR available. Once we thought we heard a tank's engine; but no convoy or tanks ever appeared. "3-6" meant third platoon leader.]

1915 hrs. Our platoon made a recon to the east today. First and third platoons captured some VC. The interrogators beat the hell out of the VC who confessed.

Saturday, May 25

0910 hrs. It's hot. The CO and first and third platoons are sweeping the area. They were sniped at. Right now, they are calling in an air strike. Last night we got sniped at and shot at by M-79 grenade launchers. Sgt. Simms and I had a run-in today about my radio.

[I don't remember what Sgt. Simms and I hassled about, but we didn't like each other anyway. He got killed later.]

1110 hrs. Our FO called in firecracker rounds (multiple explosions) on the bay. Braun fired the 90 mm at the bunkers to the northeast.

[Firecracker rounds were a type of "cofram"—controlled fragmentation munitions. The artillery fired rounds which exploded in aerial bursts dispersing hundreds of explosive "bomblets" over some large ponds. We saw the multiple submunitions pepper the water.]

Sunday, May 26

1137 hrs. Last night my platoon went out on an ambush near a church. We were discovered, received automatic weapons fire and mortars. We moved out at night and were ambushed. No one was hurt. Today, first and third platoons are making sweeps. First platoon killed a VC woman with carbine and binoculars. Third platoon had two men wounded by a booby trap. They called in Medevac; then 30 minutes later another wounded by a booby trap. Medevac called in.

Monday, May 27

1150 hrs. Yesterday, one of the men injured died. One of my men was his close friend and I tried to comfort him. I almost cried myself seeing the anguish this man had. We moved yesterday to here (more sand). We'll be air assaulted to another area. We were mortared today about three or four rounds. We fired back and some villagers (old man, women, and children) came to us for medical aid. The hell with them. They hide the VC; let them shoot at us; we return fire; they want aid. I sent first squad to look for a better PZ (pickup zone).

It is difficult to adequately explain the emotions of the time, but my entry—"The hell with them"—denotes a frustration and an acquired callousness toward those who would harm me or "mine." By contrast there is another story of my mood this day which may partially explain my "hell with them" diary entry.

Specialist Daws was a big, powerful young Black man in my platoon. It was his very close friend in the other platoon who died. When the suspected VC were captured and being interrogated (slapped around by our ARVN interpreter), I saw Daws approach the people who had custody of the suspects and demand that they step away. Daws pointed his M-16 at the interrogators and the captured VC. He intended to kill the captives.

I walked up to him slowly, stood in front of his gun, gambling he wasn't angry at me, and talked him into lowering the gun. He was sobbing and in great emotional pain. I walked him back to where my poncho liner, set up as a sun shade, was tied down. We sat under the poncho liner; I had my arm around him with his head on my shoulder as he sobbed like a baby. His anguish was palpable. Some things I will never forget.

Tuesday, May 28

0700 hrs. Today we'll air assault farther east. Last night we heard of a mission to go to Hue, but luckily it was canceled. Second platoon will air assault today. I had another disciplinary problem with Sgt. Blanko yesterday so I had him transferred to third platoon. Today's Dad's birthday and I can't even say Happy Birthday.

1715 hrs. I'm in an old French twin steeple church. We air assaulted today and got mortared and sniped at while doing it. Today my platoon found some refugees. It rained very hard as we moved. Some ARVNs are working with us. I had the interpreter with me so he helped talk to the refugees and the ARVNs. We'll camp around this church area tonight.

Wednesday, May 29

1925 hrs. It's getting dark. Today, first and second platoon with ARVNs moved east about one click. We got ambushed across the rice paddies. One of the ARVNs with my platoon got hit in the head. It was just a graze and he was Medevaced. We captured three POWs. One is a confirmed VC. We put the 90 mm and the ARA on the tree line to the front where we received fire. Rifle grenades landed close and so did small arms automatic weapons fire. We checked the area later and found it was way well shot up. We evacuated the refugees we sent to this church from here to a refugee camp. We'll move out tomorrow.

[POWs were usually taken back to a higher headquarters

for interrogation. We did not keep them with us as we conducted tactical operations.]

Thursday, May 30

0730 hrs. Last night my first squad heard movement very close to their area in the brush. They threw a grenade and heard VC (?) cut out. Last night tapping (metallic) was also heard. Today we'll move out to a different location. One of the other companies was in contact where we're going. Some ARVNs are cooking some rice and meat here. I like working with them and using the interpreter and speaking my little Vietnamese. I surely hope I get that staff job soon.

Friday, May 31

1530 hrs. It just poured. Monsoon rains. We saw five VC last night and my second squad today flushed some onto the sand. The CO did not pay any attention to my advice and info. Today the ARVNs beat and kicked the hell out of a young VC mother (suckling her baby). We had 38 refugees when the CO made us sweep a village. They (refugees) went away. I'm waiting to go in to see about another job.

My platoon was working with an ARVN platoon commanded by a sergeant (*Trungsi* in Vietnamese). There were "Psyops" (psychological operations) helicopters flying around with loudspeakers encouraging VC to give up (*chieu hoi* or "open arms") and villagers to gather to be sent to district headquarters.

There was a stone house surrounded by vegetation in the middle of a large rice paddy. My platoon and an ARVN platoon went to the house which had some adjacent out buildings. There was a small stream running between the buildings and within the surrounding vegetation, bamboo, and trees. We set up a perimeter defense, cleared fields of fire, and dug in as we normally would do. As the men cut the bamboo, bamboo vipers, one of the deadliest snakes in the world, fell out of the vegetation almost on top of the troops, and then just slithered away.

I went to the main building and Trungsi and I planned how we were going to secure the perimeter and deal with the refugees who came to our location to be relocated. After a while, I heard someone screaming outside the one-room building I was in and went to check it out. There was a young, pretty Vietnamese girl, maybe 20 years old, on her knees with her hands tied behind her back.

Trungsi, with an M-1 carbine pointed at her, was yelling at her in Vietnamese; I couldn't tell what he was saying but it sounded enraged and very accusatory. He looked at me and said, "*Co*, VC." ("The girl is Vietcong.") She apparently was a recent mother, and two older women were holding her baby. The front of her blouse was sufficiently low cut to see she had breasts which appeared to be full of milk.

Trungsi kept yelling at her, and then he kicked her right in the face with his black combat boot, breaking her nose. She fell to the side. I grabbed Trungsi and yelled "No!", realizing he had a rifle platoon working with mine, and I did not want to exacerbate an already bad situation: There were enemy troops in the area; numerous refugees with more coming; an ARVN platoon working with mine; and now this.

I went back inside the stone structure, and I heard more screaming. Trungsi had taken the "VC" girl over by the stream and placed her on her back with her hands still tied behind her. He put a board on her milk-filled breasts and kneeled on it, causing her pain. He also put wild chili peppers (some of the hottest I have ever eaten) into a handkerchief, dipped it into the stream, and twisted the handkerchief to squeeze chili juice into her eyes.

I saw this and pulled him off of the girl. I took the girl back to the older women who gave her the baby which she cuddled. We moved out with 38 refugees and our soldiers. The CO ordered us to sweep a village with the refugees with us—a really bad order. I moved my men out on line, with the refugees interspersed with the troops. I did this for control and in hopes that the "bad guys" wouldn't shoot at Vietnamese. The "VC" girl was falling behind as we traveled along; my platoon sergeant yelled to me that she was; I just let it go. I don't know if she was a Vietcong, but I thought she had suffered enough.

June, 1968

Saturday, June 1

1412 hrs. It's raining again. I'm in a poncho tent hooch. I went in last night and saw the col. (battalion CO). He told me I'm tops for consideration for the Assistant-4 job. I'll go in approximately 2 weeks. We're still working with the ARVNs. Third platoon got some more prisoners and weapons. The CO and some others are giving me a bad time for some reason. My platoon sgt., Sgt. Links, says it's because of my education and the others are envious. It's not my fault and I never mention my education. I've got a good platoon.

[Part of the "cold shoulder" may have been I was leaving the unit—getting out of the field—and there may have been some envy. But I had paid my dues.]

Sunday, June 2

0912 hrs. Last night my platoon had to go back to the same area we were at a few days ago. We spotted three VC in the goat site and five VC on the sands. I called artillery in on the five VC. I disobeyed an order to set out a squad in the village. The CO was "messing" with my platoon and me. I told him the area was no good for an ambush, but he ignored my on-the-spot observation.

[By now, it was obvious to me that Capt. Swenson was playing very dangerous games with my platoon and me. I was not going to send a squad into the village without having more "intel." This was deadly serious business, and the CO didn't care about us. Before, I thought he was just incompetent, but now I sensed it was personal.]

Monday, June 3

1140 hrs. Last night the CO had my platoon go almost 3 clicks back to the twin steeple church for a goat. None of the other platoons have been going as far at night. We saw about eight VC and the CO would not give me an artillery fire mission. I talked to him today. He's trying to undermine everything I do. I'm going to have to talk to the battalion CO.

[Going out on a goat three clicks at night was not normal procedure. I felt like this CO was trying to get us, or ME, killed. It's not paranoia if people really are trying to kill you.]

Tuesday, June 4

1237 hrs. We took Chinooks back to LZ Jeannie (on the sand). We'll be here a few days. I told the Protestant chaplain about my problem with the CO. He said he'd keep it confidential. It rained somewhat. It will rain later (cloudy sky).

```
     1710 hrs. Dear Mom and Dad,
     We've just ended another successful operation
along the coast (Gulf of Tonkin) north of Camp
Evans. We're resting a few days and then back
again. I talked to the battalion commander who
said I'd probably get the assistant S-4 job
around 20 June. If I live that long I'll be
relatively safe from getting shot at after that.
Actually, we've been chasing VC rather than NVA
```

lately so it hasn't been too bad. I believe I'll have to postpone my R&R because of taking over the new job. It shouldn't be any problem. I don't have this job guaranteed yet, but I was told from reliable sources that it looks very good. Even if for some reason I may not get this one, I'll get another one very soon after. I've been in the field 5 months now so I know what goes on. I've done and seen a lot and I am ready for a change. I just hope all goes well and I can finish law school. I hope all is well with you people. Tell Bob he doesn't know what he's missing.
    Joe

Wednesday, June 5

0950 hrs. It's a cloudy breezy day. Most of my platoon is just lying around writing letters, sleeping, or listening to a radio. I have one squad patrolling the firebase perimeter. I got a letter from Mary yesterday.

1830 hrs. I got one package from Kathleen and two packages from Mom and Dad today. I hope we stay here a few more days so I don't have to carry this stuff. I heard on the radio that Kennedy was shot in the head. He is still in critical condition. The sky has heavy clouds and it looks like rain. The word is that our company will be in the field until 15 June. I can hardly believe that it is June already.

[Bobby Kennedy was assassinated.]

1340 hrs. Dear Mom and Dad,
We're still resting here north of Camp Evans on the sands at LZ Jeannie. Today, I got two packages from you. I've got loads of goodies here. Thank you very much. All of this stuff will

be well used. I remember how I didn't care for sardines in mustard too much, but now they're great. Last week when I had a Vietnamese platoon working with mine, we were separated from the company and we couldn't get any log ship with food. The Vietnamese went into a bombed-out village and caught some wild chickens. Also they threw hand grenades into a stream and killed fish. I ate half-cooked chicken and fish and of course rice and bamboo sprouts. Actually, it wasn't too bad. Maybe when I get a "back in the rear" job, I can eat better and take it easy. It should be in a couple of weeks. Now I'm just sitting on the sand. The sky is cloudy. I sent a squad out to check the perimeter. We'll be here a few days. Thanks again for the goodies.

    Your son, Joe

Thursday, June 6

1237 hrs. Another overcast day. I walked to the stream just outside the perimeter and took a bath. It's useless to try to stay clean because sand is blown all around whenever a chopper lands. Lieut. Colby, first platoon leader, is acting CO as Capt. Swenson is sick and went back to Camp Evans. Lieut. Cobby will make capt. soon. Rumor is that we'll go to An Khe soon. I still think about telling the battalion CO about certain harassment to my platoon. The VC which I reported before to the CO near the twin steeple church turned out to be something, and the company which replaced us is running into VC and NVA in that area.

2150 hrs. It's dark as I write. The radio said Kennedy died today.

Friday, June 7
0920 hrs. Dear Mom and Dad,
I received both of your letters. Dad, I'd like for you to hold on to these checks a while as they may get wet while I'm still out in the field. I should go in, in less than two weeks. Because my R&R would be at the same time as my taking this new job, the col. asked me to postpone it for a while. I'll be going probably in August now. Mom, as for the pearls, I'll try to get the very best. That's why I wanted about $800 because of shopping as well as entertainment expenses. I want to buy clothes and a tape recorder, and these will probably cost a lot. I hope Bob knows what he's doing with the reserves. Has he got a degree yet or what? There is rumor that my unit will go to An Khe for a while and then to the Mekong Delta area. We'll see. All is the same here. Thanks for the packages.
Your son, Joe

1625 hrs. I'm sitting in the bunker. It's hot out. Sgt. Lews (my third squad leader) and I gave classes on the 90 mm and M72 LAWs. The battalion CO is on the LZ. I guess that means we'll move out tomorrow. I got two letters from Mom and Dad which I wrote replies to in one letter today. We'll probably work the coast again if and when we go out.

Saturday, June 8

0900 hrs. The CO came out yesterday. I finished a book—"The Challenge of Abundance" by Robert Theobald. I just sent a squad out on a patrol around the perimeter of the LZ. The rumor about going to An Khe sounds better all the time.

Sunday, June 9

0800 hrs. Today, we are supposed to go work the coastal villages again. Specialist 4 Brand goes on R&R today. I brought Specialist 4 Earlson up as an RTO. Specialist 4 Sands came back to the platoon yesterday from leadership school. He was disappointed that a new E-6 was running his squad. There will be conflict for a while, but I hope the problem will resolve itself. Jim Khan wrote me and told me that Jim Muir was KIA. Kathleen wrote and said her husband is leaving her.

1422 hrs. We're along the road farther east than we were before. We're at an old bombed-out schoolhouse. A nearby temple has a life-size Buddha made of gold. If I could steal that, it's worth a fortune. One of my squads is up the road. We're trying to get a Medevac for an old woman with a partially amputated finger with gangrene.

Monday, June 10

0755 hrs. We're at our last night's goat location. A Buddhist temple is across the road about 150 m. The CO told me they wanted me in for the S-4 job today. I'll go in this evening. It's difficult to believe I'm getting out of the field. I'll miss my platoon. Several of them came up to talk to me last night. Right now some of the men are cooking ducks they found.

I got the Assistant S-4 job. My RTOs manning the radios heard the news. A squad of my men went into the village to retrieve a large Buddhist incense burner (almost two feet high from the base to the top of the lid handle). It took three guys to carry the lid, burner, and base. It was a going away present.

Several of my guys came to wish me well my last day in the field. I grew attached to my platoon—we saw a lot of action together, but we performed our missions well. I had some guys wounded, but none of my men were killed when they were under my command. There is nothing as precious as human life, and the greatest accomplishment I have ever achieved in my entire life is not having lost any of my men in combat during the bloodiest year of the Vietnam War, in the unit that had the most casualties.

2030 hrs. Well, I finally made it out of the field. I'll be working with the battalion supply. I am at my company supply now. I'll sleep here for a few days. I hated to leave my platoon because I really grew attached to them, but then again I'm glad I have this job.

2322 hrs. I went to bed but couldn't sleep. The guys here at supply are playing cards. Well, I did it. I went through my tour in the field and never lost a man. None killed.

Tuesday, June 11

1745 hrs. I spent most of the day at S-4 going over the books. Sgt. Links, the new 2-6, is here to check on an admin problem. The 4-A (assistant S-4) job will be a challenge. I'm looking forward to the work. It is hot and humid here at Camp Evans during the day. Right now it's cool. Tomorrow I'll take an inventory of the S-4 equipment.

Wednesday, June 12

1235 hrs. I'm in the S-4 office reading regulations on supply. This job will be a real challenge. I'm looking forward to it. I have a brass Buddhist incense burner which I want to send home today. I got another radio from Dad yesterday.

```
     1606 hrs. Dear Mom and Dad,
     Well I'm in, in Camp Evans that is. I spent
my time in the field and now I get to be what is
called "rear echelon." I'll be the 4-A (called
the 4-alpha) which is the assistant S-4. Capt.
```

Rapper, my old company commander, is the S-4. I have checked in and signed for much of the battalion's property already. It'll be a big responsibility if anything winds up missing or stolen--I'm responsible. A lot of bookkeeping and accounting are involved. Normally, I have a warrant officer who handles the technician aspect of the job, but the one there now is leaving soon, and I have to learn his job also until the new warrant officer comes in. I'll be supervising the logistic chopper runs to the companies in the field. Also I'll be very much involved in all the supply distribution requisition in the battalion. It will be a challenge and an excellent business training opportunity in a very important if not the most important staff position in the battalion. I'll work here at Camp Evans with occasional trips to other cities on business (requisition, etc.). The most I'll get shot at is mortars and rockets coming in to here, but we all live in bunkers.

    Dad, I got the radio yesterday. Thanks. It's great. As for my R&R, I'll submit for it for July or August. I'll keep you informed so we can coordinate on the money I'll need. By the way I opened my duffel bag and found the checkbook you gave me when I came over here. I got a letter from Jim Khan. Do you remember Jim Muir (played quarterback at Rincon my senior year)? Well, Jim Khan told me that Muir got hit leading an assault on an NVA trench line. Jim Khan said his tank carried Muir back to the rear. Later he found out that Muir died. You can't believe how I've made myself immune to death and misery I've seen here, but every once in a while I think about it and it makes me sick.

    Well, I've done it. I spent about 5½ months in

the field as a combat platoon leader; I've hit the hot spots; been artilleried, rocketed, mortared, sniped at, ambushed, defended against as I've assaulted--and I haven't lost one of my men. I really grew attached to my platoon, and several of them told me they hated to see me go, but they were glad I got the job in the rear area. One of my RTOs (radio man) was talking to another and I heard him say, "He's the only one I've seen walk out of ambushes with everyone alive." I guess Somebody up there does like me. I hope all stays well. The weather here at Camp Evans is very humid. It rains occasionally in the afternoons.

    Mom, I got a Buddhist incense burner which I'll send home in a crate if it'll make it. I'll let you know after I mail it. Also, enclosed in the crate will be a Buddhist flag (green), a red vestment, a red tablecloth, a cap which I wore in the picture I sent home, and a burlap vest the ARVNs wear occasionally. Bob can use it for hunting. If and when this incense burner gets to you, I want Bob to clean it and polish it and assemble it. It has sand on it so maybe the Vietnamese buried it at one time. It may take a long time for the crate to get to you, but if it does, now you know what I'm talking about.

    Enclosed is another one of my pay vouchers. Well, give everyone my regards. I hope all stays okay. I can hardly believe that about one-half of my tour is up.

    Your son, Joe

Thursday, June 13

1235 hrs. I'm in the S-4 office. I'm still checking things. I've got a meeting to attend at 1320 at brigade headquarters. I cleaned my .45 caliber pistol. I got some clean fatigues today. I sent a brass Buddhist incense burner home to my mom today. For some reason I detect a cold atmosphere for me by some of my fellow officers. I've neither said nor did anything offensive to anyone. I believe it's the education bit again.

[I now carried a .45 caliber pistol. I liked the M-16, but it was too long and big to carry while I was doing S-4 business. Regarding relationships with other officers—the other platoon leaders may have been envious that I got the staff job with the help of my former CO, Captain Rapper. The platoon leaders were still working for my "good buddy," Captain Swenson—the one who called artillery in on me; the one who sent me 3 clicks out on a night "goat"; and the one who had me conduct a tactical sweep of a village with 38 Vietnamese refugees. Maybe I was just being supersensitive, but I don't think so.]

Friday, June 14

1710 hrs. I signed for Lieut. James' property today. Now I own all the battalion's property. Lieut. Lutstein is my new headquarters CO. He's a lot friendlier than he used to be. I got another 30-round magazine for my AK today. The weapon is really sharp. I hope to get it back home.

Saturday, June 15

1330 hrs. It's hot out. The sky is pale blue with scattered clouds (light and rain-gray inside). I've been working with the books in S-4. I signed for everything, and am now discovering discrepancies. My problems lie in that I am signed for the warrant officer and service platoon leader. I'm assuming two jobs rather than one. I think I can straighten out everything.

2055 hrs. Dear Mom and Dad,
    I am sitting here at the S-4 office which is a large bunker beneath the ground with wooden paneling, floor and roof; the clerks, Capt. Rapper, and the warrant officer are all sitting around, also. We have some fans so it's relatively cool. Anywhere else it is extremely hot and humid. Today it was 130°.
    I'm sleeping at D Company orderly room as the warrant officer will be leaving Monday, and I'll move in then. My position here is extremely important, and the responsibility is the most I've ever had--property wise--not human lives as I had as a platoon leader. It seems that I am now discovering discrepancies as I become more familiar with the books, but it's too late now as I've already signed for *all* the property in the battalion. My job is two-fold. I'm supposed to be the service platoon leader which means I supervise supply and maintenance functions. I'm responsible for seeing that the log ships get the necessary supplies to the companies in the field. I work with the S-4 who is the supply staff officer to the col.--the battalion commander.
    My other job is that of property book officer. This job is supposed to be done by a warrant officer, but he is leaving and I have to take his place until a replacement comes in. The problem is that he (property book officer--PBO) signs for everything which is what I did. I also am responsible for making the books jive which is a real accounting task. Fortunately I have a supply sgt. to assist me. Anyway, the job will be interesting, important to the troops, and a real challenge. It's a good job comfort wise and "connection wise" as I may be able to connive

excuses to go to other cities on business. In fact I know I will.

    Mother, I sent home a box. I sent it by boat, 4th class, so it may take a while to reach you. Inside the box you will find a hat, the same hat I had on in the picture I sent home. Also there is a burlap vest which the ARVNs make and wear. Maybe Bob can use it for hunting. There are also 3 cloths. One red cloth has Chinese writing on it and it is a Buddhist vestment of some sort. The other red cloth is a drapery or long tablecloth. The green flag with the white emblem on it is a Buddhist flag. An ARVN interpreter told me that the white object is a Lotus and symbolizes peace or heaven or something like that. Now the main attraction is the big vase, actually a Buddhist incense burner. The legs and handles to the base can be assembled. The lid has a figurine which needs a similar screw type object to fit the lid to the figurine. The other object is a base or stand on which the vase is placed.

    As you see, there appears to be sand around the inside of the base. It was probably buried and then dug up and placed in the Buddhist temple where I found it. I got the vase the last day I served in the field before taking over the staff job. Our company had been operating in an area where the villagers wanted to harvest the rice, and we protected them from the VC. My platoon moved about 3 clicks from the company perimeter and set up along the road near this Buddhist temple. Temples are a common sight and are in various conditions usually badly shot up or rocketed as the VC like to hide out in them. This temple was in good shape and I saw the vase. I moved my platoon to our perimeter site for the platoon and sent one squad back to get

Buddhist incense burner.

the base. Three men had to carry the different pieces--stand, base, and lid. Anyway, I got it and carried it back here to Evans where I came in by chopper. I finally mailed it. Please take care of all the stuff I sent home as it all has value to me. If you would, the base can be cleaned up and "Brassoed." Bob can assemble it when it comes in and he should be able to find a bolt to put through the lid to the figurine. Please don't sell or give this object away. Ma, you can put it in the front room if you wish as it certainly would be a conversation piece. It can be a cookie- or candy dish. If Bob wants it and talks you into keeping it somewhere else, I want the thing taken care of.

If anyone asks about the propriety of taking a Buddhist incense burning vase, just tell them that although it's religious, the VC hang around the temples a lot. The village was well shot up and deserted by civilians. Also my platoon was ambushed about 3 clicks from the area previously, and I just didn't give a damn as to whom it belonged. I just consider it a going away present from my platoon. Well, the package probably won't get there for a while--possibly never, but I insured it for $15--the maximum for items declared of "no value." I declared "no value" rather than pay duty.

How is Bob doing in summer school? Is he going into the reserves this summer? I hope he doesn't wind up over here. There are better things in life. I am at about the halfway mark in my tour over here and now I have many administration problems; at least I won't be getting shot at quite as much.

Dad, I'm sending home another voucher. I'm taking $30 now instead of $50 as before. There's nothing to spend money on unless I can swing some trips to Da Nang which I'll work on. Did I write in the last letter that I got the radio? It's a good little radio.

Mom and Dad, how about another care package same as last time? I like sardines in tomato sauce better than mustard. The green chili was good, too. The mixed nuts were great, but just peanuts would be fine. Well, same old stuff. I'll get this letter off. All is okay.

Your son, Joe

Sunday, June 16

1530 hrs. It's hot again today. I believe I am finally getting the hand receipts squared away. The warrant officer leaves tomorrow so I'll move in then. I believe I'll build my own hooch. Building materials are hard to get, one of my men says he has a way.

Monday, June 17

1250 hrs. I moved into the large S-4 bunker today. Capt. Rapper (S-4) said we (he and I) can build another bunker. One of my men got the materials. Last night I found a contact where I believe I'll be able to buy beer in large quantities.

[The S-4 bunker was huge and could sleep several of us. It was below ground and had large timbers to support a roof which was covered with a couple layers of sandbags. The S-4 was the battalion supply officer and had access to these resources—timbers, sandbags, PSP, construction equipment, etc.]

Tuesday, June 18

2010 hrs. Today I drove to Phong Dien—the town outside Evans. I bought a little plastic basin for shaving. I saw a girl, Lynn, whom I met when my platoon was on the bridges. Right now Capt. Rapper is cleaning a weapon one of the men gave him. I met the new warrant officer tonight. He reports here tomorrow or the next day.

Wednesday, June 19

1600 hrs. I can see that this job is going to give me much spare time. At times I'm very busy in spurts and if the battalion has *to move, I'll be real busy; but so far this section is a real fun section. The S-4 section reminds me of "McHale's Navy" on TV where everyone is a loafer and schemer. That's us.*

That probably was not a fair evaluation of the supply section and personnel. The pace and intensity of being in supply was different than being a combat unit commander, and there was not always that immediate "high" and sense of danger in the S-4. But when the field troops needed whatever they needed (food, ammo, other supplies), the S-4 section was hopping, taking care of business. Since we requisitioned supplies and had to sometimes be creative to get what was needed, I referred to some as a "schemer."

> Thursday, June 20
> 1050 hrs. Dear Mom and Dad,
> The new battalion commander came in today and we showed him the S-4 section. I'm the service platoon leader so I'm in charge of the supply section and maintenance section (I'm also motor officer). In other words I handle all logistic support to the battalion. The S-4, Capt. Rapper, my boss and the one who got me this job, actually is directly responsible to the battalion commander for all the S-4 planning and logistical functioning, but I wind up doing the planning and work. This job will really be interesting and fun. Being in charge of the battalion property, I have a lot of power. Dad, you know what I mean --people want things. You know the TV shows of *Sgt. Bilko* and *McHale's Navy*, etc.,--well that's what this S-4 section is like. We work when we have to, but most of the time we just mess around. Everyone in here is a bullshitter and con artist. Right now, Capt. Rapper, the S-4, my boss, hopped a chopper and went swimming at a nearby beach. After I get settled, I'll be going

on these runs and also to other cities to get supplies (bullshit!). Beer around here is hard to get unless you know someone. I've already made contact and have purchased a pallet (80 cases). In fact they'll even deliver it for me.

    The picture of me is outside my S-4 bunker. The bell in the background is one D Company (mine, when I was in the field) sent in. We found it in a temple and called a chopper to pick it up. The Jeep is the S-4 Jeep (mine). It's a brand-new Jeep.

    Capt. Rapper and I are going to build a smaller bunker behind this big S-4 bunker. We've already scrounged the materials. Mom, I haven't received the Syrian goodies yet but could you please send some items: popcorn (in tinfoil ready to heat and pop), canned oysters, canned fruit (preferably apricots), and crackers. I can set this stuff in one place now that I'm stationary.

    About my sunglasses, I've been wearing prescription sunglasses which I got through the Army. I broke my clear glasses, but I have other glasses on order.

    Well, I have got to try and get about 5000 sandbags, about 200 metal covers, and about 100 eight-foot metal engineer stakes so I guess I'll

Buddhist gong (bell) captured by our battalion (closeup) and in front of the S-4 entrance with my hooch under construction in the background.

close for now. I'm in a safer situation. I'm not out in the boonies, but we still get rocketed and mortared here. Everyone sleeps in bunkers. About my R&R, I still don't have one rescheduled, yet, but I figure it'll be around August. I'll keep you all posted when I get the orders for the R&R.

Your son, Joe

Thursday, June 20, (cont.)

1840 hrs. The new battalion CO came in today. I've been busy all day. I went to G-4 and got a briefing and some equipment. Then Lieut. Gaylord (D Company) had an ammo problem, which I solved since I'm also battalion ammo officer. Also I've been writing up a skit today for Col. Robinson's going away.

Colonel Robinson was a great battalion commander. He was the CO of 2/7 Cavalry when it cleared Route 9 and led the relief column into Khe Sanh. He later became a four-star general. His battalion was the lead battalion to clear Route 9 in the relief of the siege at Khe Sanh. I wonder if the fact he was Black at that period in our country influenced why that action did not get more recognition than it did. The civil rights movement was raging.

Friday, June 21

1800 hrs. I just got done playing volleyball. Today I took two of my men in the Jeep and went outside the camp to the bridge my platoon used to man. We had the Jeep washed there. I saw Lynn and she gave me a free Coke. The Vietnamese are money hungry and can make as much money as one dollar off Cokes. Then we took Lynn back to the village and bought ice. A large block cost $10 but I traded two C-ration cases for it. The col. is having a going away party tonight.

Saturday, June 22

1215 hrs. The party was good last night. We had very good steaks. After the party, Capt. Rapper and I took the Jeep to the MARS station where he called his wife. I got assigned a LOD investigation to do.

[The MARS station was where we could call back to the U.S. We didn't have cell phones or the Internet in those days. A Line of Duty investigation (LOD) is to determine if an injured soldier was injured in the line of duty doing his duty or injured by his own misconduct. The results have consequences for disability compensation later on. My one year of law school helped me.]

2030 hrs. We played several volleyball games. My team kept winning. I showered afterwards. We have field showers. Capt. Rapper, about four men, and I took a 2½-ton truck and swiped about $300 worth of plywood. It's hard to get but I've always liked night patrols.

Sunday, June 23

1230 hrs. I finished reading "For the New Intellectual" by Ayn Rand last night.

Monday, June 24

1940 hrs. Today Lieut. James, Specialist 4 Lord, and I went to the river (by the bridge). An MP gave Lieut. James a bad time for not having a flak jacket on. I saw Lynn at the river. She fascinates me by her oriental shyness. Today I had a four-hour class on supply procedures. It was informative. I'm going to try to learn the job rather than just get by.

Joe in front of S-4 Operations bunker in volleyball attire.

Tuesday, June 25
1830 hrs. Dear Mom and Dad,
Here is a picture of me in front of the S-4 bunker. We play volleyball each evening and I had cut up some khaki pants to make shorts. I wear my prescription sunglasses all the time. In the background you see a mound of dirt behind the bunker. I'll build a hooch there. In the left background is a shower frame with a canvas bucket hanging down.
Well, Mom, thanks for the pictures. Everyone looks good. Uncle Fred's house is beautiful.
I still haven't received the pastries. What I really like is the mixed nuts or peanuts. I have contacts where I can buy beer by the pallet so beer and nuts go together well. Half of my tour

is up. I hope the other half goes quickly. If I stay busy it should. I have to wheel and deal getting supplies and equipment for the battalion. I still respect the possibility of danger, but I am a little more relaxed now. We have a new battalion commander, and he's for rebuilding all our area. Thus, I have to work harder to get the already scarce supplies.

Mom, enclosed is a pin with the 1st Cav Patch insignia and the Garry Owen insignia. Garry Owen was supposed to have fought with or had something to do with General Custer at the Little Bighorn. The 2/7 Cav is Custer's old outfit. Anyway, Mom, I thought you might like the insignia pin to show off your son's outfit in Vietnam.

Dad, I'm debating what to do about a camera. There are so many pictures I should be taking. Do you think it would be worthwhile to send me your movie camera with loads of film? I'll shoot the film and send it back for you to develop and run off and let me know how it turned out. Our PX here is very small (no cameras now), but if I go pick up lumber in Hue or Da Nang, or go on R&R, I could buy all the really fine cameras I want. Why don't you send me the movie camera, Dad, and I'll shoot a lot of shots of Camp Evans and the choppers, etc. I'll send home a description of what's happening so you can label the film.

Well I've got a staff meeting in 15 minutes. All is the same. I miss home. I'm glad Bob is in school.

Your son, Joe

[Garry Owen was not a person but a place. It was a pub in Ireland, literally translated as "John's garden" due to the proximity to John's castle in Ireland. Regarding the movie camera, my dad had a Super 8 movie camera which I had asked for to take movies in Vietnam. I made still photos from those movies for inclusion in this book.]

Tuesday, June 25

2107 hrs. I came through today. A 2½-ton truck rolled up in front of S-4 and delivered one pallet (80 cases) of beer. Beer is hard to get around here, but all went well. Major Monburg (battalion XO) gave me a bunch of stuff to do for tomorrow. I'll shower now.

[The shower was a 55-gallon drum filled with water propped up on a canvas enclosed frame with a wood pallet as a floor. We pulled a cord which released the water, and we showered. That was a luxury.]

Wednesday, June 26

1845 hrs. Today, I took a log bird to LZ Jeannie to check their supply requirements. I rode back in the CC (called Charlie-Charlie) meaning command control—the battalion CO's chopper. I've really been busy lately. I've got a meeting in 15 minutes.

2300 hrs. I just finished reading "Broken Arrow" by Elliott Arnold. It was about Cochise and Tom Jeffords in the Tucson

Hueys on log pad readied for a mission.

area. Specialist 5 McNider (Spanky), my clerk, and I are still reading.

Thursday, June 27

2145 hrs. Lieut. Randy James, the old service platoon leader, left today for U.S.A. I moved my bunk around. I built a wooden shelf. The battalion CO has really kept me busy lately. I've been getting the supplies he wanted out to LZ Jeannie. I'm tired. I flew out to LZ Jeannie again today. I love to fly. I wish I had a camera. I guess I'll read awhile and then go to sleep.

Friday, June 28

2020 hrs. It was another busy day. I'll be glad when Capt. Rapper gets back from Da Nang. I went to a G-4 meeting today for all the supply honchos in the division. It was a three-hour meeting. I learned a lot about supply problems, etc. From info I gathered, I believe we'll be here awhile. We'll be getting ice machines and other installation of equipment.

Saturday, June 29

2210 hrs. I just attended a meeting for Capt. Rapper. It was a staff briefing on an operation. We'll be working with combat engineers, learning the area along the "Street" as we call it. The S-4 will be involved a lot for logistical support as we'll probably have to get POL out to large earthmoving machinery.

[The S-4's job was to provide needed logistics (supplies) to the battalion. We transported and distributed troops, food, ammunition, weapons, vehicles, generators, clothing, and POL (petroleum, oil, and lubricants).]

Sunday, June 30

1500 hrs. I am now at Phu Bai (outside Hue) sitting on a cardboard box waiting for Sgt. Dirk to get the supplies we need. We stopped in Hue on the way up and we took turns patronizing the prostitute facilities there. I walked onto a boat and the girl came up in a little sampan. Then we drove here to Phu Bai where I bought some beer and Cokes for Major Monburg, our battalion XO. Hue is a pretty city with many reminders of war—bullet-riddled and bombed (mortared) buildings.

July, 1968

Monday, July 1

1536 hrs. I am at LZ Jeannie waiting for a log bird to pick me up. I came out here to check on the supplies and building program here. My platoon got me a metal vase from another temple. I guess I'll give it to Capt. Rapper.

1805 hrs. Dear Mom and Dad,
Enclosed are some pictures taken with a Polaroid "Instamatic." Some of my S-4 section and I are just clowning around. I'm still trying to get some pictures of me when I was in the field. I go out and see my old platoon once in a while. Also enclosed is a pay voucher. Effective 1 July 68 (today), there is another pay raise.

Dad, I do hope you decide to send the movie camera. Whenever I get in the helicopter and go to LZ Jeanne, I can get movies of Camp Evans and the beach area near the Gulf of Tonkin. Evans is growing. Now that I'm working in the rear area, I'll have a lot to do with this growth especially since I'm in the S-4 (supply section).

I went to Phu Bai (other side of Hue) yesterday. Beer and Coke are scarce at times and I scrounged some up there. I took just my driver and me in a Jeep. There is danger from mines and snipers, but otherwise we have U.S. checkpoints along the way. Anyway, I've been requisitioning, scrounging, and stealing all equipment and supplies we need. I've been busy. Some trips to Da Nang are in store to get lumber for building a mess hall and some BOQs (bachelor officer quarters). I'm in a perfect position to watch Camp Evans grow and I'd like to photograph (movies) of what's happening.

Our PX is not big here. I went to the PX in Phu Bai and they had a nice movie camera for about $98.00, but I may never use it again. I'm waiting to go on R&R to Singapore to buy most of what I want for myself and for gifts. I saw a Saks Hong Kong outfit at Phu Bai selling suits and sports coats custom made. This Saks is of Saks 5th Avenue of New York except the Hong Kong branch. I may buy some stuff there. Mom, I know you want those pearls so I'm waiting until Singapore. I believe it's duty free.

Well, I guess I'm still a little heavy in the gut, but that seems to be the downfall of all ex-wrestlers who once were used to good stomach muscle tone. I got a letter from Aunt Jay today. She said a girl had written to me, but I never got the letter. I'll write back and tell her. You know how easy it is for mail to get screwed up over here. By the way, my address is now HHC 2/7 CAV rather

Joe (second from right standing) and S-4 team in bunker.

than D/2/7 CAV. HHC stands for Headquarters and Headquarters Company. Mom, I got that box of sweets. They were and are delicious. I don't know how they lasted. I've still got some. They all crumbled but I squeezed the crumbs together and ate them. I gave them to some of the guys and they loved the sweets.

I've been busy lately. I have several duties which is typical of any staff or assistant staff officer. I'm also the motor officer for all the vehicles; I'm responsible for maintenance of all vehicles. I'm in charge of the log pad (where the choppers pick up supplies and take to the field); I'm in charge of the supply section. But I guess my main job is chief scrounger getting whatever I can for the battalion in the way of supplies. Well, again, all is well so far.

Love, Joe

Tuesday, July 2

2111 hrs. It's very hot and humid. I went to the brigade ammo dump to check on 90 mm recoilless rifle beehive rounds. I think I can order some for the battalion's mission. We are escorting bulldozers and road plows to level the village along the road where we've been receiving fire. One of the dozers hit an 8-inch shell booby trap. It killed a man on the dozer.

Bulldozer at Camp Evans.

Wednesday, July 3

1903 hrs. It's been another hot day. I had the usual busy running around day. The monsoon season should begin about the end of the month beginning of August. I'm very tired now.

Thursday, July 4

1800 hrs. Last night I finished a book "Courtroom USA I" by Rupert Turneaux, and now I'm reading the II version, different book but with similar cases. Today I went to Phu Bai. I checked on equipment we need. I got some. Tonight we have another officers' party.

Friday, July 5

1907 hrs. Another hot and dusty day. The dust is always bad as the vehicles ground the dirt to powder. We played some more volleyball today. The operations with the dozers clearing the village area along the "Street" continue. Capt. Rapper is on another one of his trips to Da Nang. He flies up and our trucks meet him there. He's on a lumber run this time as we want to build a battalion mess hall.

Battalion motor pool area.

[I eventually took over the task of building the mess hall.]

Saturday, July 6

2000 hrs. We've been improving the area around the S-4 bunker. Today we moved the volleyball court behind the S-4 bunker. The motor pool area was fixed up today—sandbags were laid out to show the parking area.

Sunday, July 7

2100 hrs. Lieut. Lawson (third platoon leader, D Company) came in from the field. He'll be working with us. Today the water point broke down. We couldn't get water to the company at the dozers. I went to LZ Jeannie today. Spanky is trying to talk me into promoting a book written from my diary.

[Almost a half a century later, I worked on writing this book.]

Monday, July 8

1635 hrs. Here I am in An Khe. Lieut. Lawson is here, too, as he is getting a MACV assignment. We've been through Khe Sanh and A Shau together. I just checked on my baggage. I brought too much to RVN.

[MACV (Military Advisory Command Vietnam) was a major headquarters in Saigon. An assignment to MACV took one out of the field.]

2137 hrs. Lieut. Lawson, Lieut. Lockerby, two other lieutenants, and I are here at the Can Do Officers' Club, drinking. They have MACV assignments. I'm on a refrigerator mission.

Tuesday, July 9

1527 hrs. I'm sitting here at the R&R BOQ. Lieut. Lawson and I just came back from An Khe (the city itself). We got haircuts, shines, steam baths, massages, and "lays." I checked on a refrigerator at the PX today. The last shipment was sold out so I'll go back empty-handed. Specialist 4 Pogue, who came with me, and I will have to head back tonight or tomorrow.

2228 hrs. I left Lieut. Lawson and Lieut. Lockerby at the club. I've got to get up early to catch a plane. I just finished reading "Courtroom II." Time for bed.

Wednesday, July 10

1615 hrs. I'm back at LZ Evans. It's hot and humid. It looks like rain. I got a new wallet with a 1st Cav insignia.

Thursday, July 11

1650 hrs. I'm on our log pad waiting to go to LZ Jeannie to see what building materials they need. They say they need more PSP, but I don't think so. It's cloudy and windy now. The breeze feels good. I'm sitting on top of some 81 mm ammo boxes now. A Chinook just was lumbering into the sky.

[PSP is perforated steel planking—steel planks with holes used for aircraft runways or for placing on bunkers to make very strong overhead cover.]

2127 hrs. I didn't go to the LZ because the log bird took too long to return. I just finished an outstanding book—"The Age of the Junkman" by P.D. Ballard.

Friday, July 12

2220 hrs. I'm writing by flashlight. It rained today. I worked on a movement transportation requirement plan all day today. I needed a lot of info and statistics concerning battalion equipment—vehicles, ammo, etc. It's good experience to work on projects like that. It rained today. The monsoon season will be coming in soon. I miss being in the U.S. and having little comforts I once took for granted.

Saturday, July 13

1945 hrs. It poured today. We went outside in the downpour and dug trenches for water runoff. We got soaked. Tomorrow I've got to get the money as I'm pay officer.

2220 hrs. Dear Mom and Dad,
Here's another book about the 1st Cav. Things are going fine here. Capt. Rapper, the S-4, is leaving soon, and he just told me he told the battalion CO that I'd do a fine job as the S-4 (a captain's slot). It's another good experience for me--working with property (at battalion) and vehicles, and of course working with people. It rained hard today. The monsoon season is on its way.

Dad, if you have that old movie camera, or if Bob has it, how about letting me use it before the weather gets so lousy that I can't take pictures? Still no word on my R&R. I'll probably be on September's allocations for R&R. Thanks for the last batch of goodies. Mom, I don't need so much chili. How about more sardines or oysters? Also, I believe there's a salami that can be sent.

I'm also sending a clipping I kept on Khe

Sanh. Also, I'm sending a map of where I operated in the A Shau Valley operation. It's been hot and humid during the days and our generators (our source of electricity) were out so our fans didn't work. With the coming rains, it should cool off.

How's Bob doing in whatever he's doing? Is he in summer school? Time flies. Just think, tomorrow I'll be 25 years old. Mom, I got your message about Aunt Jay; I wrote her (Aunt Jay) already.

Well, I guess that's it again. I guess I'll hit the rack now as I'll get up early tomorrow.

Your son Joe

Sunday, July 14

1934 hrs. Today I'm 25 years old. Lares (my driver), Sgt. Wilson, and I went to Utah or Wonder Beach. We took a Jeep and a lowboy (truck). We got four pallets (80 bags) of cement.

I am getting into my jeep.

[Wonder Beach was up near Dong Ha—the last major city before one got to the DMZ. It was a Navy "port" or unloading site of sorts. We needed the cement for a pad for the battalion mess hall, so I traded lots of captured weapons to these "supply types" to get what I needed. I can't criticize the "supply types" too much since I became one. At least I did my time as a grunt in the boonies.]

Monday, July 15

1910 hrs. I'm pay officer for HHC this month. I drew about $8000 and paid most of it today. Tomorrow I'll go to LZ Jeannie to pay some troops there. We've been improving the area around the S-4. We also leveled the ground for the mess hall. It should be nice when completed.

[The troops were paid in cash. I signed for the money, sat at a table, and paid the troops who showed identification to receive pay. The trooper would approach my table, and state, "Private so-and-so reporting for pay, sir," while rendering a hand salute.]

Tuesday, July 16

2135 hrs. We just had another going away party for officers. We had barbecued chicken which was delicious. Our 2½-ton truck made a run to Phu Bai and came back with a 2½-ton water trailer. I went to LZ Jeannie to pay some troops. I'll probably go there again tomorrow.

Wednesday, July 17

1010 hrs. I'm on the sands north of Camp Evans at A Company's location. I came up to pay the medics. I'm sitting on a case of smoke grenades. It's hot. On the way here I saw an air strike from the air. It was fantastic. I wish I had a movie camera to record it. Lieut. Stoner is acting CO here right now.

2025 hrs. Dear Mom and Dad,

Thank you for your card. Enclosed are a couple of snapshots. We built an entrance to the S-4 bunker as you see. In one picture I'm having a beer; and in the other, you see the way I dress every day. I carry a .45 caliber pistol. Sometimes when I visit a unit in the field, I carry the AK-47 automatic rifle I captured on the way into Khe Sanh. I wear the sunglasses all the time; it's too dusty to wear contacts. Also enclosed is another pay voucher.

Dad, how about another money breakdown for me--savings account, checking account, interests and receiving--everything? Also, Dad, if you can and if they are not too expensive now, I'd like some more shares in the Old Tucson movie set. I believe that will be (if not is) a good investment. See what you can get me for $100. I'm very serious, Dad. I remember when Shelton was selling at one dollar per share. I'll bet the price is up. I read an article in *Stars & Stripes*--Army newspaper--about the set and Hollywood's investment in Arizona for movie sets, soundstages, etc. Just purchase me $100 worth of shares and let me forget about

Joe in front of S-4 bunker in duty uniform.

the investment for a while. Also, see if you can send me info on the movie set--business wise.

Well, all is the same. We're improving our area here at Camp Evans. We're building a mess hall. When Capt. Rapper leaves in about two weeks, I'll be the S-4 until a captain comes in. Do you remember Walt Bert from Fort Polk? Well, he is in Korea and he's dropped me a couple of letters. He was a good buddy. I'm glad he's had a good, safe job. I guess that's it for now.

    Love, Joe

Joe with a beer in front of S-4 bunker entrance.

Thursday, July 18

1920 hrs. I went to D Company to pay the medics today. Last night, Sgt. Ross, one of my old squad leaders, was killed. Sgt. Blanko told me this morning that it was a hand grenade which hit a tree and bounced back. I went out to the field and saw that it's flat sand and no trees around. I was told by my old platoon men that he was shot by a man in third platoon who was "scare shooting." Lieut. Gaylord went out there to investigate and got it to be a ricochet or a VC bullet. He's covering his and the company's asses. It disgusts me to see it distorted so obviously even though it probably was an accident.

[As I look back, I ask myself—"What should have been done? Have a long, drawn-out investigation? Take the man out of the field, leaving the unit short a man? Court-martial him?" No. It was an accident. There was nothing else to do. As I have learned many years later practicing law—sometimes there are wrongs without remedies.]

Friday, July 19

2015 hrs. I made a quick trip to Wonder Beach (by Jeep) today and picked up three more pallets of cement. Intelligence reports predict an attack on Camp Evans soon (19 July to 21 July). Our battalion's operation along the beach has also brought in a squadron of armored cavalry (tanks and APCs). This is more supply work, but it's important.

Saturday, July 20

2037 hrs. Sgt. Doxel is helping me build a hooch today. It's going along pretty well. I got a movie camera from Dad today; it's a really sharp one.

My hooch under construction.

Sunday, July 21

2155 hrs. Sgt. Doxel and I went to the 14th Engineers area and saw a show they hired consisting of a band and some exotic dancers. I've been building a hooch which should be done tomorrow. We got more lumber in today. I believe we'll build a supply room which at present is a tent.

2105 hrs. Dear Mom and Dad,

This is just a quick note to say thanks for the camera. Dad, it's great. I'll try and get some good shots and then mail them home for development.

Mom, I appreciate any and all goodies you may send to eat. Sardines, oysters, or even some canned things to heat would be all right as we have a hot plate here. Sgt. Doxel, one of my men, and I are building an 8' x 8' plywood hooch for me. It should be finished soon. It rained today. The monsoons are on the way. All is pretty much the same. I've been really busy.

Dad, how much money can I write a check for? If I'm at a PX somewhere and I want to buy a tape recorder, speakers, etc., how much am I covered for by check? Please try and send me some kind of financial statement if you can.

Your son, Joe

Tuesday, July 23

Late entry—0705 hrs. I took some movies with my movie camera. We laid more cement for the mess hall.

2055 hrs. I flew to Wonder Beach today and scrounged some more cement. Bates and I swam in the Gulf of Tonkin. There were jellyfish in the water. The water was an aqua color. We moved the supply tent today. We're flooring it. We got a typhoon warning for tomorrow.

Wednesday, July 24

2135 hrs. We had another officer's going away party. Capt. Rapper was honored tonight. He got a Bronze Star and Air Medal, but I believe he should have gotten more. The award system is political also. We didn't get a typhoon today. It rained most of the day. I got to go to An Khe to turn in the money to finance.

[As pay officer, I pay the troops; but if some went on leave or were in the hospital or were otherwise not at the site for payment, I had to return the unpaid amount to finance.]

Thursday, July 25

1605 hrs. I'm here in An Khe sitting on a bunker at the DEROS Center. I brought Spec. 4 Norse with me. It's raining outside. I'll count the money at finance at 1800. I want to get to the PX to buy a stereo tuner-amplifier.

[The 1st Cav administrative headquarter was at An Khe. The tactical operations and headquarters operated out of Camp Evans. When troops went on R&R or were about to ETS (Estimated Term of Service), they went to the DEROS (Date of Estimated Return from Overseas) Center.]

2150 hrs. I got the payroll turned in without any problems. I hope to get a Jeep tomorrow. I believe I'll buy the stereo set I want tomorrow. I saw Capt. Dana and Lieut. Gaylord here. They are DEROSing.

Friday, July 26

1137 hrs. Specialist 4 Norse and I are sitting out front of the PX here at An Khe. I bought the sound equipment I want. It should be sharp. We're waiting for the Jeep to return. I hope to catch a 3:30 VIP flight back to Camp Evans today.

1730 hrs. I'm here at the Red Cross center shooting pool with Lieut. Dave Kinder. Specialist 4 Norse and I went to An Khe (city) today where we got steam baths, massages, and "lays." I had the same girl as last time. Her name is Lan and she looks part Chinese.

Saturday, July 27

0936 hrs. I've been waiting here since 0630 to get a flight back to Camp Evans. Replacements have priority so I'm still waiting for a plane to come in. Last night Lieut. Kendall and I went to the officers' club which had a floor show—a band with two go-go dancers. It was great.

2007 hrs. Dear Mom and Dad,
This is just a quick note to say all is well. Enclosed is a picture of me at An Khe where I went to turn in the payroll. I am also HQ company pay officer. Dad, while in An Khe I ordered a sound set for myself and wrote a check. Please make sure it's covered right away for $563.50. This includes shipping from Japan. I ordered the set through the An Khe PX. This whole outfit is well worth over $1000 in the States. When it is shipped home please let me know. Just store it for me. Mom, enclosed is this picture. I've still got a gut which I hope to lose. My job is keeping me busy and is very interesting. I get to travel once in a while. In the future, I'll send some of the movies home for development. I may not write a note; if you get them please have them developed; run them; and tell me how they came out. I've used two roles already. Ma, did you assemble that Buddhist incense burner? Is it polished?
Love, Joe

Sunday, July 28

2209 hrs. Capt. Rapper and WO Stern went to Da Nang today. I worked on my hooch. It's almost done and it looks sharp. I bought a Polaroid Swinger for $5. It's in good shape. I've got to get to Wonder Beach tomorrow to get more cement.

Monday, July 29

1520 hrs. Sgt. Doxel and I went to Wonder Beach today to get some cement. There was none, but I did get some screen for the mess hall. Right now I'm sitting in the Jeep just inside the Camp Evans gate. The fuel pump in the Jeep is not working.

2020 hrs. I just finished reading a book, "Men and War" by M Jerry Weiss, editor. It was a compilation of poems, speeches, excerpts of novels, etc., about war.

I'm at An Khe outside a Bachelor Officers Quarters.

Wednesday, July 31

Sgt. Doxel and I went to Hue and Phu Bai today. I stopped at the sampans. We were looking for a ceramic elephant for Capt. Rapper. We got a new S-4 today, Capt. Grange. He seems to be pretty sharp.

August, 1968

Thursday, August 1

1945 hrs. I got done playing volleyball. The col. inspected the whole S-4 area today. We looked pretty good, but the motor pool area needs to be improved. I'm almost done with my hooch.

[Being a rear echelon soldier was not as dangerous or as exciting as being a combat platoon leader. Although safer, it was an anticlimactic experience.]

Friday, August 2

1735 hrs. It's cloudy today. I got the Pena-prime machine to work on the log pad. A forklift picked up extra concertina wire in the area. The monsoon season is coming on. I am somewhat disappointed that the col. wouldn't let me leave the battalion to take a general's aide job in Saigon. I was the only man eligible in the brigade, but we're already short of officers. My job sure makes the time go by fast.

[Pena-prime is an oil substance sprayed on the ground to bond with the dirt to keep the dust down.]

Saturday, August 3

1930 hrs. Today, I got interviewed for General Tabor's aide de camp. I will represent the 1st Air Cavalry Division. I'll go to Saigon to be interviewed by him.

2116 hrs. Dear Mom and Dad,
I'm sending home these 3 roles for development. Sgt. Doxel and Specialist 4 Nate (backseat of Jeep--has mustache) and I went to Wonder Beach. I took pictures as we moved along the road. I'm afraid I may have wasted much of the film from bumping along or moving scenes too fast. We drove from Camp Evans through various villages until we got to the white sands of the beach. Let me know how the movies are coming out.

Tomorrow, I'm flying to Da Nang to get some supplies. One of our trucks and a Jeep with a trailer will meet me there. Today, I got interviewed by brigade for a job as an aide de camp to General Tabor, USARV Chief of Staff. On 10 August I fly to Saigon to be interviewed by him. I'll be representing the 1st Air Cavalry Division for the job. Other divisions in Vietnam will send representatives. It's an honor to even be considered for the job. I'll let you know how I come out. I believe I'll have a problem though because I'm not a career officer and of course they prefer someone who wants this experience for his Army career. I may extend a year if necessary to get the general's aide job. I still want to study law. Maybe I can do it through the Army.

Well, give my regards to everyone. Dad, did you cover my check for $563.50 on my stereo equipment? How's the rest of my money? Why so long in replying? As you can see on my pay voucher, I make $600 per month. I should have a lot of money saved up by now. Mom, I go on R&R next month unless I get the general's aide job and then I'll have to go on another roster again for R&R. I'll get your pearls then.

    Love, Joe

Sunday, August 4

1415 hrs. We're on the road on the way to Da Nang. The view is beautiful as we get up high at the passes and look out at the South China Sea. The road is narrow and winding and mountainous.

[I looked out at the South China Sea from the top of the pass in the mountains and said, "Someday, Hilton or somebody is going to build a beautiful hotel here."]

Monday, August 5

1835 hrs. I'm in Lieut. Dundee's (CO of HHC, 15 TC at Da Nang) tent having a beer. Today I went around Da Nang to various places. I patronized a girl near the 15 TC area. My Vietnamese is passable. It's hot and humid. I should have my business taken care of tomorrow.

[The 15 TC was the 15th Transportation Corps—it was the 1st Cavalry's HQ for the large aviation assets—Chinooks and flying cranes (CH-54s).]

Tuesday, August 6

0850 hrs. Today, I'm going to try to get a great deal of lumber. We needed to build sleeping quarters. Last night the 15th TC O Club had a good floor show.

Top: Chinooks at Da Nang; Right: Hueys behind the parapet, and flying crane. Bottom: 15th TC parapet at Da Nang.

Wednesday, August 7

1520 hrs. I got the lumber requisitions approved which was a chore in itself. It seems NSA (Naval Support Activity) doesn't want to release the lumber as most of it will go to Camp Evans anyway. It's hot and humid. I went swimming in the ocean nearby. Hope to get back to Camp Evans today.

Mess Hall

[Captain Rapper knew a colonel in the supply system at Da Nang. I went to him and used Rapper's name. I got two deuce and a halves (trucks) full of plywood which was like gold in Vietnam. Two trucks I had sent from Camp Evans to Da Nang loaded up and took the plywood back to Camp Evans up Highway 1—a dangerous route. We eventually built the mess hall with that plywood.]

Thursday, August 8
1236 hrs. Dear Mom and Dad,
I bought this album for only a buck. It's worth more. Use it as you wish--maybe to put the pictures I send you in or for any clippings or both purposes. Dad, I got your letter with the accounting of my money. Thank you. Enclosed in the box is a map. It's the map I used the 6 months I was a combat platoon leader. It has certain locations marked on it which I'll explain later. I'll also be sending home some film. Some of it is already paid for, for developing. I built a little 8' x 8' hooch out of plywood. It's comfortable and will keep me dry during monsoon

season. I go on R&R to Singapore on 13 September. Dad, is there anything special you want? Ask Bob for me, too. Also, I can get things extremely cheap through the PX.

Love, Joe

Thursday, August 8, (cont.)

2055 hrs. I moved into my hooch last night. It's pretty comfortable. I have a fan in here, too. I was selected a few days back to represent the 1st Air Cavalry to compete for the job of general's aide in Saigon. I was honest to certain people and told them I was planning to get out of the Army. Now I hear the interview with the general is off. I believe it is to be because of my not being career. Now I'm determined to ETS. I'll serve my time and get out.

My hooch after completion.

It finally dawned on me that I was not in "tight" with the corporation. My not being a career officer would impact future assignments, awards and decorations, and other administrative actions. Honesty is not always the best policy. I decided that I would not consider staying in the Army beyond my Estimated Term of Service (ETS).

Saturday, August 10

1100 hrs. Today was the day I was supposed to fly to Saigon to be interviewed by Gen. Tabor to be his aide. I was informed a few days ago I need not go as he got someone already. I believe this occurred as I am not a career officer. Such is life.

Sunday, August 11

2000 hrs. We worked on the motor pool today. I got assigned a LOD, also. Time flies when I'm busy.

[An LOD means Line of Duty investigation. When a soldier is injured, the Army wants to know if it was an injury incurred in the line of duty, thereby entitling him to compensation from the government; or if his injury was due to negligence or misconduct, thereby mitigating or negating any government compensation.]

Monday, August 12

2030 hrs. I got out of doing the LOD. We worked some more on the motor pool. Being motor officer is going to keep me busy. Tomorrow, we'll build a shed for maintenance. I got the frontloader today. There's a possibility we may be called upon to operate at Da Nang.

Tuesday, August 13

1943 hrs. It rained most of the day. We're using 8" x12" timbers for our maintenance area, and they are too big. We'll have to saw them. I think the XO is pissed off because I let the motor pool have plywood to build pretty nice living quarters.

Wednesday, August 14

0730 hrs. I finished reading "Poems of François Villon" translated by Norman Cameron. They were poems from a man who lived in France during the 15th century.

Wednesday, August 14, (cont.)

2045 hrs. I traded the 8" x 12" timbers for 4" x 4" lumber for the motor pool shed. I also picked up the payroll. I always seem to have many things to do. The motor pool area is coming along fine.

Thursday, August 15

1940 hrs. I did some paying today. The motor pool is shaping up. I've been really busy. At least time is flying faster.

```
2105 hrs. Dear Mom and Dad and Bob,
    Mom and Dad, I don't know if you're on your
trip yet so, Bob, if you are taking in the mail
you can relay the info. I got the goodies you all
sent and they were great. Please thank Schaeffer
for the beef jerky and salami. They were really
great.
    I made a little 8' x 8' plywood hooch which
is quite neat and comfortable. It's starting the
rainy season again so I prepared for it this
time. Enclosed is another pay receipt. I'll get
the voucher with total payments at the end of the
month. I go on R&R to Singapore 13 September 68.
What I think I'll do is write checks or maybe get
money orders.
    We have been building up Camp Evans a great
deal. We got a new captain for the S-4 so I'm
the assistant S-4 or service platoon leader. I'm
also motor officer which means I'm in charge of
all the battalion's vehicles. We've been building
a maintenance area and I have been scrounging
all sorts of supplies and heavy equipment such
as road graders, bulldozers, etc., to do work in
the area. I took two men and a Jeep and drove
```

to Da Nang which is about 3 hours away. We're supposed to go by convoy, but we took off on our own. We were lucky we didn't get ambushed or hit by a landmine. I got some pictures with a movie camera driving up and some pictures flying back in a Chinook helicopter. I took pictures of the door gunners firing the M-60 machine gun outside down at the ocean. I've been really busy lately so the time has been going by fast.

Bob, if you're receiving this mail, could you please develop the film I sent home and tell me how it is? Some of it will be fast and jerky, but it's from riding in the Jeep. Most of the pictures will be of the countryside, or people or vehicles, or buildings around Hue and Da Nang.

Well, that's about all for now. I'm looking forward to R&R in September and hopefully getting home by or just before Christmas. Give my regards to everyone.

Love, Joe

Friday, August 16

2230 hrs. Another busy day has gone by. We finished the shed today; it looks good. The whole motor pool is shaping up. I'm still paying the troops when I can. Tonight the major (Monburg) and HQ CO emphasized base defense—the ready reaction platoon. An LZ nearby got overrun and several Americans were killed. With the bad weather seems to come the more bitter conflicts and probes from the VC and NVA.

Saturday, August 17

2015 hrs. About one-half of the battalion's vehicles came in for cleaning and spot painting. Sgt. Hage, my motor sgt., is pissing me off. He's very lazy, not a leader, and an alcoholic.

Tomorrow, I'm supposed to be interviewed for Gen. Davis's aide. I found out that Col. Dennis wrote a letter requesting I not be taken as General Tabor's aide because I was needed in this battalion. I hope I get this job.

2120 hrs. I just heard shots about five minutes ago. I turned out my lights and got my .45 caliber pistol. I couldn't find anything. There may be an infiltration as occurred on LZ Nancy night before last.

[The shots could have been an actual penetration by NVA or VC, or it could have been some moron popping off rounds while "scare shooting."]

Sunday, August 18

1720 hrs. I was interviewed by Gen. Davis today for aide de camp. He chose someone else.

> 1720 hrs. Dear Mom and Dad,
> I got the last letter about the movies. I was afraid they might come out bad. I'll try to improve them. I probably won't take too many shots of myself; I'm more interested in the natives, equipment, scenery, structures, and things in general showing the war here. About the deal of being a general's aide, I was told later by my battalion that I needed to go for an interview with him. I discovered later that my battalion commander wrote a letter saying how much he needed me here in the battalion. A funny thing happened though. It turned out that General Davis, Assistant Division Commander here on Evans, needed an aide. I was interviewed by him today, but he selected another guy. I told him that I was not a career officer so that hurt

me, I'm sure. It's been an honor though to be selected to compete for general's aide twice. I just wish I even had the chance to be interviewed in Saigon by the general there.

Well, it's the rainy season again. We really got some today. I go on R&R 13 September 68. Should I get gifts for my aunts and if so what? Ma, I know you want the pearl necklace. Dad, what do you and Bob want?

Love, Joe

P. S. I should be home by 3 January unless I get a Christmas drop, maybe by 23 December.

Monday, August 19

2422 hrs. I'm up late getting prepared to fly to Da Nang later today. Spec 4 Lares and I will take a Jeep and trailer to get supplies. We'll go by Chinook. Later I'll go to An Khe to turn in the money I got as pay officer. The motor pool area is really looking much better.

[I always thought it ironic that I was and still am very unmechanically inclined, but I was the motor officer. This reinforced the old saying, "The right way; the wrong way; and the Army way."]

Tuesday, August 20

1150 hrs. I'm sitting in my Jeep with Spec 4 Lares here in Da Nang at the 95th Evac Hospital. I'm waiting for a nurse (Jan) to take her to lunch and have a few drinks.

[I met the nurse at the hospital, struck up a conversation, and asked her out. It was so refreshing to meet an American girl to just visit with. The short chance encounter helped me forget about the bloodiest year of the war for a short time.]

1830 hrs. Lieut. Jan Burrows and I had dinner at the Stone Elephant. We had a few drinks in the lounge, and I took her back to the hospital.

Wednesday, August 21

1900 hrs. It's hot and humid. I'm back here at Red Beach (15 TC). Today I swung a deal for eight bundles of three-quarter inch plywood. I've now got the problem of getting it back to Camp Evans. Also I've got to fly to An Khe to turn in the payroll. I've been driving all around Da Nang observing the people, the historic and sometimes beautiful buildings, the peasants, the ARVNs, our own troops, everything in general.

2145 hrs. I just finished reading Management Uses of the Computer by Irving I. Solomon and Lawrence O. Weingart. It's an interesting book about computers and their uses.

Thursday, August 22

2140 hrs. I'm sitting in an Armed Forces police station in downtown Da Nang. I'm trying to retrieve an M-2 carbine (sawed-off stock) that was confiscated. WO Danny James (from Tucson) is with me. It's hot and humid. I hope I can get the weapon as the trucks will leave by convoy tomorrow. I haven't decided whether or not to stay downtown for a while. An attack is expected.

[I don't remember exactly why I was trying to get the confiscated weapon back, but I think it was the warrant officer's weapon. It was unauthorized, but its shortened length would make it easier to carry in a helicopter, and I think James was an aviator. I was just trying to use my rank and influence to help him get his weapon of choice back.]

Friday, August 23

0830 hrs. Last night I got the weapon back. Then the two warrant officers and I went to the Stone Elephant Club. Then we walked around the block to the MACV Club. We came back last night while the 15th TC compound was on alert. At about 0300, I woke up to an explosion and a flash of light I saw through the open tent flap. We got mortared heavily (103 rounds total). Lieut. Daniels and I hit the floor off our cots and then went outside near some sandbags. The rounds just kept dropping all around us. I hugged the ground where I was rather than run to the bunker another 30 m away. The 15th TC battalion commander's office was hit (only 50 m away). I sent my trucks on convoy today.

Even after I got out of the field (so to speak) and was on a supply run to Da Nang, I still had to worry about getting mortared. I spent the night at Da Nang and got to sleep on a cot in a GP medium tent on a wooden floor. The side flaps were rolled up and I saw the flash of mortar impacts around us. We could hear the *thoomping* of several mortars firing from the vicinity of Monkey Mountain. I rolled off my cot down to the floor, got up, tripped and fell once I got up, and then I stumbled trying to get out of the tent, following others to a nearby bunker. I found some sandbags and stayed behind them. It's difficult to describe the terror I felt knowing there were scores of high explosive mortar rounds capable of making many shrapnel fragments on impact flying through the air, possibly going to drop on me. I finally heard an all clear siren. The next day the S-3 of the 15th TC and I checked the area and he told me there were 103 mortar impacts.

Saturday, August 24

0650 hrs. I'm sitting on a PSP chopper landing pad facing the ocean. The sun just came up and I can see some U.S. ships in the ocean. This early in the morning all is quiet, and it seems as though there is no war. Specialist 4 Norse and I tried to get back to Evans, but we got bumped from the chopper by some brass. The lumber and self-service supplies got back to Evans okay.

Sunday, August 25

1647 hrs. I got to An Khe where I am now today and turned in the payroll with no problems. I finished reading "The Year of the Rat" by Mladin Zarubica. It's about a World War II plot which deceived the Nazi high command and led to an Allied victory.

Monday, August 26

1430 hrs. I took care of some business today. Last night Lieut. Joyner (Bernie) and I saw a movie at the club, and we had quite a few drinks. I'm tired so I'll read on this bunk and maybe lie down. I'll go back to Camp Evans tomorrow.

2130 hrs. I just got back from the Can Do Club. They had a movie—"The Double Man" with Yul Brenner and Britt Ekland. I can hear a tape recorder next door playing "Monday, Monday" by the Mamas and Papas. I'm really homesick. I've got to get up at 0500 to catch the plane back to Camp Evans.

Tuesday, August 27

1645 hrs. I got back here to Evans this morning. We're still building and improving the area. It's hot and humid. The plywood I got will come in handy for many building projects. I signed for an M-16 today. It's an old one.

2111 hrs. Dear Mom and Dad,
I hope you are home in time to receive this letter. I'll be going on R&R to Singapore the 13th through 18th of September. I'll leave here from Camp Evans 10 September to go to An Khe to prepare for R&R. As soon as you receive this letter could you please get me some postal money orders as soon as possible? The finance office is not supposed to cash checks. Do money orders work in foreign ports? I'll need probably about $500. I want to buy presents and some clothes. Mom, please specify what type pearls you want again. What would make good gifts for Aunt Lorraine and Aunt Jo, Ma? Dad, what do you and Bob want? If for some reason I don't get a reply before I go to An Khe, I'll see if I can get a partial payment from finance or write checks or something. Please write back as soon as possible.

I just got back from An Khe returning payroll. Before that I just got back from Da Nang where I got supplies and made a deal which got battalion 8 bundles of plywood which is hard to get. We've been trying to build up Evans before the rains really get bad. Some mortaring and rocketing has increased with the bad weather. I should be home by Christmas. I'm still careful and aware of ever-present danger. All is okay. I'm looking forward to going on R&R.

Love Joe

[As I reflect on the correlation between the increased mortaring and rocketing and the bad weather—I think bad weather decreased the sorties of aviation aerial observation. This allowed the VC and NVA to do more mischief.]

Wednesday, August 28

2120 hrs. Another typical day. Today, I went to the Brigade S-1 to see about a job as assistant adjutant. I may get a job. I hope so. I'm tired with the battalion now. I need a change. Specialist 4 Tinser, one of my truck drivers, is in here reading my Vietnamese language handbook.

Thursday, August 29

1930 hrs. We inspected all the vehicles today. They needed parts badly. I wrote a letter to Aunt Lorraine today. I should write some more letters. I guess I'll shower now.

Friday, August 30

1955 hrs. I'm listening to Humphrey speak on the radio. He sounds so phony—typical political speech. Today we had a meeting with the motor pool to iron out some difficulties. I am getting tired of this place. I need a change

I deeply resented the politics of the Democratic Party and the antiwar protesters. I felt then, and feel even more so today, that they were dupes for the Communists. Their naïve, disingenuous, political antics put our lives in great danger. I remember that I got to vote by proxy while I was there in Vietnam. I voted for Richard Nixon while sitting on a bunker. To put things in perspective more recently, I deeply resented the politics of the Republican Party who were dupes for the ideologues, Religious Right and others. Their naïve, disingenuous, political antics put others' lives in great danger with almost no justification in the Middle East.

Saturday, August 31

1850 hrs. We're having a going away party tonight for Capt. Study. Col. Dennis will inspect our area tomorrow. The brigade S-1 told our S-1 that brigade can't have an assistant S-1.

2130 hrs. I just got a call from our S-1. He sent a report to G-1 tomorrow for a mission involving 60 days TDY. It sounds so mysterious. I won't know what I'll be doing until tomorrow.

[TDY meant a temporary duty assignment.]

September, 1968

Sunday, September 1

1525 hrs. I took an LOH here to Hue MACV compound. I was informed I was getting a liaison officer job, but I see that I am to go back to the field with an ARVN unit. I made calls to try and straighten it out.

[An LOH (or "Loach") is a light observation helicopter—an OH-6, one of the best helicopters ever made. They would go out with the Cobras (attack helicopters) in "hunter-killer teams" and flush out and kill the "bad guys." I let it be known that I wanted a change, and they were going to reassign me to advise an ARVN unit. Although I needed a change, I still wanted to be with the "Cav."]

Monday, September 2

1125 hrs. I'm sitting waiting for a confirmation that I do or do not have to be an ARVN advisor. I am really getting screwed.

```
    1325 hrs. Dear Mom and Dad,
    What a life! I am at the MACV compound
(Military Advisory Command Vietnam) HQ where I
was informed by my battalion that I would be
taking a liaison officer job. When I got here I
```

was informed by MACV that I would be an ARVN advisor which means I would go back out to the field with Vietnamese troops. I made calls back to Camp Evans and it has supposedly been worked out where I go back to Evans. This was to be a good deal but it didn't turn out that way. Also, reference the general's aide job for General Tabor, my battalion cmdr. wrote a letter to him stating that the battalion needed me so I was informed that I needn't show up for the interview. I was interviewed by General Davis, but he chose another man (he was a career officer). My name was submitted for General Forsythe's aide (new division commander), but I was supposed to get this "good" job instead. Well, I think everything will work out all right.

    I'm supposed to go on R&R 13 September to 18 September to Singapore. By the time you receive this letter it will be too late for you to reply to this letter. I sent a letter earlier requesting money orders. I hope I get a reply on that in time. If not, I'll see what checks they'll cash. I've got 4 months left in country. I wish the time would fly. I got your letter, Mom, from Fort Wayne. I'm glad you and Dad had a good time. I hope to be back at Camp Evans by tomorrow. If any changes of any kind in my status come up, I'll inform you.

    By the way, Ma, are you sure Grandpa was in the 2/7 Cav? How are things going at home? Is Bob in school; did he graduate? Is Dad still practice teaching? Dad, how is that Caddy holding up?

    Love, Joe

My grandpa had run away from home and joined the Army because his father chopped up a bicycle grandpa bought with earnings he failed to share with his family. Grandpa had been part of General "Black Jack" Pershing's military expedition to chase Poncho Villa who crossed the U.S.-Mexico border in 1916 and raided Columbus, New Mexico. I used to see the "doughboy" helmet in Grandpa's closet. The helmet is on a mannequin now in the Arizona Military Museum in the Papago Park Military Reservation in Phoenix, Arizona. The lettering on the helmet says: "1st US CAV." A half a century later, I was in the "Cav." Grandpa and his troopers used horses; we used helicopters. My grandpa used to tell me that, "Your two best friends are your rifle and your horse," and "If you have a little bit of water in your canteen, give it to your horse first." Take care of your horse and it will take care of you. That was how my grandpa, a real horse cavalryman, thought.

Monday, September 2, (cont.)

1745 hrs. I just finished reading "The Memoirs of Casanova" translated and abridged by Lowell Bair. It was really interesting. Still no final word on my status.

Tuesday, September 3

1115 hrs. I got a ride from the MACV compound to the hospital log pad inside the "old" walled city of Hue. A Marine chopper just brought in a dead woman. I'm waiting for a chopper going to Dong Ha to drop me off at Camp Evans. Maj. Monburg, battalion XO, told me all was taken care of. I'm sitting on a table near the log pad looking at a pond on one side and a canal on the other. Vietnam is really beautiful in some places, but the filth and the scars of war detract from the beauty. Some of the Vietnamese women are really beautiful.

[I still think that one of the most beautiful women in the world is Eurasian—half Vietnamese and half French.]

Wednesday, September 4

1040 hrs. It's rained all morning. All is rectified reference the assignment problem I had. I'm back to Camp Evans in the S-4 shop. Lieut. Berg will go to the advisory team job. Last night we had a party in the BOQ tent. It was pretty good. Capt. Grange is driving to Phu Bai today with Lares. The roads are wet and slippery.

2155 hrs. I was over in Lieut. Joyner's hooch. We drank some bourbon and Coke which is unauthorized. It rained all day today. The lights just went out so now I'm using a flashlight to see by. The rain just started up again. My hooch leaks but it's still fairly comfortable. I go on R&R in six days. Soon I'll be home. I guess I'll go to sleep now.

Thursday, September 5

0445 hrs. It's rained all night and is pouring now. Everyone is up on a typhoon alert; typhoon to hit at 0600. I walked the battalion area to check the strength of the bunkers. I'm soaked.

[The roof of my 8' x 8' plywood hooch leaked when it rained. I had screen up high on the side walls and the wind blew the rain in there, too. The hooch looked like an outhouse, but it was mine. I built it aboveground and took my chances with potential incoming mortar- or rocket fire. I slept on a cot with a poncho liner, and the hooch gave me privacy.]

Friday, September 6

1335 hrs. We've been in the midst of the edge of a typhoon. It's been raining constantly. The winds have been strong. My hooch leaks. Everything is wet. The rain is just a drizzle now.

2035 hrs. Things are drying out. It stopped raining. I'm drying clothes in my hooch. I hope to get some letters from home soon. Planes haven't been taking off and landing for the past few days because of the weather. Tomorrow I'll try to repair my hooch (fix the leaks).

Saturday, September 7

2025 hrs. It drizzled today. The motor pool has been keeping me really busy. We have a problem getting parts here in Vietnam. Today, I put some different covers over the screen area of my hooch. There's still a leak in the roof. I bought a Swinger camera for five dollars from one of the men. It's almost brand-new.

Sunday, September 8

1820 hrs. I got a letter from Mom and Dad today. Tomorrow, I'll go on R&R. I've got to get some things squared away in An Khe, such as finance and getting khakis cleaned. It's hot and humid. I dispatched several vehicles today for various missions.

2115 hrs. We got mortared a couple of hours ago. The rounds landed near brigade—about 500 m away.

[Camp Evans was a large division compound, and whenever any mortars landed anywhere in the perimeter the impacts made distinct pounding sounds unless you were very close, and then you heard and possibly saw the loud explosions. Sirens then went off.]

Monday, September 9

1150 hrs. I took a Caribou here to An Khe. I'm at the air terminal waiting for the bus to the R&R center. The sky is cloudy and there's a gentle cool breeze blowing. I'm finally going on R&R.

[A Caribou is a twin-engine cargo plane that can take off and land on short runways. It belonged to the Army, not the Air Force, in those days.]

Tuesday, September 10

1445 hrs. Last night I saw a movie at the Can Do Club. It was "How to Save a Marriage and Ruin Your Life" with Dean Martin and Stella Stevens. I believe there's a floor show tonight. Today I went to the city of An Khe. I looked for this girl I would always visit but I couldn't find her. I found another girl who was cute soliciting outside. When I told her I wanted her, she acted surprised. She stepped to the back of the shop looking for someone and then motioned to me to go to her. Her room was neat and clean and very orderly, not at all like a prostitute's room one finds in Vietnam. While I was with her in her room she would signal for me not to make a noise. She was cute, clean, and well built; she was 19 years old.

Wednesday, September 11

0920 hrs. The club had a floor show last night. They were Koreans and were good. I'm sitting on a bunk at the DEROS Center listening to some tapes being played in the building next door. I just finished reading "The Insanity Defense" by Abraham S Goldstein. Kathleen sent me the book. It was very informative and interesting. I believe I'd like to be a criminal lawyer.

1110 hrs. Dear Mom and Dad,

I'm in An Khe at a Red Cross ctr. I'm shooting pool and killing time. Tomorrow, I'll go to Cam Ranh Bay and then to Singapore for R&R. I got your letter before I left. I got a partial payment of $200 from finance which comes off my next month's check. I've also cashed two $50 checks at the PX, and I'll cash 1 or 2 more if I can. If I don't take as much money as I want, I'll just budget. There won't be any problem. Mom, I'll try and get the things you asked for. Enclosed are my partial payment voucher and my last month's pay voucher.

We had a typhoon warning the other day, but just bad winds and rains resulted. Evans is growing and getting more statesidelike with rules and regulations of dress and behavior, etc., even though we're near the DMZ in a combat zone. I hope to be home by New Year's Day at least. Maybe, Christmas, but doubtful. I could extend, but instead I think I'll bum around until school starts. I've still got to check with ASU. They probably won't accept me, and U of A will accept me only on probation. I'll check it out later.

I've only got about 100 days left in Vietnam. I'm getting "short" as the expression goes. Have you received my stereo equipment from the Pacex outfit yet? Dad, has anyone cashed my check for $563? It takes about 2 months to get the stuff. Maybe it's on the way. It's my turn at the pool table so I'll close.

Love Joe

[Although I was back in good standing for law school, I wasn't sure whether to go back to the University of Arizona or attend Arizona State University. I went back to the U of A, and the professors were very nice to me. I got good grades. Maybe the newspaper clippings about my platoon leading the relief into Khe Sanh had something to do with it.]

Thursday, September 12

1255 hrs. I'm at Cam Ranh Bay R&R processing area. I saw Paul Milton at An Khe. He was a crew chief—1/9 Cav. DEROSs in about 30 days. I'm waiting to process now.

[The DEROS Center at An Khe was where we out-processed from the Cav.]

1830 hrs. I am in a little billet for officers at Cam Ranh Bay. I ate and went to the officers' club for a couple of drinks. I'll shower now and get ready for tomorrow. By this time tomorrow, I should be in Singapore.

2140 hrs. I just finished reading "The Ugly American" by William J Lederer and Eugene Burdick. It's an outstanding book and I'm sorry to say for the most part accurate in the portrayal of American diplomacy, especially in Southeast Asia.

Friday, September 13

1237 hrs. Well, here I am in the Serene Hotel in Singapore. I got a double at single-room prices. There is piped-in music. I'll change clothes and then check out the area. It's nice here.

Saturday, September 14

2130 hrs. I'm in my room. I had a girl yesterday and I have a different one tonight. She's in the lounge now. The girls are called "hostesses." There's a girl, June, who is assistant manager. She is Chinese and a real entrepreneur. She's intelligent and Orientally beautiful. I called home yesterday and talked to Ma.

It was kind of interesting how one could select a sexual partner. Several girls would come to the lounge in their finest silk flowing apparel, and the client would select whom he wanted—just like buying a suit of clothes. Our values and language are often hypocritical. Profanity is omitted from public broadcasting, but photos of death and destruction as in war are okay. Some people don't like "bad words," but they have no problem killing innocent men, women, and children in Iraq. I am reminded of that line that Colonel Kurtz said in *Apocalypse Now*: "They teach young men to drop fire on people, but they won't let them write 'fuck' on their airplanes because it's obscene."

Monday, September 16

1715 hrs. I bought a lot of things today. I spent a great deal of money. I bought gems and pearls and ivory and silk, etc. I hope I don't regret it, but I think they make beautiful gifts.

Ivory I purchased.

DEAR MOM AND DAD, LOVE FROM VIETNAM | 221

My mother has since passed away, but my wife has the pearls I bought for my mother. I still have the several various ivory figurines I bought in Singapore and Vietnam. The silk tablecloths were given to various aunts. One aunt who was a seamstress made a beautiful afghan out of the silk tablecloth I gave her.

Monday, September 16, (cont.)

Late entry—We, Capt. Dave Loader, our girls, and I went downtown to Chinatown area and ate authentic Chinese food. We ate shark fin soup, crab claws, fried rice, octopus, and sweet-and-sour pork. Everything was absolutely delicious. I have a Malaysian girl who waits on me hand and foot.

[That was a fantastic meal. Our "hostesses" for the evening were Chinese and knew where to go and what to order. We went to a market area and saw the various wares on sale in the shops, and we got to the area where chickens and ducks and other produce were hanging in the open on racks. I had never eaten shark fin soup or octopus before. It was all delicious.]

Tuesday, September 17

1650 hrs. We go back to Cam Ranh Bay tomorrow. It's been interesting. I've been able to buy gifts and clothes at very low prices. I've been entertained by girls whose job it was to please me in any way possible. I've been on two tours—the one today, we went on a boat. I've taken film which I hope is all right. I called home twice since I left the U.S.A. nine months ago.

[The Tiger Balm Gardens was interesting, as was the boat ride. There was a "snake charmer" with deadly snakes, and I petted a king cobra just to prove I could do it.]

Large statue of a tiger.

Boat type used for the cruise.

I'm holding the basket with a Cobra snake.

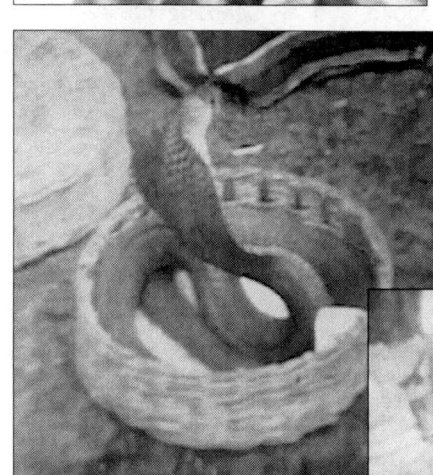

Cobra snake.

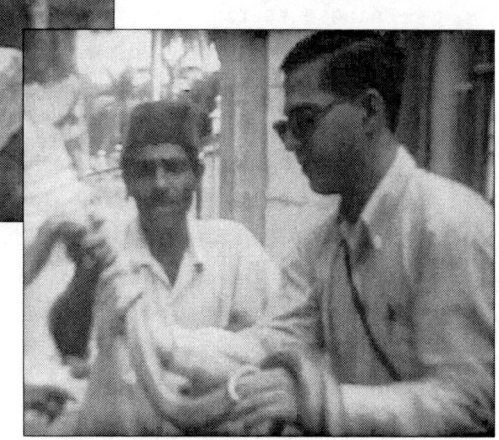

I'm holding the Cobra.

Wednesday, September 18

0850 hrs. Today, we go back to Vietnam. We are to assemble at the hotel here at 1000. We'll get to Cam Ranh Bay today and maybe An Khe, too. I hate to go back to Evans. I wonder if my hooch got flooded out while I was gone.

Thursday, September 19

1253 hrs. I'm back at An Khe now. I mailed my suits and gifts home. I sent a jade bracelet to Kathleen; I hope it gets there all right. It's really hot and humid.

    1410 hrs. Dear Mom and Dad,
    I am now at An Khe. I'm writing now so I don't forget certain instructions pertaining to the things I bought in Singapore and am sending home. Dad, please make sure that the bank covers me up to around $800 in checks. I don't believe I wrote that much, however. Singapore was beautiful. It's the 4th largest port in the world. I stayed in a nice hotel and this capt. and I took some tours around the city. We took some girls to eat in the Chinese section of town one night. We ate shark fin soup, octopus, fried rice, sweet-and-sour pork, and some fried crab claws. Everything was delicious.
    Mom, I bought many items which I sent home and I want you to be looking for them. I just mailed a box in Cam Ranh Bay, RVN, to home in Tucson. In it are two suits and a burgundy sports jacket with black pants. All three outfits together cost me $140 American money. Also in the box are a jade ring (for Dad), a Seiko watch (for Bob), and a pearl necklace (for Mom). Ma, the pearls are Mikimoto cultured pearls--the best. Dad,

also in a small envelope wrapped in cotton are 5 black star sapphires--each 4 points. I paid $4 for each carat for them in Singapore money. Singapore money is $3 to our one dollar. Dad, you can do with these sapphires what you want. I would recommend making a ring or necktie clasp or cuff links. They are for the family so whoever wants something made with any of them--go ahead. I looked at jade, but I wasn't sure what to buy. The box with these items should get to you in about 10 days or the end of the month.

   I'm also having sent another box which should get to you in about 3 or 4 weeks. In this set of items I got five silk tablecloths or bedspreads, one ivory Buddha, one ivory bridge, one ivory pillar with an ivory ball of balls carved inside of it, and one intricately carved ivory boat. I got all of that for about $117 American money. Ma, I want one each of the tablecloths to go to Aunt Lorraine, Aunt Josephine, Aunt Mary Lou, Aunt Jamelia, and to Grandma. I know you probably want one, but I'll get similar items later. You can't imagine all the stuff I could've bought, but I had to hold myself back. Keep the other ivory pieces in the house and don't give them away. They are real ivory. These last goods I mention are from the Bonyear Trading Company and should arrive in 3 to 4 weeks. Keep me informed as to the status of these goods. Oh! Also in the box with my suits, I sent six roles of movie film. I hope customs didn't x-ray the box as the film may be ruined. I had the captain take some movies of me playing with a cobra snake. I hope they come out. None of my movies will have meaning unless I narrate them.

Well, I'll go back to Evans tomorrow. I may have some mail there from you. I really enjoyed talking to both of you on the telephone. I'll enclose the receipts of the things I have bought so they are around for reference. Don't be alarmed at the prices; they are Singapore prices, so if something says $300, it's $100 U.S. money. Well, that's about it. Give my regards to everyone. Tell Bob to keep plugging away because although there's some good excitement and enjoyment over here, most of it is bullshit.

Love Joe

Friday, September 20

0120 hrs. I'm at the dispensary here at An Khe. I'm checking on my foot (toe) again. Lieut. Joyner is also here at An Khe. We'll go to the PX later and then to the city, An Khe. I don't believe I'll extend after all. I saw Capt. Stoneman, Bob Stoneman—my first FO—last night at the Can Do Officers' Club. I really like him. He and I took that small daytime patrol out at the bridges. He was also with me on February 27 when we hit the big shit.

1535 hrs. I went to sin city (An Khe). I made love to a pretty Vietnamese girl whose family has a shop on the main street. She's really pretty. I went to the bar section and a cute Chinese-looking girl caught my eye and she cost me another five dollars. What a life!

[I was young, single, and didn't know if I'd be alive the next day, so I lived life intensely.]

Saturday, September 21

1940 hrs. Lieut. Joyner and I got back to Camp Evans today. We're now having motor stables which means I hold a meeting, checking that each driver checks his vehicle. Everything seems to be getting more petty, but I'll stick it out for about 100 more days. I got a lot of mail when I came back.

Sunday, September 22

1930 hrs. It rained all day today. I feel sick. I have what feels like a chest cold and the flu combined. My hooch still leaks. I wrote a letter to Lieut. Ron James, my predecessor here as service platoon leader. I've got to write Mary and Kathleen, Aunt Lorraine, and Aunt Jay. The col. seems to have so many projects for the motor pool. We have a CMMI day after tomorrow. This is a big inspection. We have the IG next month so everyone is hopping.

Medical tent or aid station.

Monday, September 23

1015 hrs. I went to the aid station today as I felt sick. I vomited twice last night, and today my temperature was 103°. I'm out at the 15th Medical Battalion ward where I'll be overnight. The doctor thinks I have spiraled bronchitis. I feel lousy all over.

Tuesday, September 24

1435 hrs. I'm still at 15th medical. I feel lousy. My temperature hit 104° last night. I haven't eaten anything yesterday or today. I don't have malaria—just a bad chest cold. I called the S-4 shop to see how the CMMI came out. Capt. Grange wasn't around. I may go back to work tomorrow, but I don't really see how. I feel so lousy.

Wednesday, September 25

0900 hrs. My chest feels congested. I keep coughing. I'll go back to work tomorrow. It rained some more today. I've definitely got to fix my hooch so it doesn't leak.

Thursday, September 26

2047 hrs. I returned to the 2/7 Cav area today. I feel better. I went to brigade today and was accepted as the brigade R&R officer. This is an outstanding idea for morale and I'll be OIC (officer in charge).

As a morale booster and "perk" for troops coming in from the field, someone came up with the idea to create a Brigade R&R Center right there at Camp Evans. It was to have billets with cots and a small PX and other accommodations for the troops. I was to put it all together and run it.

Friday, September 27

2145 hrs. I saw the R&R center site. It's right on the other side of the log pad. It's going to really be outstanding. The buildings are being built now. This job will be interesting and a challenge and a good way to speed the time. I've got about 97 days left in country.

Saturday, September 28

1915 hrs. I went over to Capt. Stoneman's (Bob) artillery battery today. We just talked about the Army in general. He's a really nice guy. Today, I also checked the R&R area again. It's progressing pretty well. I got a package of various candies from Kathleen.

R&R Center under construction.

Sunday, September 29

1955 hrs. The R&R area is slowly but surely coming along. It rained today. I've still been coughing. My lungs are still irritated, but I guess I'll be all right. I'm looking forward to working at this new job. It will be a challenge, but it's an outstanding idea. Troops really need their morale boosted.

Monday, September 30

1935 hrs. I've decided to move my hooch down by the R&R Center. I'm listening to my portable radio now. It's a little weak. The R&R Center is improving. It'll be a problem at first, but it should turn out all right. Capt. Grange wants to use my hooch for a dispatch hooch, but I need a place to stay so I'll take this.

```
Dear Mom and Dad,
    Well, I've got 94 days left in Vietnam and
maybe less if I can get some kind of a holiday
drop. I've been back here at Camp Evans for a
while and a lot has been happening. When I first
got back, I got very sick with viral bronchitis.
I'm still coughing, but I was in the ward for 3
days. I had 104° temperature. I finally got a job
close to like what I was wanting. The 3rd Brigade
(ours) is building an R&R center right here on
Camp Evans. It's got the highest priority in the
brigade now. There will be a PX, a Vietnamese
gift shop, a barbershop, a dayroom, an admin
building, a mess hall, a snack bar, volleyball
court, basketball court, and billets to sleep one
```

company at a time from the field. I am the OIC--officer in charge of the whole operation. Major Black, a colored major, the Brigade S-1, is the man who got me the job. He says it'll be a lot of responsibility and a real challenge, but I had told him before I'd like a job with a lot of administration. This is it.

Well, the monsoon season is here. Rain every day. I sent home another one of my big blue suitcases yesterday. It'll still take about 30 days to get home. Remember to be checking on my box of suits (and gifts) and be on the lookout for other merchandise coming in. I hope time flies for these last 3 months. I put in for a seven-day leave to Australia around 7 November to 14 November. For my passport, I need a $12 U.S. Postal money order payable to the American Embassy. Dad, could you send me this? I'm looking out the front door of my hooch and the rain is coming down.

Well that's all for now. My new address will be HHC 3rd Brigade now, but I'll check on my mail here for a while. I'm pretty enthusiastic about this R&R center as it will really be something, and it has top priority in the brigade at the present time. It's more good business experience. Keep me posted on what's happening at home.

Love, Joe

October, 1968

Tuesday, October 1

1745 hrs. The R&R site is still improving. All the billets' roofs have tin on them. I'll move my hooch down to the R&R area tomorrow. I tried to get a detail to move it today, but they couldn't handle it. Right now I'm sitting in the briefing tent at the brigade TOC. I'm waiting for the briefing and then chow. Capt. Grange was pissed that I was taking my hooch, but that's too bad. Chief Stepson tried to get into the act, but the XO already okayed my taking the hooch. How petty people can be.

Thursday, October 3

0740 hrs. On 2 October I got a forklift and moved my hooch to the R&R Center area. I wrote a letter to Aunt Lorraine and a letter to Aunt Jamelia.

1740 hrs. I got orders today to serve as a defense counsel on a court-martial. The defendant is charged on three counts, each a different offense; and this case looks bleak. It'll still be good experience for me, as I'll try to give him the best possible defense. I got a dozer at the R&R Center area today, and the area was cleared nicely. The place is shaping up. I have been walking a lot lately as I don't have a vehicle. I'm still waiting to sign over my property at the 2/7 Cav.

[I guess I can consider this my first criminal case in more than 40 years of practicing criminal law.]

Friday, October 4

1105 hrs. Today, I have 90 days left in RVN. Lieut. Mobis and I have been flying around to ARVN compounds trying to get weapons (SKS). I'm in the chopper now at Hue at the MACV compound.

Saturday, October 5

1307 hrs. I'm in Da Nang at the USO waiting for a ride. I came here with a Lieut. John Dale who is to help me get the funds to start the PX at the R&R Center. Yesterday, I told Maj. Black, the Brigade S-1, that I didn't want the case because the man had gone AWOL from my platoon. But I talked to Specialist Gaines and I believe he is innocent, and I will defend him. He has three charges against him, but I'll do my best.

[Gaines was charged with AWOL, Sleeping on Guard, and Possession of Marijuana.]

This was an awkward situation for me. Major Black got me the job as OIC of the R&R Center. He was a Black man. Gaines was a Black man and had been in MY platoon when he allegedly went AWOL when we were going into Khe Sanh. I should have been a witness against Gaines rather than representing him. I told Black and he was pissed and told me to get the hell out. Sergeant Links, my last platoon sergeant, also a Black man, brought Gaines to my hooch. I decided to represent Gaines as I thought he was innocent and was getting screwed. This was 1968, and the "Negro" did not always get fair treatment. Gaines was an excellent "point man" in my platoon, and I felt I owed it to him to represent him in his trial.

Sunday, October 6

0945 hrs. Lieut. Dale and I got civilian clothes and stayed in a hotel last night in Da Nang. I had a girl all night. It's real morale booster to have female companionship once in a while. We'll go back to Evans today. I have $3000 in cash in a suitcase.

[The $3000 was start-up money for the R&R Center's PX. I would buy items to stock up.]

Monday, October 7

2102 hrs. I'm in the admin hooch. We have a generator and electricity. I was listening to the Kinks on a tape recorder. I think I'll like this job. 1st Sgt. Mimms and I are discussing our needs for tomorrow. The day room and gift shop are ready for operation.

[I'm now in my R&R Center. We're planning and waiting for troops to arrive. A "day room" is a recreation room.]

Tuesday, October 8

1730 hrs. I got a letter from Kathleen and one from home. Everyone got the gifts I sent. Col. Cox, Col. Gore, Col. Harden, and Major Skelly all checked out the R&R Center today. Everyone is impressed. Col. Harden commented on the policing of the area though. Hell! My people have been doing an outstanding job. I've been working on the defense for Specialist Gaines. It's going to be tough. The trial counsel is evasive on many things. I called Long Bien to get a statement from a witness. The guy is in jail there. It's hot and humid.

["Policing" an area means cleaning it up, picking up cigarette butts or trash or weeds, etc. This was not usually a priority in combat zones.]

Thursday, October 10

0715 hrs. On 9 October, Col. Gore had a meeting with Major Skelly, Mr. Oswald (food service advisor), Maj. Black, and me. The R&R center is to open up Monday, 14 October 68.

0716 hrs. I just made the entry above. I'm at the air terminal now waiting to manifest to An Khe. I've got to get records to clear my defendant.

[I wanted to see what the MP reports said. It's a good thing I did because I knew the government's case later on better than the government's counsel did. A manifest is the roster of passengers on an aircraft. I used the word as a verb.]

1530 hrs. I got to An Khe, got the medical statement, and missed the flight to Qui Nhon. I'm waiting for an MP gun Jeep to take me to Qui Nhon. I believe I can prove Spec 4 Gaines' innocence.

[Part of Gaines' defense was he went for medical treatment and that treatment and the availability of transport were the reasons for his absence from duty with my platoon.]

Friday, October 11

0650 hrs. I'm waiting in an MP Jeep here in Qui Nhon to shuttle rides back to An Khe. Last night I got some info at the 504th MP station reference Spec 4 Gaines' marijuana charge. I rode shotgun this morning as we patrolled the streets in the dark to get to this MP station. The court-martial is tomorrow and the trial counsel has not done anything to get evidence or witnesses. I have a million things to do.

0915 hrs. I got to the top of An Khe Pass when we had to turn around and chase 10 speeding 2½-ton trucks in convoy. The MPs are citing the drivers now. The sky is cloudy, and it is starting to get hot already.

Saturday, October 12

1737 hrs. Today, I bought some items for the PX. While I was gone, the CG inspected the Garry Owen VIP Center as it is now called. I've been extremely busy the past few days. Col. Gore, Brigade XO, told me that the CG was pleased. I'll buy some electronic equipment from the main PX for my PX tomorrow.

I felt I was doing something good for the troops initiating and running the R&R Center, but it was anticlimactic activity compared to when I was a combat unit commander. We changed the name to VIP Center. The Commanding General of the 1st Cavalry Division was impressed with the Garry Owen VIP Center.

Sunday, October 13

1320 hrs. I'm at Snoopy Pad (1/9 Cav) ready to board a chopper to Da Nang to pick up more items for the PX. I bought over $1000 worth of watches and electronic equipment today.

Monday, October 14

2222 hrs. We opened the VIP Center today. It rained all day; I'm soaked. There were little problems with the company, but we'll iron them out. We had hot coffee, dry clothes, and good chow for the troops when they came in. General Forsythe visited us twice today.

Tuesday, October 15

1900 hrs. Today Spec 4 Gaines had his court-martial. He was charged with 3 charges—(1) AWOL (2) marijuana (3) sleeping on guard. The last charge was dropped. I got the 2nd charge thrown out today because the MPs' statements were hearsay. The 1st charge was reduced to a lesser offense—failure to repair to place of duty. Gaines was lucky. Well, the VIP Center is running okay. The PX sold a lot of items.

That was my first criminal trial. I really wanted to win that case. I fought hard. At the end of the trial when we got the decision, one of the legal clerks said to me that nobody ever fights that hard in these trials. It made me wonder if the military courts weren't simply "show trials" or kangaroo courts. After the war, I've practiced criminal law and military law since 1971.

> 2133 hrs. Dear Mom and Dad,
> I got the latest letter from home yesterday. It was raining and I got it wet, but I could still read it. It's been raining heavily here every day. I really got a neat job here. The Commanding General has a special interest in the center as it is for the troops' welfare. We have a gift shop run by Vietnamese, a PX which I stock and run, a snack bar which sells beer and Coke, a mess hall, a dayroom, and billets for the field troops to sleep in and be dry. I'm due to go home 4 January 69 but I keep hoping for a Christmas drop to around 20 December 68.
> It's raining again very heavily right now. Now it just let up. The rains here are very sporadic. I'm glad to hear everyone liked the presents. I hope to get a leave in the latter part of November to Hong Kong. Maybe I can get more gifts. Dad, would you please send me some more

checks? Just a few blank checks in an envelope will do.

So my brother's thinking of marriage. Maybe it will do him good. I just hope Bob finishes school because a college degree is a must today. No matter how many units he has, he's got to get a degree for show. Well, that's up to him. Ma, don't worry about my health. I just got run down when I got sick. It's amazing how I get drenched almost every day and still not get sick. When I got sick, it was the first time that I've been sick here.

Well, I've got to check the PX inventory. I've got a lot of property and money that I'm responsible for. My last job, I was responsible for a lot of property, but now I'm dealing with money, too. I'll write when I can. I've been very busy lately.

Love, Joe

Wednesday, October 16

1755 hrs. I bought more electronic equipment for the PX today. It sells fast. I'm having problems balancing my sales, purchases, and inventory figures. I guess it will come out okay. The first company we had at the Garry Owen VIP Center left today. We get another one tomorrow.

Thursday, October 17

2126 hrs. Today Col. Gore told me that Lieut. Kinder would take my place as OIC of the VIP Center. I will take his place as the liaison officer for the 2/7 Cav at Phong Dien just outside of Camp Evans. I think I'll like that job. Apparently Col. Gore was pissed off at me because the bunkers weren't being built as fast as he wanted. He checked on our area all the time making comments on what he didn't know about. Anyway, I talked to Col. Cox tonight, brigade CO, and he said not to worry about it. He told me that I did an outstanding job and that Col. Gore probably preferred someone else. Well, such is life.

[In a way I was glad to escape the headaches of running the VIP Center, but I was also pissed at what I thought was Colonel Gore's lack of appreciation for my building the center, putting it together, buying the inventory—making it all work.]

Friday, October 18

1400 hrs. I'm in a chopper on the way to Da Nang. We're flying low over the rough ocean along the beach. I can see boats lined up on the sand (a beach). The waves are rough. It's cloudy and visibility is limited for the pilots. Lieut. Kinder is with me.

1715 hrs. I transferred the PX account to Lieut. Kinder. We're sitting in the chopper at Da Nang. It's raining and the sky is heavily clouded. I believe we'll be stranded here tonight.

Saturday, October 19

2030 hrs. I'm at an ARVN compound at Phong Dien. I'm working with a MACV team. I am the 2/7 Cav liaison officer. I'll be around a lot more Vietnamese now. A Vietnamese 1/Lieut. invited 3 of us lieutenants to dinner at his house tomorrow night for a Vietnamese dinner. I think this will be an outstanding job.

[I was assigned to be the battalion's liaison officer to the MACV team to coordinate intelligence info.]

Sunday, October 20

2100 hrs. Lieut. Evers, Lieut. David, Lieut. Walt, Capt. Blancer, and I just came back from the Artillery Vietnamese 1/Lt's area where we had dinner. The Vietnamese spoke French with the captain, and I spoke broken Vietnamese to the Vietnamese. He gave me a 1st lieutenant's rank insignia (Vietnamese). I like working with the people. I fired my AK-47 today. It's a sharp weapon.

ARVN 1st Lieutenant rank insignia and Artillery patch the ARVN Lieutenant gave me.

I distinctly remember having chicken. It was the worst chicken I ever had in my life. It gave true meaning to the expression "rubber chicken." It was really tough and hard to chew. I really wanted to eat some good chicken but had maybe only one piece. One has seen in the movies where a person is eating some food and they can't stand it, but they just don't let on to the host—that was it. But I liked the Vietnamese ARVN 1st Lieutenant. He was quite personal. He had fought the Viet Minh, and was about 40 years old or so.

Monday, October 21

2110 hrs. Tungwi—ARVN artillery 1st Lieut.—had us over at his area in the compound this evening for another Vietnamese dinner. We always take our interpreter with us. I speak a little Vietnamese and he speaks a little English. Capt. Blancer speaks French to Tungwi and I catch a few of the words from my Spanish training. I guess I'll shower now and then take my shift on radio watch. I test-fired my .45 caliber pistol and AK-47 today.

I'm with my AK-47 at a French bunker.

2235 hrs. Dear Mom and Dad,
Well, my experience here in Vietnam is always exciting and interesting. In my last letter, I told you about being OIC of the VIP Ctr. Well, just a couple of days ago, I got another job which is probably the best I've had since I've been in Vietnam. A few miles outside of Camp Evans is an ARVN compound. It has old French buildings and bunkers and newer sandbagged bunkers and rows and rows of protective barbed wire around it. The 2/7 Cav is to have one liaison officer at this compound to coordinate with the ARVN troops for the 2/7 Cav. Well, I'm that liaison officer. I have an RTO--radio-telephone operator--and we live in a building with MACV personnel. There are about 10 of us Americans all total working, living, and eating with the Vietnamese troops in the compound. Tonight, an ARVN artillery 1st/Lieut. invited the other officers and me to his place to eat a

Vietnamese meal. I've taught myself to speak a little Vietnamese and it comes in handy.

Right now I'm monitoring the radio on a two-hour shift. I really have hardly anything to do on this job except pass on important information to the battalion commander.

If I get a Christmas drop to December 20, I have less than 60 days left in Vietnam. If I go to 4 Jan as I'm expecting, I have less than 75 days left in Vietnam. Have the items I bought (ivory, silk) in Singapore reached Tucson yet? They are due by now. If I don't receive orders for Christmas drop by next month, then I won't be home until around the first week in January.

Enclosed are some more of my pay vouchers. Dad, how is my money doing? I know I spent a lot but my pay should have just about balanced it out by now. How is business, Dad? Have you made any good deals lately? Well, I've got a relatively short time to go. I'm fairly secure where I'm at but there is always danger in the area. The

I'm in front of French bunker at Phong Dien.

monsoons have hindered the VC a great deal but they occasionally rocket Camp Evans. This ARVN compound has been mortared before, but we have good bunkers. I guess I'll just stay careful until I get home.

Love, Joe

P. S. Mom, please send me a box of tinfoil as soon as possible? I have a use for it.

Tuesday, October 22

2053 hrs. Nothing exciting happened today. Col. Cox came here to Phong Dien. He would like to set up a TOC here for operations with the RFs, PFs, and ARVNs. My nose is running. I guess I have an allergy. I hope not too much action occurs here at this ARVN compound until I leave. I'm too short for anymore of that kind of stuff.

[TOC means tactical operation center. RF means regional force; PF means popular force (like a militia). I was working with MACV, and we coordinated with the Vietnamese forces. Being "short" meant having a short time left in Vietnam.]

Wednesday, October 23

1245 hrs. Today was a nice day as was yesterday. Right now, though, the sky is getting a little darker with clouds. 2/7 Cav, B Company CO called in and wants me to bring Lieut. Walt to the bridge to deal with a problem. I'm waiting for a Jeep. I practiced with my .45 caliber today. I'm becoming a pretty fair pistol shot.

1902 hrs. Lieut. Walt and I checked out an accident in front of the refugee village between Camp Evans and here. A 5-year-old boy was hit by a truck and killed. Later we went to the 1st bridge where I talked to Capt. Myra—CO of B Company. I think we can help him on his problem.

Thursday, October 24

1220 hrs. It's a nice sunny day. The nights are getting cooler. I just finished reading "Anyone Can Make A Million" by Morton Shulman. It was very informative on stocks and bonds and other investments.

2048 hrs. The "tungwi" (pronounced "chungwi") of artillery is going up to Quang Tri. The new ARVN speaks English pretty well. I mailed home some film today.

Friday, October 25

2030 hrs. Lieut. Evers, Lieut. David, and I played Scrabble this evening. I lost. It's starting to get cooler. Tungwi Hung left today for Quang Tri. A new ARVN artillery unit is in. I went to the village today and got a haircut. I need to buy a footlocker.

2140 hrs. I just finished reading "Rosemary's Baby" by Ira Levin. It was outstanding. A really well-written book.

Saturday, October 26
0235 hrs. Dear Dad,
I got your letter yesterday with the money order. I'm sending it back as I don't need it now. I had to cancel my leave request to Australia as it was taken off the list of authorized leave sites. I resubmitted a leave request to Hong Kong which I hope I can get before I rotate back to the U.S.A. Reference the other merchandise I bought in Singapore, I wrote them a letter yesterday requesting that they

check on the status of my purchase. They told me it may take 3 to 4 weeks for delivery so anytime now the goods are due. I'm glad you all liked your gifts. You'll never believe how much I spent for the ring and watch and pearls. If I remember correctly, I didn't pay more than $35 for any one of the 3. There are fantastic buys to be had in the Orient. Right now, I've got only about $30 on me, but I may cash checks at the PX. I have 3 checks left and I'll need more if my leave for Hong Kong comes through. There are so many things I'd like to buy while I'm here because of the fantastic buys.

I'm still taking pictures with my Super 8. I really like it. I'm glad the pictures are a little better. I'm going to take more pictures of this ARVN compound. This job here as liaison officer is extremely interesting. I can speak enough Vietnamese to carry on small conversations with the ARVN troops and villagers. I am called Tungwi (pronounced chungwi) which means "first lieut." I taught myself Vietnamese when I was in the field as we sometimes worked with the ARVNs (Army Republic of Vietnam) or PFs (popular forces from villages) or RFs (regional forces from the provinces). All I do all day is hang around this compound and gather as much intelligence information as I can, and then I inform my battalion.

Dad, do you know of any way to get Super 8 film wholesale as it costs me $3.95 a roll including processing which I don't use. Is it cheaper to buy as I am now or can you do better and send me several boxes for these last few months? Tell Ma that I finally got the last two letters she wrote. The mail gets jumbled around here once in a while. Also tell her to tell Mary Lou I send my sympathy reference her mother's death. My address again is HHC 2/7Cav. I get my mail when a Jeep comes out this way or if a chopper brings a visitor. I guess that's it for now, Dad. I hope I still have money left after my checks for Singapore. As I said, I'll need more for Hong Kong if I go.

    Love, Joe

Saturday, October 26, (cont.)

2320 hrs. The generator is off so I'm writing by flashlight. Today a Land Rover used as an ambulance got stuck in the mud and Lieut. Jim David and I helped get it out. PFC Conner, my RTO, and I got the word we are to move out tomorrow. We are to be packed and ready to go back to LZ Evans by daylight.

Sunday, October 27

1240 hrs. I'm back at the 2/7 Cav TOC. I'll work with Major McGivers in the S-3 shop. We're going near Saigon. There are four NVA divisions and the situation is extremely dangerous. This will be an extremely dangerous area.

[We got the word that the 2/7 Cav—our battalion—was moving down south to III Corps. I was pulled back from Phong Dien and had to be ready to move ASAP. I helped organize the loading requirements, which was a monumental task. We had to move an entire air mobile battalion. I helped to calculate the capacities and weight of the Conex containers.]

2130 hrs. I'll get up early tomorrow. We should get to our new AO tomorrow. This is my 4th big move with Cav. Fate is so unpredictable.

> Monday, October 28
>
> 1315 hrs. What a day! I've been shuttling troops to the airport to fly to our new AO. I am in one of the staff hooches at the 2/7 Cav TOC. It's funny how I think I'll miss Camp Evans. I've been here 10 months now. I just hope the move will make the time go by faster now.
>
> **[I helped move an entire air mobile battalion (troops and equipment) from Camp Evans in I Corps to Quan Loi in III Corps. It was a monumental logistical feat.]**
>
> Tuesday, October 29
>
> 1010 hrs. We're at our new AO location. Their area is really set up. We have clubs and nice buildings to live and work in. I'm at the airport acting as liaison to get the troops to their new areas. PFC Donnell, my RTO at Phong Dien, is with me with a radio. Yesterday, I got here at 2000 hrs. There are a lot of trees, rubber plantations, and dust.

We were at Quan Loi, not far from An Loc. Four years later in 1972, the battle of An Loc was one of the greatest battles of the war. An Loc was 3 kilometers west of Quan Loi where the NVA broke through and captured Saigon on April 30, 1975. Many years after the war, I realized how important it was to secure this area. Our new AO (area of operations) was a built-up area with tent structures with wooden floors, and other buildings. It was better than sleeping on the ground or in bunkers or in my often rain-soaked hooch I had at Camp Evans.

> 1935 hrs. I'm on a perimeter defense now with about 55 men positioned hastily on the perimeter. The only commo I have is with the CP (radio) and the whole defense is inadequate. I don't know whether I'll be on base defense for a while or if I'll go to a jump CP.

Left: Quan Loi battalion CP area.
Right: I'm with landline handsets on my perimeter defense.

[The battalion had a command post (CP) which I communicated with by a PRC-25 radio at my CP bunker at the base of one of the perimeter towers. The defensive perimeter was not as fortified as I would have liked it. We weren't dug in—we just had sandbag fighting positions. A jump CP would be a forward command post in the field.]

```
Wednesday, October 30
1235 hrs. Dear Mom and Dad,
    Well, here we are again with another change.
By the time this letter reaches you the news may
have told of the 1st Cav's move down south near
Saigon. We got here day before yesterday. I had
to pack my stuff and get ready to go on the spot.
Our battalion led the move. I'm working in the
S-3 operations section as a staff liaison officer.
Last night I helped to coordinate base defense of
our area.
    We are at a place called Quan Loi.
Intelligence reports say that 5 NVA divisions are
poised to attack. We are to defend this area.
You may be interested in knowing that the famous
woman who predicted among many things Kennedy's
assassination also predicted that this very
```

place, Quan Loi, would be overrun by the NVA on or about 7 November. We shall see. With less than 2 months left in country, I'm put back in danger again, but as always I'll be careful.

I wrote to Singapore about those goods I bought. I'm waiting for reply from the merchants. Also, I sent home a big blue suitcase by boat about a month ago. Has it ever reached home? Also, I sent home a wooden footlocker before we moved down here. I packed it hurriedly but I hope it gets home. Other than being busy getting oriented here, much is the same. This is my 4th big move with the Cav. I'm one of the old-timers, officer wise, in the battalion. Well, so much for everything. I'll write more once I get settled.

Love, Joe

[Because of the short notice of the move, I put the AK-47 I got at Khe Sanh in the footlocker. I didn't have time to go through proper channels to send it back home.]

Left: Joe at a base defense perimeter tower. Right: Joe in tower with .50 cal. machinegun.

Wednesday, October 30, (cont.)

1845 hrs. I'm on this perimeter again tonight. We're supposed to be hit harder sometime before 7 November. Doc Henderson, my old platoon medic, is with me tonight. The dust around here is really bad. I'm really dirty. I wrote a letter home today.

[Being a base defense sector commander was not as glamorous as leading a rifle platoon conducting combat air assaults and search and destroy operations, but it was important to protect the battalion headquarters and our sector of Quan Loi, which had an airfield.]

Thursday, October 31

0740 hrs. Another night on the perimeter defense has elapsed. I'm really filthy. The dust is very bad. I'll wash up now and tend to some chores later today. Today is Halloween day. Tomorrow is the 1st November.

Left: View from perimeter road looking at a watch tower. Right: .50 cal. machinegun overlooking perimeter area.

November, 1968

Friday, November 1

0847 hrs. Last night there was a lot of scare shooting on the perimeter. My sector only fired once, and that was because there was a trip flare ignited in the concertina wire. The battalion is sending out a forward CP today. The dust here is atrocious.

Saturday, November 2

0800 hrs. I had perimeter defense last night. There was a lot more scare shooting around the perimeter, except in my sector. I told my men not to shoot unless they could produce a body the next day. Yesterday morning after I made my diary entry, I heard on the radio Johnson's bombing halt declaration. I hope we don't suffer. Also yesterday, the battalion sent out a forward CP to operate companies closer to Cambodia.

The forward CP or "jump CP" was a CP closer to the operating subordinate units. The Ho Chi Minh Trail ran along the Laos and Cambodia borders to the west of the Vietnam border. The "trail" was not a true trail—it was an axis of advance or movement of large quantities of troops and supplies by the NVA who could cross the border at will and wreak havoc in Vietnam. Quan Loi and An Loc were susceptible to attacks as the 1972 battle at An Loc and the ultimate invasion and capture of Saigon in 1975 later showed.

Sunday, November 3

0730 hrs. Capt. Myra, CO, B Company was killed yesterday. One of the captains at LZ Billy may have to take his place and I may go out to LZ Billy. The LZ is near Cambodia. There are many NVA. The 2/7 Cav just began LZ Billy yesterday.

2240 hrs. I'm on base defense now. The mosquitoes are bad. I expect to go to the jump CP—LZ Billy—anytime soon.

Monday, November 4

1330 hrs. I'm at the S-3 operations hooch here at Quan Loi. I'm monitoring the radio. So far our battalion has set up a firebase—LZ Billy—5 clicks south of the Cambodian border. I'm still waiting to be sent forward to act as liaison between the battalion and brigade. So far, back here, I've been helping Lieut. Jim Shell with perimeter guard. LZ Billy is being built up and our companies are sweeping the surrounding area. Brigade has put many exterior and interior guard commitments which we must keep.

[Security was a consideration for the battalion CP (interior guard commitment) and for the perimeter defense line (exterior guard commitment) which the Cav had around Quan Loi.]

Tuesday, November 5

0800 hrs. I am at Snoopy pad sitting on the CC chopper. I'm going out to LZ Billy to get info to take to brigade. Lieut. Dan Gonzales and Chief Stern and I went to the O club and had a few drinks last night. Yesterday I met a really cute Vietnamese girl named Khan who lives at An Loc down the road. She rode

> a Honda here and we talked for a while. She said she'd take me to the village to see the area but it's OFF LIMITS to us now.
>
> 2045 hrs. I flew to LZ Billy and stayed there all day. It's an open field surrounded by wood lines all the way around. I'll work as the LNO (liaison officer) in the operation section, assisting in coordinating air strikes, Medevacs, artillery and ARA support, and anything which aids our operations. I'll fly to LZ Billy in the mornings and return in the evenings unless something develops. Col. Cox got a Silver Star for retrieving Capt. Myra's body.

In the daytime, I acted as a liaison officer for the S-3 section (operations). At night, I was a base defense sector commander on the perimeter with troops manning bunkers and towers. One might ask, "When did I sleep?" The answer is, "Whenever I could for a few hours in the daytime." The politics of the awards process was epitomized by the colonel receiving a Silver Star for taking the battalion out to retrieve a dead body.

> **Wednesday, November 6**
>
> 1637 hrs. I'm at LZ Billy now. A Chinook is hovering about 30 m away blowing a strong wind. Jets are conducting an air strike about 3 clicks away as D Company got into contact to the north of LZ Billy. I've been monitoring the radios. I just heard the "hum" sound of the jets' guns. The ground shakes as the bombs hit. I can see the smoke from the bombs' impacts rise above the trees. Trees surround this LZ which looks like a rough, huge football field with guns and bunkers.

This was a bad day for D Company, my old company. I was monitoring a radio while at Quan Loi and heard from the transmissions some of what was going on in real time. The company air assaulted into an open area along the Cambodian border. The

LZ was triangulated with three .51 caliber machine guns, and NVA troops were in the surrounding tree lines. It was a devastating ambush.

There was some high, dry grass so that tracers ignited it and a prairie-type fire engulfed much of D Company. Men took off their blouses (shirts), stood up, and tried to beat down the flames through the smoke and incoming fire. They were cut down. I heard Medevac transmissions in which the pilots radioed that some choppers were shot up and others couldn't get to the killed or wounded.

The company suffered 50% casualties. That meant for every two soldiers, one of them was killed or wounded. I was personally infuriated at President Johnson for halting the bombing along the Cambodian border. That was when I probably first realized the politics of war.

Wednesday, November 6, (cont.)

1900 hrs. D Company hit many NVA today. Capt. Seeden got killed. Many of D Company are wounded. I guess I'll go in tonight. Most of the battalion, including leaders, is inexperienced, and they all want glory.

Thursday, November 7

0755 hrs. I'm in the CC with Major McGivers and Capt. Ord. We have 2 companies and Col. Dennison on the ground near where D Company got it yesterday. We still want to recover Capt. Seeden's and the medic's bodies. We're flying high and I can see the FAC plane marking the spot on the ground for an air strike. I slept on the ground last night at LZ Billy.

The CC or "Charlie-Charlie"—the military phonetic alphabet, referred to the Command and Control helicopter which flew above the troops and coordinated the maneuverability of the ground troops. We were monitoring the ground action where the battalion commander was leading two companies to look for the dead company commander's and the medic's bodies. We were going to call in an air strike, and a FAC (forward air controller) was "on station" to mark where the jets would drop their ordnance.

1000 hrs. I just finished reading "Age of the Wife Swappers" by John T Warren. I came back to LZ Billy. The 2 companies are checking yesterday's area of contact.

2103 hrs. I'm back at Quan Loi now. All the companies are on LZ Billy. B-52 strikes will hit the objective and our companies will check it out tomorrow. I heard that an NVA set up a Claymore beside Capt. Seeden's body and blew him to kingdom come. His body and the medic's body were never found. Col. Dennis made a good move pulling back and putting in B-52 strikes.

Friday, November 8

1330 hrs. I'm at LZ Billy. The sun is bright. We had 4 NVA artillery rounds impact outside of our LZ. I hope I get a leave to Hong Kong.

1455 hrs. Pony teams (C Company) just made contact. We got some incoming stray small arms fire. The contact is not far outside our perimeter. Major McGivers and Capt. Ord are in the CC.

1735 hrs. I rode a Chinook back here to Quan Loi. About 5 minutes ago one end of the runway took a barrage of enemy mortars. Our headquarters here is just across the street but at the other end of the runway which was hit.

1850 hrs. My mail is finally catching up with me. I got several letters yesterday and today. I got a "Snoopy" stuffed dog from Kathleen and a book, Ben Franklin's "Wit and Wisdom" from Mary.

Saturday, November 9

1440 hrs. We just put an air strike in on the objective area of contact. It's hot and sunny again today. Three of our companies conducted local patrols of the LZ. I monitored the radio awhile.

Sunday, November 10

1315 hrs. Yesterday, Capt. Seeden's and the medic's bodies were recovered. They were decayed and putrid. Their dental plates will have to be checked for official identification. Three of our companies are going to recon the area of contact today. The col. and S-3 will stay out overnight with the companies and come back tomorrow.

```
    1515 hrs. Dear Mom and Dad,
    Well, I'm at a firebase we set up called LZ
Billy. It's only five clicks south of Cambodia.
I commute from Quan Loi to here each day acting
as a liaison between our rear area and here.
Our companies have been hitting NVA units near
Cambodia every time they go out. We've only
been at this LZ for about eight days and we've
got many wounded and two captains--company
commanders--killed.
    Dad, I got your letter today with my money
accounting and the checks. Actually, for a year,
I haven't spent much. Almost $600 alone went for
my stereo equipment. The rest was my R&R and
buying presents. Thank you for the tinfoil, Dad.
Well, I wrote to Singapore and got a reply about
the merchandise I bought. If it's not home by
about the 15th or 16th of November, let me know;
and I'll write again.
    Well, I put in for a leave to Hong Kong for
```

on or about 20 November. If approved, I should
be going soon. It could be disapproved though as
the tactical situation changes and the battalion
may need me around. I have got checks to cover me
so I should be okay, I hope. The reason I lost
$40 on my last paycheck is because I took $200
advance pay for my R&R. The Army is probably
taking it out for that reason. I'll check on it.
There is rumor that we may even move again from
this place. Maybe all this stuff is a final big
push. Has my blue suitcase ever gotten home? I
had a bugle in it--the one I captured and blew
on the way into Khe Sanh when we liberated the
Marines. Also, I've recently sent home a wooden
foot locker. I hope it makes it with no trouble.
Well, so much for now. I am fine and still
cautious, as I'm still in some danger. I guess
life anywhere is hazardous. All is well. I'll be
home within 56 days from today.
    Love, Joe

2050 hrs. I moved into a BOQ hooch. I hear we may move again. I hope I go on leave soon. I have 56 days left in RVN. I hope all goes well.

Monday, November 11

1120 hrs. I've already been to LZ Billy and back this morning. I'm in a "hook" to go back now. Our companies found some dead NVA and some bicycles. I wrote to Kathleen this morning.

["Hook" was a nickname for the Chinook helicopter. Another nickname was "shit hook."]

1822 hrs. I just saw 5 bursts of antiaircraft fire about 5 clicks north of here near the Cambodian border. The NVA were shooting at one of our jets. I'm waiting for a chopper to go back to Quan Loi.

1845 hrs. That jet made two more passes and got fired on both times about six rounds each. It's getting dark now and there's a whistling sound of the approaching night—the sounds of insects.

Tuesday, November 12

1230 hrs. I'm at the S-2/3 billets here at Quan Loi. My leave was disapproved by the col. because of a shortage of officers. I'm waiting to take a log bird to LZ Billy.

1854 hrs. I flew in on a LOH. They are fun to ride in as I ride up front next to the pilot. It had a minigun on it. I got a letter from home that my AK-47 was found. I hope I don't get into too much trouble. I wanted to get it to the VFW but I didn't have time to send it through S-2 channels. What a life!

[A minigun is a gattling gun with several rotating barrels which fire 6000 rounds a minute. The AK-47 I sent home was discovered. This began the saga of the AK-47, which was to cause me much concern until I DEROSed.]

    2025 hrs. Dear Mom and Dad,
    I am back here at Quan Loi now. Dad, I got your letter today about the AK-47. My platoon captured this with many other weapons when we rescued Khe Sanh from that two-month siege. I planned on getting it through proper channels to the Tucson VFW to display as a war trophy, but our move from Camp Evans to here was secret and sudden; so I threw it in the footlocker. I

didn't have time to mail it otherwise. I'll just have to face the consequences. As for my moving around--S-3 is "Operations." I am working close with the battalion S-3, Maj. McGivers, and the battalion commander, acting as their liaison officer. I'm a courier and a troubleshooter so to speak. We've been working just five clicks south of Cambodia with Quan Loi, our rear area. I fly out each morning to the forward LZ (landing zone) and back in the evening to here at Quan Loi. The battalion XO just told me that tomorrow I'll go to a Special Forces camp to check the area out. Our battalion will move there in a few days and I'm to go there first to coordinate certain things. I don't know what my mission is yet. I'll be told tomorrow. Our battalion is air mobile so that's why we move a lot. There is still danger so I'm not out of all this stuff yet. I've applied for leave, but the col. said he couldn't let me go because of the shortage of officers. We lost two captains in four days--both killed.

    The Special Forces camp should be interesting. I've really done some interesting and exciting things since I've been in the Army and especially here. I hope all turns out okay. As for the gun problem--it's a possible $500 fine and/or prison term. I'm worried. Well, as I said, I'll just have to face up to whatever happens. It's starting to get "crappy" around here and I'm getting so close to getting home. Don't worry; I'll be careful. Dad, thanks for the checks. I guess I won't use too many of them now. Mom, please keep up the prayers.

    Love, Joe

Wednesday, November 13

1407 hrs. I'm at Tong Le Chan. It is a Special Forces compound with an airstrip outside of it. There is also an artillery battery outside of it. I came by Chinook this morning bringing demolitions which the engineers are using to blow down trees. We will move our own 105 howitzer battery in our battalion here in a few days. I've come to coordinate the movement here.

[The Chinook which brought me was filled with high explosives. I remember thinking that a well-placed tracer round would have caused me to be vaporized. There was C-4 and various types of ammunition.]

Thursday, November 14

0905 hrs. Last night I slept on the ground with my poncho liner. It rained and I got soaked as I used to when I was in the field. Also last night, LZ Dot, which is 6 clicks to the northwest of here, got hit heavily by an NVA attack. I could hear them calling for artillery on the radio. Today they are still being hit by rockets. Our choppers have also spotted a lot of .50 caliber machine guns on the ground. Our engineers are still blowing down trees to clear an area for our 105 howitzers. I'm still trying to get a dozer.

I stayed the night at the Special Forces location sleeping on the ground near a 155 mm howitzer battery. It had fire missions all night, which almost deafened me because I slept so close to the guns. It was cold, wet, uncomfortable, and deafeningly noisy; and I had little sleep. I remember being afraid we would get overrun.

Friday, November 15

1817 hrs. I'm here at Quan Loi. I'm on the perimeter now with Spec 4 James (used to be in my old rifle platoon) and Sgt.

Garza, a medic. I'll be in charge of base defense. When I was at Than Le Chan, we were mortared on the airstrip about 300 m away--I later found out. The sun is almost down now. I hope I don't get into too much trouble over the AK-47. I paid part of HHC today as I am pay officer. I'll have to go to the field and pay the rest of HHC.

Saturday, November 16

1100 hrs. I'm sitting on the log pad (runway) waiting for a Chinook to LZ Billy to go pay the troops and talk to the col. about my AK-47 problem. The S-1 told me that the col. told the XO to court-martial me. If I can't get support from the col., I'm in trouble.

The S-1 and I did not like each other. I think he relished the idea that I was worried about the AK-47 situation. He told me the colonel wanted to court-martial me, but when I talked to the colonel later, I learned that was not the case. The S-1 was an obnoxious, arrogant asshole.

1645 hrs. I went to LZ Billy and paid the HHC troops there. I talked to the col. He said he wouldn't court-martial me, but that everything is out of his hands anyway. He said I'd probably get a fine.

Sunday, November 17

0805 hrs. The POL point was hit last night by either rockets or artillery. I could see the explosions and fire from my CP on the perimeter. Today I'll go to LZ Jake (Tong Le Chan) to finish paying.

Even though I was not leading a platoon in the field now, I was still subjected to rocket and mortar attacks. That was the nature of the Vietnam War. There was no "safe" area. I felt the safest when I was in the field with my platoon which I controlled and knew about how they operated.

> **Monday, November 18**
>
> 0735 hrs. I'm waiting by my CP on the perimeter until 0800 to go back to the battalion area. I'm sector commander of 2/7 Cav sector on the green line as the perimeter is called. I'll have to fix up our sector. Also, today I got to do more paying. I'm waiting for any day now to hear about the weapon.

That was my last official duty in Vietnam—base defense sector commander. Quan Loi had an airstrip near where our battalion headquarters was. The perimeter went around the battalion HQ, sleeping billets, other assets of the battalion, and some very nice homes (mansions) of the French plantation owners. Quan Loi was in the rubber plantation region. The ARVNs had responsibility for defense of one-third of the perimeter; another Army unit had another sector; and the 2/7 Cav had the other third sector. I was the 2/7 Cav's base defense sector commander. I took personnel from various units to man bunkers and towers on the perimeter at night. I slept during the day, if I could. I obviously wasn't sleeping that day D Company landed in that "hot LZ" along the Cambodian border.

> **Tuesday, November 19**
>
> 0730 hrs. I'm at my CP again. I guess we'll have to stand guard until 0800 each day. Yesterday, I paid more of the troops. Today, I'll pay again; I guess I'll go to the new LZ we made—LZ Sue. I'll have to turn in the extra payroll to Phuoc Vinh. I'm still concerned about the weapon problem. I'm curious who will do what. My battalion CO is not too cooperative, it seems to me.
>
> ```
>      1040 hrs. Dear Mom and Dad,
>      I've received both of your last letters. I
> talked to the battalion CO about the problem and
> ```

I showed him the letter from the post office. He said it was out of his hands and just to wait. He said he wouldn't court-martial me and to expect possibly a fine. I don't know what to expect the way I've seen some things operate over here so I'm just waiting. Notification through channels may come down any day. I'm very concerned because now they're cracking down on sending firearms. My sole intent was to get it to one of the museums, preferably VFW downtown near the courthouse, but the quick move impelled me to send it home as I did. I hope the CID's notification to the 1st Cav Division gets lost. I'm just waiting and worrying.

Enclosed is a picture of me playing volleyball. I'm at the far left of the picture. Ma, in the suitcase, is there a bugle? That's important! Also, will you reply quickly and tell me if the items from Singapore have still not arrived? I'll write one more time to them if they aren't in Tucson by your next letter. Also enclosed is a clipping about the R&R or VIP center that I started at Camp Evans. Also enclosed are my pay vouchers. I had my leave request disapproved because of shortage of officers, but the col. said I still may be able to go. I surely hope a drop for Christmas comes up out of the clear blue sky.

Well, I'm our base defense commander. I'm in charge of the 2/7 Cav sector defense here at Quan Loi. I man the perimeter at night and still work during the day. I'm in the process of paying HHC troops right now so I'll go to a forward LZ and pay them. We built another one--LZ Sue. CBS News may have it on TV.

Well, Mom and Dad, I hope all goes well. I've still got my worries, but I think I can pull

through. Give my regards to everyone. I hope all is well with you two.
    Love, Joe

Tuesday, November 19, (cont.)

1635 hrs. I'm taking a crap right now so I'll make an entry. The guards will be forming up in about 25 minutes. I went to LZ Sue today to finish pay. As we were landing, I could see everyone was down in a foxhole. The LZ had just received sniper fire before my chopper landed.

[I went to LZ Sue to pay the troops. When I was pay officer, I'd draw thousands of dollars, put the money in an ammunition can, and go to the field to pay the troops. I had to account for every dollar. When my chopper approached LZ Sue, I saw that the troops had gotten down, avoiding enemy fire. We weren't fired at, but even being a pay officer could be "interesting" and tense.]

Wednesday, November 20

1347 hrs. We have intelligence reports that Quan Loi is highly subject to attack during the next 4 days. Col. Gore, Brigade XO, wants us to improve our perimeter sectors of defense. He came to my CP last night and asked me many questions about my sector. There was a base defense meeting today and as usual there are many requirements and little support. I counted the money today and I'm short. I hope it comes out all right at finance. I've still not received word about the AK problem.

Thursday, November 21

1120 hrs. I'm here at the air terminal at Phuoc Vinh. I turned in the payroll and it came out even. I stopped by JAGC and talked to a capt. there. He said the CID would probably be looking me up soon. I hope nothing goes bad on my record—civilian or military record. The JAGC officer said I'd probably get an article 15, but I could get a court-martial.

Friday, November 22

2022 hrs. I am inside my CP bunker, number 69. I'm going to Long Bien to check my toe again. I got a letter from Mary today. I wonder what kind of a job she will get. I still haven't heard word about the AK-47 problem. I'm still waiting. It is very dark and quiet outside except for the crickets and occasional thunderous boom of the 155 howitzers. We've been on alert for an attack for the past few days. Everyone is worried. Since the French houses are in my sector, I'm not too worried as they have never been hit; and I believe they are paying a bribe to the VC and NVA not to hit this sector. We'll see.

French mansion behind my CP watch tower.

The French houses of the rubber plantation owners were beautiful mansions. My CP was at the end of a vast front yard of one of the mansions. It never got mortared. I think there was some kind of an "understanding" between the VC or NVA and these plantation owners.

Saturday, November 23

1030 hrs. I'm at Lai Khe waiting for a Medevac chopper to go to Long Bien—93rd Evac Hospital. I took a Medevac chopper to here, and it was a cool ride. I rode next to the right door gunner. I left the base defense problems to Sgt. Tagg, my NCO for the orange sector. He's a good NCO.

Sunday, November 24

0745 hrs. We had another alert last night. All these alerts do is scare people. It rained last night and the sky is cloudy today.

0910 hrs. It's sprinkling now. I'm at our BOQ. Being commander of the 2/7 Orange Sector means I work at night and can rest during the day, but usually I still work during the day. Last night I drove up and down the perimeter road-checking my bunkers. It's dangerous but necessary.

1830 hrs. It's getting dark. Sgt. Tagg just checked the perimeter. Lieut. Joyner came back from R&R after being gone 30 days.

Monday, November 25

0730 hrs. I'm waiting at my CP for Sgt. Tagg to bring the tower guards back. I sent most of the men back to garrison while I'm waiting around. I put in for leave to Hong Kong again. I'm curious to see what happens.

Tuesday, November 26

0900 hrs. I bought two Seiko watches yesterday—one for Dad and one for me. Lieut. Taggett is stalling around on my leave. It's supposed to go to the field today for the col.'s approval. I may get to Hong Kong yet. Still no word about the AK 47 incident.

1235 hrs. Lt. Taggett told me that Col. Cox disapproved my leave due to "job requirements."

Wednesday, November 27

1230 hrs. Nothing new today except we had a base defense meeting and discussed 5/7 sector firing and causing a false alarm last night. I'll write home now.

[The "5/7 sector" referred to the 5th Battalion, 7th Cavalry sector. There were three battalions in the 3rd Brigade of the 1st Cavalry in 1968. They were the 1/7, 2/7 (mine), and 5/7. When I previously referred to the 2/7 having one-third of the entire responsibility for the perimeter defense of Quan Loi, actually the 3rd Brigade must have had the responsibility with its battalions providing the manpower.]

1231 hrs. Dear Mom and Dad,
I still haven't received any word about the AK-47 problem. Col. Cox leaves 1 December 68, so I don't know how the new battalion commander will look on the whole thing if it is presented to him. Col. Harden will be our new battalion commander. He is the present brigade deputy commander. He was the one who interviewed me and accepted me to represent the 1st Cav to compete for General Tabor's aide. Col. Cox wrote a letter and said he couldn't afford to lose me, so I didn't get to go. Anyway, about the goods in the box, that felt-lined box is what I got your pearl necklace in, Ma. I just saved the box. Both a movie camera and a Polaroid Swinger should be with my items, also a lamp. Nothing else was of any real value--except the AK-47 which I would not have sold for $500 because of what I believe to be the sentimental and historical value. I'm really worried about the whole thing because one never knows how the thing will turn out. Even if the Army doesn't deal with me before I get

out, the matter might be turned back over to the postal authorities, and I may get prosecuted by the federal government for a federal offense. I'm still waiting and worrying.

I'm still working as our sector base defense commander on the perimeter of Quan Loi. There is always the threat of being overrun by the NVA, but I have my HQ near a French mansion. The few French around here have not been bothered, and I believe it's because they are paying taxes to the NVA and VC. I put in for a leave to Hong Kong; Col. Dennis disapproved because of "job requirements." Maybe the new commander will let me have a leave. I only have about 40 days until I'm home anyway. I wrote a letter yesterday urging some type of explanation from that Singapore store. About the only recourse I have is their honesty, or to have it blacklisted at the R&R hotels. Maybe I can get my money back. I'll wait for their reply. The sky looks like rain. I guess I'll mail this letter.
    Love, Joe

Wednesday, November 27, (cont.)

1812 hrs. My perimeter is set up again. I am at my CP now. Last night in front of my bunker 64, the NCO heard a high-pitched sound like a radio transmitting. I went to the bunker and heard it, too. It may be a radio transmitter; I'll be listening for it tonight.

Thursday, November 28

1430 hrs. Today we had a fantastic Thanksgiving dinner. Shortly thereafter, I got word to man our defense sector because a report of 750 VC three clicks northeast of here—LZ

Andy. This morning, Lieut. Gonzales and I went to An Loc to get paper to decorate the mess hall. I bought some Vietnamese Christmas cards there.

Friday, November 29

1820 hrs. I got packages from Mom today with candy, sardines in tomato sauce, and assorted cheeses. I also got popcorn which I have here at my CP now. Today, Sgt. Tagg and Specialist 4 Reevers (Maj. Byrne's driver) and I test-fired a .50 caliber machine gun which we now mounted here at tower 4. It's an impressive weapon. Well I'm getting closer to getting home.

Saturday, November 30

1800 hrs. I'm at my CP now. I just briefed the guards, and they are now in position. I sent the Jeep back to battalion garrison area to have the radio fixed. I'm getting guards from other units including 15th Medical Battalion, and the medics don't want to pull guard. We're all pulling guard.

December, 1968

Sunday, December 1

1415 hrs. We had the change of command ceremony this morning. I wished Col. Cox "farewell and good luck." Col. Harden is my new battalion cmdr. I just finished reading a really fantastic book—"The Jury Returns" by Lewis Nizer. I hope I'm as enthusiastic about reading about law later as I am now. Still no word about the AK-47 incident. Lieut. Gonzales is teasing me about going to jail. It's not funny.

Monday, December 2

1750 hrs. I'm at my base defense CP. The guards are in and I'm waiting for the sun to go down. I got letters from Mary and Kathleen today. I wrote each one a Christmas card. I started reading a novel today. I guess I'll try again for a leave to Hong Kong. I've got the Jeep parked here at bunker 69. The radio is on loud so we can monitor based defense push. I'd like to buy some Christmas gifts. Lieut. Joyner and I played Crazy Eights today.

Tuesday, December 3

0940 hrs. I'm in my room at the BOQ. Chief Stern just gave me a statement for report of survey I'm doing. Last night tower

> 4 (next to my CP) saw an object inside the fence which looked like a person. I saw it, too, through the starlight scope after climbing up into the tower at 0300. I fired three M-79 rounds at it and the 3rd shot set off a trip flare which showed sandbags or something only looking like a person. I put in another leave request to see Col. Harden's policy on leave for officers. If it's "no" this time—that's it.

My sector of the perimeter included a tower and several bunkers or fighting positions. In front of our locations was a road—the perimeter road—obviously running along our perimeter defensive line. To our front was an area of cleared or chopped-down grass and other vegetation to clear fields of fire. Then there was a fence with a gate and a road that exited the defensive perimeter to go outside the wire (fence). We saw something on the ground on that road just inside the perimeter wire. The M-79 is a 40 millimeter grenade launcher. We determined it was a false alarm, but if it were a "bad guy" with an RPG (rocket launcher)—it could have been a serious problem.

> 1300 hrs. Dear Mom and Dad,
> Well, Maj. Byrne, our battalion executive officer, told me that he got word that I am to be "flagged" until further investigation of the AK-47 problem. I'll wait about four or five days to see if CID contacts me about it; then I'll try and expedite whatever action is to be taken so I get home close to my normal DEROS date. Being "flagged" means being held up on my DEROS or rotation date. As you can imagine, I'm worried about the whole thing because the action--flagging action--is being initiated by USARV (which is for US Army Republic Vietnam), not just at division level. I don't want a court-martial or dishonorable discharge or have to resign from service. When the CID comes to question me, I guess I'll just tell them the truth and hope for the best. Well, this flagging action also cuts my

hopes for any leave to Hong Kong. Everything else here is okay, I guess.

I'm still our base defense commander. I sleep out on the green line (perimeter of the base) and hope we don't get hit or infiltrated or overrun. I wrote to Singapore about the items and I may have to chalk it up to a lost cause. I'm still waiting for a reply. They already told me once that they sent the items. Ma, is a bugle in that blue suitcase? That was another souvenir from Khe Sanh. Please send my field jacket and gloves back to me as soon as possible. It will be cold when I get home, and all I'll have is my short-sleeved khaki uniform. My field jacket still has my second lieutenant's rank on it, but I'll get it changed here.

Well, I guess I'm about as ready for what going to happen as I'll ever be. My HHC company commander, Ben Gonzales, says not to worry about it. I'm worried because I'm getting out of the Army, and Army people act differently toward such people. I'm enclosing this note in a Vietnamese Christmas card which I bought in a nearby village.

Dad, why don't you send me my camera and film, too? I can take movies here before I leave. I've still got a month. Maybe longer. I'm expecting the worst and hoping for the best.

Love, Joe

1355 hrs. I got word from Maj. Byrne that I'm flagged for investigation on the AK-47 incident.

[The "flagging" of records means that all personnel actions—leaves, promotions, reassignments, etc.—are suspended.]

1835 hrs. D Company hit some NVA today and they have many KIA and WIA (U.S.).

Wednesday, December 4

1740 hrs. I got 4 brand-new radios from brigade which I gave to our battalion, for 5 old radios for base defense. I also called a CID man to come over and I told him about my problem. He said he would check it out ASAP and then get a statement from me. Lieut. Gonzales told me that HHC had to cut my flagging orders on me today. I got so damn many problems—being here on the perimeter all night; wondering about the outcome of this AK-47 incident; and hoping to get home for my normal DEROS. I got a delicious fruitcake from Mary today. Sgt. Tagg and the driver are checking our landline commo right now. The end of the day is nigh.

Thursday, December 5

1705 hrs. I am at my CP. Specialist 5 Disaunt (used to be my clerk in S-4) is my driver tonight. I'm still waiting for word on my investigation and flagging action. I mailed a nightgown-type dress (Vietnamese) to Kathleen today. I bought a Vietnamese (smoking jacket) jacket for Bob. I'll mail it later. I've still got to get something for Mom. I already sent Dad the watch. Sgt. Kuhn is assigning the guards their bunkers now. Sgt. Kuhn and Sgt. Tagg rotate each night as my NCOIC.

Friday, December 6

0942 hrs. Last night my tower 3 took three mortar rounds to its rear. Enemy mortar rounds impacted at other points in the perimeter. D Company's contact a few days ago caused the company about 50% casualties. 22 men were KIA, a couple from my old platoon. They were damn good men, too. 100 dead NVA or VC isn't worth one dead GI as far as I'm concerned.

[That was the action when D Company landed in that hot LZ.]

1755 hrs. I'm at my CP again. Bert (Lieut. Joyner) and I played Crazy Eights today. I talked to the girls who work at the Vietnamese laundry in our battalion area. I read to them the expressions I learned in my Vietnamese phrasebook, and they think I speak well.

Saturday, December 7

0730 hrs. My sector of the perimeter got hit twice last night by rockets. The first time about 8 to 10 rounds landed about one click from tower 3's front; the second time about 3 rounds landed about 300 m to tower 3's front. Both tower 3 and 4 called in artillery and ARA on the origin of fire. I didn't get much sleep last night.

1550 hrs. I went to Mass today. I bought a pearl brooch for Mom. I'm sitting in a Jeep at a Special Forces camp at An Loc. I talked to the brigade S-1 about my flagging action and he said to go to Phuoc Vinh and see JAGC.

1750 hrs. I'm at my CP. Lieut. Gonzales, Lieut. Larry Renner and his friend, and I went to a "cat house." We all drank beer and I had a nice-looking girl.

Monday, December 9

1126 hrs. I'm at Phuoc Vinh at the JAGC office getting legal assistance on this AK-47 problem. I'll make a statement to my attorney and we'll save it if anything develops. I've got two concerns—(1) getting off with nothing, or a verbal reprimand, and (2) making my DEROS date on time.

1743 hrs. I'm at my CP. I talked to both JAGC officers at Phuoc Vinh and they said to wait a while longer, and someone would come to get a statement from me. They also said that I could get an article 15 with a small fine or just a verbal reprimand. They don't believe a court-martial will arise, but I'm still worried. I hope all is resolved well soon and that I can go home on time. Ma wrote and said that the items from Singapore arrived.

Tuesday, December 10

1028 hrs. I'm at the battalion aid station waiting to soak my left foot big toe—ingrown toenail. Last night, tower 3's location took several rockets. We found the blown up rockets today and I took two of them to brigade S-2. Last night my tower 4 saw the origin of rocket fire and we called in ARA on it. I called on base defense push and had to cut in and tell them to quit "bullshitting" on the radio when a target location is being sent in. Later a captain chewed me out as he was on the radio at the time. He was still "bullshitting."

The NVA often used makeshift launching rails out of bamboo to fire 122 millimeter rockets. Two rockets impacted within the battalion's perimeter—one on the airstrip. I found the exploded, twisted rocket and took it to the S-2 (battalion intelligence officer). When the rockets ignite, you can see the fire trail, and I called helicopter gunships in on the point of origin. I had to interrupt a captain on base defense push (base defense frequency).

Wednesday, December 11

1150 hrs. All was quiet on guard last night. I just finished reading "Cat on a Hot Tin Roof" by Tennessee Williams. It was a play and well done. I still have no word from USARV CID. I saw that JAGC officer here today as he had other business here. He said to wait.

1808 hrs. I am at my CP. Sgt. Kuhn will be my NCOIC as Sgt. Tagg is going to the brigade commo section. I drove to An Loc with Lieut. Charlie Wester. We went by a cat house to see a girl I met here at Quan Loi. Co Khan is her name and she's good-looking even if she is a Vietnamese prostitute. I plan to patronize her in the near future. Some of these people are so poor; it's really pathetic. I hope someday I'll be able to visit this country under different circumstances.

Thursday, December 12

1236 hrs. All was quiet on the CP last night; Col. Gore told me that today begins the VC/NVA offensive on all military reservations and cities. Bill, Larrs, and I went to An Loc. Co Khan and I made love. She is really attractive and intelligent for an 18-year-old Vietnamese prostitute. She has short black hair and she speaks pretty fair English. She has a very nicely developed body. As we were leaving, a schoolgirl came into the house. She had some long, flowing black hair and she demurely went upstairs. I could smell pork coming in from another room.

An Loc "working" girls.

Although I related my sexual encounters with these Vietnamese girls, I want to be clear that I had great respect and understanding for the plight they were in. It was war; they were poor; and they provided a service for virile young men. I treated them with respect and tried to have conversations with the ones who learned some English other than just, "Number 1 or number 10, GI!"

Friday, December 13

1405 hrs. I'm here at the BOQ. Last night was quiet. This morning I kept the guards and had them clear fields of fire by chopping the bamboo growing along the concertina wire.

Saturday, December 14

1315 hrs. Capt. Stacey, the new HQ commandant, inspected my guard sector last night. He seemed quite satisfied. All was quiet on guard last night. I still have not received word on the AK-47 problem or my flagging action. This waiting and not knowing is a punishment in itself.

1756 hrs. We got a warning order today that we would be moving. I opened the package from Kathleen with Christmas sweets in it. Capt. Stacey told me I may get an article 15 but there's still is no official word on the AK-47 deal. I believe I'll DEROS on time, but I don't know from what LZ because of this move.

Sunday, December 15

1321 hrs. I went to Mass today. Our battalion is supposed to be prepared to move, but there is also rumor we may not move. Chief Sterns is eating some nuts at the table.

Monday, December 16

1238 hrs. All was quiet on guard last night. The bipod on one of the M-60 machine guns broke and I replaced it today. I'm reading "The Graduate" by Charles Webb. It's great.

1521 hrs. I'm sitting in the front room of this whorehouse in An Loc. Another lieut. is getting laid; I've just been. An old woman, head shaved, is singing to a baby and rocking the baby to sleep in a hammock. This house is old with cracked cement for a floor. There are wooden stairs. Co Khan was not here. The ceiling is tin.

[I saw various types of houses in Vietnam. There were huts made of vegetation; there were brick, plastered structures; there were the mansions like the ones at the French plantations; but this old house caught my attention because it had a tin roof rather than a palm or wooden or shingled roof.]

1738 hrs. I'm at my CP again. I just finished reading "The Graduate." It's a story truly of our times. I feel as though I've gotten a lot of postgraduate education also.

Tuesday, December 17

0942 hrs. Last night and tonight I called An Khe to check my records to see if I was flagged, and I'm not. Lieut. Taggett, S-1, is playing games with me as he and I hold each other in contempt. I called SJA to check with USARV CID to see if they initiated a flagging action. SJA will call me back.

Dear Mom and Dad,

Well, I've got two weeks to go before I go back to An Khe to process out of Vietnam. Col. Harden talked to me today. He told me he'd rather handle the problem, if I desired, so he could give me an article 15 (which is nothing) and I wouldn't be at the mercy of higher headquarters or the FBI. The S-1 informed me that the FBI contacted Department of Army who told USARV to flag me, and this all came down through channels. I checked with An Khe and the records clerk there said my records aren't flagged (held for disciplinary action), but I'm still checking. I might just sneak out with no problem here at all, but maybe it will catch up with me later under a federal prosecution. Col. Harden said he "holds me in high regard" so he will help me. The way he said it, I wouldn't mind if he court-martialed me--I respect him that much. I did wrong and got caught. I called SJA (staff judge advocate) and I think they will help. Meanwhile, I'm just waiting. If nothing happens, I may just head home and hope nothing follows.

Ma, Snoopy is mine. It's not for you. Have any of my packages I sent home got there? These are new ones--one for each of you--Mom, Dad, and Bob. I'm glad to hear everything else is home. I'll drop Aunt Emily a note. Dad, I wrote about $300 more in checks as I bought a TV and some clothes which will be sent home (through PX). I wanted to go to Hong Kong, but this AK-47 problem came up. Well, in a matter of about three weeks, I should be home.

I'm still our defensive perimeter commander. I've got about 50 to 60 men with 6 to 8 machine guns online, 8 radios, and other equipment to defend our sector. I believe I'll miss this life somewhat. Right now, I just want to get home. Ma, I believe you still have time to send my field jacket and my camera if you haven't already. I'm just counting the days.

Love, Joe

Tuesday, December 17, (cont.)

1720 hrs. I'm at my CP now. Col. Harden told me today he would help me and he would give me an article 15 if I wanted to have action taken so no one will mess with me later. He told me he holds me in high regard, and right now I don't care if he court-martialed me because I have the greatest respect for him. He's a West Pointer in the top 5% for a promotion to full colonel. I just want to go home.

Wednesday, December 18

1242 hrs. I'm reading while Chief Sterns, Chief Poster, and Lieut. Renner are playing cards. I called SJA last night and Capt. Ford will inform me of what action anyone is taking. Today about 25 armored personnel carriers rumbled by to go on

Armored personnel carriers at Quan Loi.

an operation. The nights are getting colder and shorter. I hope some mail comes in.

1740 hrs. I slept this afternoon. Capt. Ford came by on his way back to Phuoc Vinh. He's having the CID check out for an investigation on AK-47. Capt. Ford said not to worry about anything. I got a card from Kathleen, a card from Aunt Emily, and a letter from Mary.

Thursday, December 19

1536 hrs. Col. Gore had a base defense meeting today. General Forsythe has intelligence info of sapper attacks at various bases. Our guard is to be increased tonight, and I'm to send out an LP about 200 m outside our perimeter. Our C Company had 4 KIA today as they made contact near where D Company had their 22 KIA.

[Sappers were enemy personnel who carried satchel charges (satchels with high explosives). They would run into camps, cities, and military installations and detonate the explosives. They were almost like suicide bombers because they were not always going to escape the areas they entered. We were on alert for these attacks.]

Friday, December 20

1835 hrs. Capt. Ford said that CID and USARV have no record of a flagging action on me except initiated by here. Lieut. Taggett deliberately flagged me to prevent my taking a leave. I'm waiting until the col. comes in to tell him. Today Lieut. Gonzales and I went to An Loc. We went to a whorehouse, but we just drank beer. We're on another big alert tonight. I've got every bunker manned. I'll send out another LP tonight.

Saturday, December 21

1500 hrs. I flew to LZ Sue today to see Col. Harden. I told him that SJA informed me that I was flagged by the battalion and not USARV. The col. was unhappy that someone took it upon himself (Lieut. Taggett, the S-1) to flag me other than the col. I hope all turns out okay. I believe that the S-1 will get what he deserves. I believe all will be all right. I saw the CA (combat air assault by helicopters) being made nearby by two of our companies at LZ Sue. A CA is really impressive.

CA or Charlie Alpha or Combat (Air) Assault was the signature tactic of the 1st Air Cavalry. We'd be picked up by lift ships to go to an LZ which was usually "prepped" by artillery fire and ARA rocket and machine gun fire and we'd land, un-ass the choppers, and go out on search and destroy or search and clear missions.

Sunday, December 22

1300 hrs. I went to Mass this morning. Some of the officers are writing up awards for the move from Camp Evans to here. A lot of the awards are bullshit.

[I helped move the entire battalion, and I didn't get an award. The person processing all awards was my "buddy"—Lieutenant Taggett—the S-1. If I saved the President, I was NOT going to get an award.]

1720 hrs. Chief Poster and I went to An Loc again today checking out different whorehouses. We just drank beer. Major Byrne said he'd check on my flagging action; if nothing has developed, I should be free to DEROS on time.

It was different witnessing a combat air assault for a change rather than doing it. I took movies of the air assault which occurred outside Camp Evans and made these photos from them.

Combat Air Assault outside Camp Evans: 1. Artillery prep of LZ. 2. Hueys with troops approaching. 3. ARA gunships prep LZ. 4. Hueys get closer to LZ. 5. Gunship covers lift ships. 6. Lift ships descend to LZ. 7. White phosphorus round signals end of artillery prep. 8. Gunships cover the landing.

Monday, December 23

1420 hrs. Capt. Stacey, HQ CO, said he called division to lift my flag. I never was flagged by any USARV or higher HQ, only by here at Major Byrne's and Lieut. Taggett's orders. I can go to the IG and raise a stink about the unauthorized flagging action, but Col. Harden has been more than fair and understanding; and I believe he'll take care of any injustices. I don't believe any repercussions will follow me. The year here is almost over and I've learned a great deal about life and people. I made some real friends and worked with some outstanding people.

1610 hrs. I just finished reading (after about a month) "The Thibaults" by Roger Martin du Gard. It was a 771-page novel of the highest literary merit.

Tuesday, December 24

1410 hrs. Today is the day before Christmas and the only things reminding me of it are cards on the wall and decorations at the An Loc ARVN compound. Chief Poster and I went there and I played with some of the Vietnamese kids. They are cute. Lieut. Charlie Wester (S-5) was there, too. I'll have base defense tonight, too. I hope no problems as it's Christmas Eve. Capt. Stacey told me the col. definitely doesn't want me flagged and he will give me the necessary papers to assist my DEROS. I wrote Sgt. Tagg a letter of commendation today. Even though it's almost over, danger still lurks. Two days ago, I had to disarm a damaged, dangerous hand grenade, and last night I put a small fire out near one of my ammo bunkers, which had hand grenades, ammunition (M-16, M-60), and 90 mm recoilless rifle ammo. What a life!

Wednesday, December 25

1800 hrs. Today is Christmas. Col. Harden awarded me my bronze star and air medal. I go back to An Khe in three days. I hear that An Khe has been penetrated by VC several times who threw satchel charges in the R&R and DEROS Center. I guess I'm never safe over here, even going home for DEROS. I briefed Lieut. Shell on the defensive sector, and he has it tonight. I got my movie camera and field jacket today. Chief Stern, Lieut. Wester, and Lieut. Franco are playing cards. I'm drinking beer and writing. Lieut. Grand is reading. I can hardly wait to get home, but in a way I'll miss the battalion.

[So even out-processing to go home I had to worry about sappers with satchel charges. It is true about the camaraderie that develops among brothers in arms.]

Thursday, December 26
1038 hrs. Dear Mom and Dad,
Well, I'm in the home stretch. Day after tomorrow, I'll go to An Khe and "clear" records there. I'll be there a few days, then to Cam Ranh, then to Fort Lewis, Washington. Nothing has resulted on the AK-47 deal, and I don't believe it will. The S-1, a 1st lieutenant, wanted to make a big deal out of it, but the col. was on my side; and I'll leave and hope nothing follows. I did get screwed out of a leave to Hong Kong as a result of the unauthorized flagging action on my records; and I could go to the IG (Inspector General) and raise a stink about my rights being infringed on, but the col. has been good to me so I'll just exit the Army rapidly and quickly. I dread going back to An Khe as it was overrun by VC last week and three U.S. troops were killed

and several wounded. Even going home I have to worry about being safe.

I got the camera and field jacket. Thanks! I'll probably take some movies of the area today or tomorrow. I hope you got the present I sent you, Ma. I also sent Bob a gift, too. Enclosed are some pictures of me by one of my base defense towers. Well, wish me luck getting home. This will probably be my last letter until I get home. I'll call when I get to the States. Tell Aunt Jay I got a letter from her two days ago that she mailed in November.

Love, Joe

Thursday, December 26

1810 hrs. I went to An Loc today and took some movies of An Loc and Quan Loi (here). I patronized another brothel and drank beer with two EM (enlisted men) and Lieut. Gonzales. The girl I had was named Tu Hong, an attractive, intelligent Vietnamese. What a life! I'm short (time in country) as the expression goes and I'm killing time. Yesterday, Specialist 4 Osterman, one of my best men in my old platoon, gave me the highest compliment. There have been six platoon leaders in charge of my old platoon since I left, and Osterman said I was the best. That means more to me than any medal or award. I've learned a lot about my fellow man this year, and a lot about myself. I believe I'll have to work for myself—be my own boss. I've got to really work hard to get through law school.

Friday, December 27

0802 hrs. I finished reading Gore Vidal's "Myra Breckinridge" last night. I clear here today and leave for An Khe tomorrow.

Friday, December 27, (cont.)

1047 hrs. Capt. Stacey showed me a copy of the CID report which came down on my AK-47. He said it's a late Christmas present and that he won't "have received it" until I've gone, and nothing should follow.

[That was a late, great Christmas present.]

2210 hrs. A bunch of us drank beer and "BSed" tonight. I'm a little high. Ben is falling asleep on his cot. Tonight is my last night with 2/7 Cav. In a way I am sad to leave. This year's been exciting and interesting and I have learned a lot about my fellow man and myself. I've got to worry about An Khe now and then to home.

Saturday, December 28

0733 hrs. I can hardly believe it. I'm in the process of going home. Last night, I drank a lot of beer and went to sleep. Around 2330, Bill Wester woke me up and said some guys came over to see me off—they were Capt. John Marlbrand and Sgt. E-5 Jim Brakus (used to be my FO). I'm here at the Quan Loi airstrip now.

[It is true that people who share experiences together in a combat situation develop a special bond. That was true of my platoon and me, and with these guys and me.]

Sunday, December 29

1007 hrs. I got here at An Khe yesterday. I'll just kill time here until my name is called to manifest to Cam Ranh Bay.

1851 hrs. I'm at the Can Do Club having a few drinks with a guy named Jim Turner. He will DEROS soon, too. He's been telling me about his wife and how he really misses her. I guess being married can really be great, but it just isn't for me right now. I believe a wife would hinder me in my endeavors now. I hope I can attend law school at ASU, but I'm not counting on it. I really want to be an attorney.

Monday, December 30

1819 hrs. Jim and I went to "Sin City" today. I took some movies. I met a cute girl who I just made out with. I may make love to her tomorrow. I bought some ivory figurines at the PX. The year is almost over. It's really been an exciting and enlightening year. I hope this war ends soon and that there can be peace all over the world. It sounds trite, but I really appreciate life and peace after seeing what I've seen. I've learned my strong points and my drawbacks. I guess I'll always be a free soul and independent. I believe law is for me as I can express myself through it and serve my fellow man (and myself). I could write so much about this year, but I'd need volumes of paper. I'm thankful that God or Someone has watched over me and allowed me to accomplish the missions I've done and still keep my men alive. When I go home, I'll have to really work.

[I was very "short" as the expression went. I had a very short time left to be in country. I guess I was reflecting on a very eventful, exciting, and dangerous year.]

Tuesday, December 31

1607 hrs. Today, the last day of an extremely exciting year, Lieut. Dick Vineyard and I went to An Khe village. I patronized a pretty Vietnamese girl. It's a shame to see poverty drive people to do the things they do, especially here. We Americans are so lucky. I hope this war ends soon. Today the Can Do Club will have a floor show. I cleared finance and AG records today. I'm just waiting to board the plane to Cam Ranh Bay. I hope next year finds the world resolving its many conflicts. Peace really means a lot to me now. I also hope this year brings me closer to the things I want; I hope I can work for and deserve them.

The last girl I encountered in Vietnam. She was not one of the prostitutes. Her family owned the shop and "brothel." We went through the jungle to her house away from the "business" area. We just hit it off, and I wanted to have sex with her. I may have been her "first." She was so pretty, so young, so fresh, so innocent; and I have often wondered what happened to her after the Communists took over.

2238 hrs. The club show was interesting. I can't think of anything profound to close out this diary, so I'll just hope for a better world and peace and prosperity for everyone. I should be in Cam Ranh Bay day after tomorrow, stay overnight, and then to U.S.A.

The last girl I encountered in Vietnam was not one of the prostitutes.

I got on the commercial flight to go home, and when the plane's wheels lifted off the ground, all the guys cheered. An interesting phenomenon occurred when we got airborne. My father had bought me a Bulova 23-jewel, self-wind wristwatch with luminous hands when I was in college. It was my "combat watch." I wore it 24 hours a day, every day—in the monsoon rains, in the scorching heat, when it hailed, on the sands, in the jungle, on the ground, in the air on combat air assaults, taking the shock of combat while being on my wrist—but the watch never failed me. When the plane got off the ground at Cam Ranh Bay to take us home, I was looking out the window; and then I glanced at my watch. It stopped for the first time, as though it knew it was okay to do so then. I still have that watch.

Both my parents have passed, and I wish they were alive to share this compilation of my previous writings, but they experienced my letters and thoughts with me. My mother told me years later that when she and my dad watched the body counts each night on television, my dad would cry. When I left for Vietnam, my ma kissed me and looked me in the eyes and told me I'd come back. She was right.

My Vietnam watch.

Epilogue

After Cam Ranh Bay, I got back to the U.S. and out-processed at Fort Lewis, Washington. I flew to Phoenix, and my mom and dad drove up from Tucson to pick me up. It was nighttime, and they met me in the terminal. I was in my khaki uniform, bloused boots, combat decorations, overseas cap, and a 1st Cav patch with a button loop on my breast pocket. There was no welcoming committee—no brass band or banners—just my ma and dad. I was glad to be home ("back in the world," as we used to say) but could barely believe it.

We drove from Phoenix to Tucson in the dark of night. Ma sat in the back seat; Dad drove. We made small talk. I remember that when we got to the area of Picacho Peak between Phoenix and Tucson we passed the pecan orchards, and I saw purplish-blue lights around the trees to keep them from freezing during the cold winter nights. It was surrealistic and consistent with the milieu of the 1960s. I kept looking out the window as we drove along, trying to convince myself that there was no threat of an ambush. I was trying to mentally convince myself that I was home and that I was safe. I was back in the world.

Dad and me after I returned home.

I reentered the University of Arizona Law School in February 1969, and I think the rigors of law school occupied my mind to help me adjust to being "back in the world." The antiwar protests were going "strong," and I spoke up for U.S. involvement in Vietnam at a law school rally and got shouted down. I remember another time being in the Student Union building across from the Law School during a lunch hour, and two Jewish law students were sitting there. They knew I was a Vietnam veteran, and as I passed their table they talked loud enough so I could hear—one said, "I would never go fight in Vietnam, but I would fight for Israel."

That statement left an indelible impression on me then, and still does today, since we send our young men and women to conduct combat actions against the "enemies" of Israel. It was difficult to accept the fact that so many draft-dodging cowards would comment on "how bad it was in Vietnam." It often seems to me that those who have never experienced actual combat and been shot at are the first to want others to go to war.

I joined the Arizona National Guard and later the Army Reserve and had an interesting military career, often intertwined with my civilian career, retiring as a Colonel (O-6). I became a lawyer, moved to Phoenix, and practiced criminal law (15 years as a county prosecutor and the rest as a defense attorney in city, state, federal, and military courts) since 1971. In 1980, I became actively involved in the Arizona Military Museum which portrays the military history of Arizona. The museum, which has earned several awards, has a large room dedicated to the Vietnam War, and is an official partner of the DoD Commemoration of the Vietnam War project. It has sponsored several major events honoring Vietnam veterans.

Running a military museum since 1980, I have encountered numerous veterans and been involved in various veterans' organizations and military-related events. As a result, I learned two things that those who served their country really want: They want their service recognized, and they want their service appreciated; hence, this book. Many proclaim that they support veterans or the "heroes who fought for freedom", but somehow the service of Vietnam veterans is not even acknowledged. I believe that this is due to a sense of national guilt from the politicians, media, and the misguided antiwar protestors who threw away and maligned Vietnam veterans' accomplishments and service.

The Vietnam War was just, legal, and truly to defend the freedom of the South Vietnamese. The American military won the Tet Offensive in 1968; brought the war to a successful end in January 1973; and left Vietnam and promised to logistically support the South Vietnamese if the North invaded again. Watergate occurred; a newly elected Democrat Congress ended all funding to south Vietnam; and the Communist North invaded and took over South Vietnam. These are facts.

In 1999, I was diagnosed with prostate cancer, attributable to my exposure to Agent Orange; hence, I get compensation for my country poisoning me. But I am not a victim. I served my country when called upon and I am proud of my service.

I've been actively involved in veterans' activities—NONE for a profit motive. Those who say they care about veterans should speak out and show their appreciation for the service of our nation's largest group of living veterans—Vietnam veterans. I have a personal mission to educate everyone about the Vietnam War—its history, its reasons, its battles, its soldiers' heroism and accomplishments, its politics, and the shameful conduct of those who maligned an entire generation who honorably served their country. The Vietnam War is still very much a part of my life.

Visit Joe Abodeely at:

www.JoeAbo.com

About the Author

Colonel Joe Abodeely, U.S. Army (Ret) lives with his wife, Donna, three dogs, and eight cats on 20 acres of desert about an hour south of Phoenix. He has practiced criminal law for over 40 years, served as a combat unit commander in Vietnam, and later served in the Arizona National Guard. He retired from the Army Reserve as Chief Legal officer for the Military Police Operations Agency at the Pentagon.

Joe writes articles and essays about terrorism, geo-politics, Middle East politics, military and international law, and the 1st Air Cavalry. Joe is the director and actively involved in the all-volunteer Arizona Military Museum, which hosts events honoring Arizona's Vietnam veterans and portrays the colorful military history of Arizona. Joe edits the museum journal. He is involved with Vietnam veterans and the local Vietnamese community in various events.

CPSIA information can be obtained
at www.ICGtesting.com
Printed in the USA
FFOW04n0747140514
5391FF